A. COOK'S PERSPECTIVE

A. COOK'S PERSPECTIVE

A Fascinating Insight into 18th-century Recipes by
Two Historic Cooks

CLARISSA F. DILLON

and

DEBORAH J. PETERSON

BROOKLINE
books
Havertown, Pennsylvania

Brookline Books is an imprint of Casemate Publishers

Published in the United States of America and Great Britain in 2023 by
CASEMATE PUBLISHERS
1950 Lawrence Road, Havertown, PA 19083, USA
and
The Old Music Hall, 106–108 Cowley Road, Oxford OX4 1JE, UK

Copyright © 2023 Clarissa F. Dillon and Deborah J. Peterson

Hardback Edition: ISBN 978-1-95504-118-8
Digital Edition: ISBN 978-1-95504-119-5

A CIP record for this book is available from the British Library

All rights reserved. No part of this book may be reproduced or transmitted in any form or by any means, electronic or mechanical including photocopying, recording or by any information storage and retrieval system, without permission from the publisher in writing.

Printed and bound in the United Kingdom by CPI Group (UK) Ltd, Croydon, CR0 4YY

Typeset in India by Lapiz Digital Services, Chennai.

For a complete list of Casemate titles, please contact:

CASEMATE PUBLISHERS (US)
Telephone (610) 853-9131
Fax (610) 853-9146
Email: casemate@casematepublishers.com
www.casematepublishers.com

CASEMATE PUBLISHERS (UK)
Telephone (0)1226 734350
Email: casemate-uk@casematepublishers.co.uk
www.casematepublishers.co.uk

Contents

Acknowledgements   vii
About the Authors   ix
Introduction   1
Ann Cook's receipts   7

Ann Cook's Professed Cookery   11
    To the Reader.   13
    An Essay on The Lady's Art of Cookery   19
    Professed Cookery   75
    Instructions for Potting Fish or Fowl   115
    Appendix   149

Glossary   163
Bibliography   183
Index of Recipes   185

Acknowledgements

We have received assistance from many. Without their help this project would not have been possible. At the top of the list, we thank Sarah Mulligan, Library Information Officer at the City Library, Newcastle-on-Tyne, UK, for all of her assistance, along with Fiona Hall and the staff on the Enquiries Desk for their help, too.

The Historical Society of Pennsylvania, Philadelphia, made it possible for us to determine which edition of Hannah Glasse's *The Art of Cookery, Made Plain and Easy* we should use.

The Library of Congress, Washington, D.C., scanned their copy of the second edition of Glasse's book for us.

Arlene Zimmerle, Humanities & Media Library at Bryn Mawr College, helped us when our computer got cranky.

Two historic sites let us use their hearths. Thanks to Neil Bobbins, Site Director at Pottsgrove Manor, Pottstown, PA and to Rich Paul and Pat Martin at The 1696 Thomas Massey House, Broomall, PA.

Thanks to:

Marc Meltonville, former food and drink historian for the Royal Palaces in the UK, who answered lots of our questions;

Barbara Corson, DVM, explained "spav'd quay" or we'd never have known;

Erwin Tschanz reproduced 18th-century apple-scoops for us to use;

Dave Hoffman made a cock's comb cutter in case we needed one;

Laura Adie took our photograph in the Miller's House at Newlin Grist Mill, Glen Mills, PA.

Our special thanks to the butcher, anonymous by request, who supplied us with interesting ingredients.

The members of Past Master in Early American Domestic Arts researched, cooked, and cheered us on.

Historic cooks Mya Sangster, Pamela Cooley, and Pat Mead shared their experiences and insights which helped enormously.

Kim Praria proof-read the index with us.

Last but not least, our heartfelt thanks to Jennifer Green, and her assistants, who shepherded this project through to publication.

About the Authors

Clarissa F. Dillon received a doctorate in History (two continents, two centuries) from Bryn Mawr College in 1986. She has been active in living history since 1973 and has produced a number of self-published "little books" as well as a cookbook, *So Serve It Up,* that provided 18th-century receipts for a meal a month for Pennsylvania residents of various economic and social levels.

Deborah J. Peterson began her living history activities with military re-enactments in 1982. She toiled as a camp-follower on many Revolutionary War sites. From 1999 to 2013, her Heirloom Pantry provided hard-to-find and well-researched ingredients and equipment.

Both Clarissa and Deborah were founding members of Past Master in Early American Domestic Arts and worked together on the group's newsletter and *The Pennsylvania Housewife*. Since the group disbanded in 2013, they have continued to work together on a variety of projects.

Introduction

Ann Cook, a little-known 18th-century cook, teacher, and author, produced only one book. That's not unusual; very little information is available about other cookbook authors like E. Smith and Martha Bradley. Her book, *Professed Cookery*, was printed in three editions. The first edition is evidently so rare it is not listed in *A Short-Title Catalogue of Household and Cookery Books*. One copy does exist—in the City Library, Newcastle-on-Tyne, UK. Clarissa was able to visit the library where Sarah Mulligan, Library Information Officer, provided the first and second editions, a desk, and a chair, and left Clarissa to enjoy herself.

Teasing out information about Ann Cook's life is challenging. She provided some tidbits in *Professed Cookery*, which could have slipped into oblivion after its appearance in the mid-18th century but for its unusual contents. Instead of the common "Introduction" found in similar volumes, it contained a very long poem, commenting scurrilously about another period cookbook, *The Art of Cookery, Made Plain and Easy*, by Hannah Glasse. Period comments about this unique feature have yet to be discovered. Cook wrote of herself:

> A profess'd cook, born in a homely Cottage,
> Beholds the Surfeit of her Meat and Pottage;
> . . . .
> Eighteen Years Cook, and Master of an Inn,
> During the Whole, encouraged not lude [lewd] Sin; (p. ix)

She wrote of working for families: "…I have acted in the Station of Cook and House-keeper, so have I been very successful in pleasing the Families I served…" (p. 194) Families…how many? How large? In what level of society? Where located? And for how long was she employed? Why did she leave? Where did she go next? All unanswerable questions. For part of her life she was an inn-keeper's wife or mistress of an inn, but things did not go well.

The first inn managed by Ann and her husband, John, was the Black Bull in Hexham, a small Northumberland town west of Newcastle-on-Tyne. While there, a problem arose concerning some wine. The incident, along with its very long aftermath, was described in an addition to the second and third printings of *Professed Cookery*. According to Cook's narrative,

> ...My Husband sent to borrow six Bottles of this great Man's Wine, telling the Chancellor whose Wine he had borrowed for him...This ...Agent...enquired of the Chancellor how he like the Wine that was sent to the Inn from Squire *Flash*. He [the Chancellor] said, 'I had no Wine but what I payed the Landlord for'... (3rd ed., p. 270)

The squire denied lending the wine, for which Cook later offered to pay, and claimed theft. In Cook's narrative, she involved herself, explaining

> As to this great Man I will write him a letter...and shew how much I love or fear him; nor will I tamely let him rob me of my Character, branded with their Father's stealing this Tyrant's Wine. (Ibid., p. 278)

The squire's response was a public declaration: "...in the open Street, that he could freely forgive my Husband, but swore to be the Destruction of the Bitch, his Wife." (p. 279)

Because of such threats, the Cooks decided to move.

> ...If I can meet with a convenient House out of his Jurisdiction, where I can receive the Fruit of my Diligence and Pains, and have a Prospect to live in Peace, I would freely leave him the Field. (p. 283)

Accordingly, when the Queen's Head Inn became available in Morpath, a small community north of Newcastle, the Cooks took it, with a bond for £369. They had, however, to retain the Black Bull for three months (p. 287). A new environment did not improve things for the Cooks; their new landlord turned out to be a cousin of Squire Flash and demanded payment of all owing, £30 of the original bond. The Cooks moved again, this time to Newcastle where they planned to open a shop; they purchased supplies on credit. After selling "£200 Worth of Furniture" to pay creditors, the Cooks were unable to pay a maltster what they owed, so John was imprisoned for debt (pp. 295–6).

What does this have to do with Hannah Glasse, target of Ann Cook's acid attacks? There were remarks like

> But does she boil; and full as ill she roasts,
> Good Meat does spoil, yet of her Cook'ry boasts. (p. iv)

In addition to the poem, there were sixty-eight pages of comments about the receipts in *The Art of Cookery*. Hannah Glasse was the illegitimate daughter of a Northumberland landowner, Isaac Allgood. She was brought up in his household with his heir, Lancelot [later Sir Lancelot] Allgood. It was this man, called Squire Flash, who charged John Cook with theft. Glasse, by virtue of her birth, was condemned along with her half-brother. The early editions of *The Art of Cookery* were authored by "A Lady," and as "The Lady," Hannah was vilified. One of Cook's complaints is what today would be called plagiarism: "She steals from every Author to her Book,…" (p. iv) Recent scholarship supports this charge (Stead, Bain). However, Glasse's "borrowing" or "stealing" was not unique; it was common in the world of 18th-century cookbooks.

This was not the only attack on Glasse. James Boswell recorded a conversation in which Charles Dilly, a publisher, stated that Sir John Hill was the author of *The Art of Cookery* (Quayle, p. 71). It is not known how widespread this thought was, nor whether Mrs Glasse ever came forward to refute it.

It might be tempting to think Cook's attacks were motivated by professional jealousy because of Glasse's success. However, at the time of her book's printings, Cook would not have known that *The Art of Cookery* would be printed thirty-seven times—well into the 19th century—accompanied by the less successful manuals, *The Compleat Confectioner*, reprinted seven times, and *The Servant's Directory*, with four printings (Maclean, pp. 59–61).

Cook laid all of her trials, tribulations, and sufferings at the feet of Sir Lancelot Allgood, who branded her husband a thief and hounded the family to ruin. It would seem that Hannah, by virtue of her birth, was to be hounded in revenge. All of Cook's complaints could have been boiled down to: "This Teacher has no Connection with the true Art of Cookery…" (p. 30) But Cook clearly enjoyed going on and on about Glasse's shortcomings.

In many ways, these women had much in common. Both had connections in the north of England. Both had other means of support besides just cooking. As mentioned earlier, Cook managed inns; Glasse worked as a dress-maker in London (Maclean, p. 60 n.1). Both wrote their books to augment family income, both had their early printings made "For the Author," and both died in poverty, the result of a series of financial reverses.

Did Cook ever confront Glasse in person, or vice versa? We don't know. It is fun to speculate about such a meeting—two cooks facing each other. They would have been sturdy women able to lift and shift heavy pots, dismember carcasses, haul firewood and water. Each would have been sure she was in the right—Cook attacking with flashing eyes and perhaps a wooden spoon at the ready, and Glasse, cool, calm, and collected, sure of her competence in the kitchen and staring down the virago in front of her. Too bad we'll never know…

* * *

While scholars have long speculated about the reasons behind Cook's criticism on Glasse's receipts, none have tested its validity. As historic cooks, we wondered whether they were accurate; so we set out to investigate, comparing Cook's comments with the results we obtained during our years as independent historic cooks as well as from our activities with Past Master in Early American Domestic Arts.

We have chosen to rely on the first edition, which had no index and no "Plan of Housekeeping." These were added to the second edition. The third edition was published in London, "Printed and sold by the Author" in 1760. The earlier editions were published in Newcastle by different printers in 1754 and 1755. The "Plan of Housekeeping" has very little housekeeping information: five pages *in toto* for keeping and caring for poultry, two pages on preserving meat, and four pages on wine-making. This material is presented more effectively in other books of the period.

We realized we would have to try and determine which edition of *The Art of Cookery* was used by Cook. In her "Essay" there are critical comments that could have been based on any one of a number of Glasse's thirty-seven editions. We went to The Historical Society of Pennsylvania and examined the fifth edition, published in 1755. We ended up realizing that it was too late, so we purchased a scanned copy of the second edition, 1747, from The Library of Congress. We believe this is the one used by Cook. There are two reasons for this. There is an appropriate amount of time between the two publications and, also, beginning on page eight, Cook began giving Glasse's page numbers for the receipts she was criticizing.

Working our way through the "Essay," we commented as we went along. It quickly became clear that we really had to try some of the dishes to determine if the criticism was valid. This also gave us the opportunity to *cook*. This adds a dimension lacking in merely scholarly discussions of the two women and their books. As you will find, a number of Cook's comments are not called for. And when you read her receipts, you'll notice that she is not always the frugal and efficient cook she describes herself to be. Just look at her very first receipt: *"A White Fricassey of* Chickens." The cook must use several different processes, some of which have several steps; it is much more complicated than Glasse's receipt (p. 23). Another example of Cook's receipts prepared hogs' ears and feet; they are stewed with spices and veal gravy, then some are fried. Glasse's receipt uses wine, ketchup, and mustard, but only stews the meat until tender. In 1997, members of the ALHFAM Historic Foodways Committee and interested conference attendees prepared the Glasse receipt, very much simplified, at the Irish Farm at the Museum of Frontier Culture in Staunton, VA. It took forever for the ears to become tender and even longer for the feet. Clarissa's thoughts about this dish ran along the lines of "waste not, want not" and "why bother?" She also wondered how often this dish would have appeared on the tables of the better sort. There are enough receipts in period cookbooks to think it might have done. A case could be made for setting this dish on the table to achieve the symmetry desired on 18th-century dinner tables; the leftovers could be enjoyed by servants after the dinner guests had departed. We don't know.

For many 18th-century housewives, a cookbook or a personal collection of receipts was not necessary for day-to-day meals. For special occasions, and perhaps for a change from the monotony of everyday meals, cookbooks provided opportunities for new dishes, and maybe a challenge for the cook. That's how we viewed it, and we hope you do too.

Ann Cook's receipts

Professed Cookery is not really a go-to volume for historic cooks. Although very few of the receipts are unique, there are directions for making unusual yellow, red, or green fricassees of chicken, for a "Pokey Tongue" which is actually lamb forcemeat in the shape of a beef tongue, and both a "sham pig" and a "sham turkey." Many receipts call for a great many ingredients prepared by different processes.

There are two questionable receipts. One is for what Cook calls "Steeple Cream." We prepared it and found it similar to "Ambassador Cream" in Ann Peckham's cookbook and "To make Cream of any preserv'd Fruit" in *The Director* by Sarah Jackson. These receipts call for an hour of beating (we took turns). After about fifty minutes, the texture and behavior of the cream changed dramatically, and at the end of the hour, it could be piled in glasses, retaining its peak. In other cookbooks that give receipts for "Steeple Cream," the cook is to use jelling agents, isinglass and hartshorn, and to spoon the cream into special molds. Hannah Glasse describes these as "… small high Gallipots, like a Sugar-loaf at Top…" (p. 281; borrowed from E. Smith, p. 187?). The other receipt is "To fry Cream." When Clarissa tried to make fry'd cream in the Palace Kitchen at Williamsburg in 2011, she used N. Bailey's receipt. She mixed cream, eggs, sugar, and spices with a small amount of flour; the mixture was to be cut into diamond shapes and fried in boiling suet. It was never stiff enough to cut into shapes, and frying produced quite a mess. Ann Cook's receipt calls for thick, round slices of bread, soaked in cream, cubed, and fried in clarified butter. It sounds like Hannah Glasse's *"Pain perdu, or cream toasts"* (p. 163; borrowed from John Nott, C, 229?). Today we call it "French Toast." Nott also had a receipt for a similar dish called "Poor Knights" (p. 193).

As historic cooks discover, sooner or later, a lot of "borrowing" went on in the world of 18th-century cookery. In many of the complaints about Hannah Glasse's receipts and borrowing, the criticism could have been, or should have been, directed at other cooks who provided similar or identical receipts.

A *sham* pig.

Steeple Cream.

Members of Past Master prepared a few receipts from *Professed Cookery*. "Sausages without guts" were on the menu for a hearth-cooking workshop at The 1696 Thomas Massey House on April 14, 2004. A demonstration at Historic Fallsington on October 8, 2011, used Cook's receipt for a boiled fowl with onions and a prune pudding. Clarissa found the pudding very different from the Glasse pudding (p. 220) of the same name. All of the results of Cook's receipts were well-received. Clarissa used Cook's sausage receipt at a cooking workshop at The Massey House in April 2004 and found them very much like "Very fine sausages" in E. Smith's *The Compleat Housewife* (p. 91). She also prepared Cook's unique pickled pumpkin at home on November 1, 2015. It was not enjoyed by children or adults, so it isn't worth doing again.

For those historic cooks making a collection of 17th- and 18th-century cookbooks, *Professed Cookery* would be a welcome addition. On the other hand, for those with a limited budget and/or shelf-space, there are other, far more useful books to be acquired. If receipts are to be demonstrated or used in cooking classes, there are many other books with tasty, workable dishes to use.

Ann Cook's
Professed Cookery

To the READER.

IF long Experience make all Fools wise,
It will enable me to criticize;
A poor Mind, if known, might be conceal'd,
Mean Poverty is shewn when its reveal'd.
A Lady claims such Skill in dressing Meat,
Prescribes to Lords and Ladies what to eat;
From what she does collect makes up a Book,
Assumes the Author and the sov'reign Cook.
Of so much Art, that each ignorant Maid
By reading it, is Mistress of the Trade;
Shall know to do the Art of Cook'ry well,
Examines not for Judgment, Taste or Smell.
Look and behold the Lady's Introduction,
Her noble Progress promis'd by Instruction,
The lower Sort makes Choice of, for to sway,
And says, will treat them in their own Way,
For such a Teacher's Reformation pray:
To fleece the poor low Servants to get Wealth,
And collect Surfeits to destroy all Health,
Can this be honesty or pelf'ring Stealth;
Robbers on the Highway may take a Purse,
But who steals away Health is ten Times worse,
Good Cooks are Blessings and bad Cooks a Curse.
Th' Cook'ry Art got Birthright and a Blessing,
Which all true *Isra'lites* are still possessing;
Jacob's good Broth, *Rebecca's* sav'ry Meat,
Sets forth the Worth of Cooks that are compleat.
She steals from ev'ry Author to her Book,
Infamously branding the pillag'd Cook,
With Trick, Booby, Juggler, Legerdemain,

Right Pages to bear up vain Glory's Train.
Can this be Honour to the *British* Nation,
To gild her Book with Defamation?
As Slander harbours in the Dunghill Kind,
So Heroines abounds in a gen'rous Mind.
If Genealogy was understood,
It's all a Farce, her Title is not good;
Can Seed of noble Blood, or renown'd Squires,
Teach Drudges to clean Spits, and build up Fires?
Two Preface Culliss's goes far to show,
Whether the Pedigree be High or Low;
Such Laws, Thrift, and meer Ostentation,
Sets for the th' great Roast-ruler of the Nation.
Well has she marketed her little Wit,
By a great Artifice link'd close to it:
Poor cunning Art sometimes finds Ways to rise
Up to such Heights as might the World surprize;
Can Cream be thought a proper Sauce for Fish,
Or Salmon bak'd in Milk a wholesome Dish?
If Epicures full of such Meat should cram,
Their Stomachs they might lose, and the Cooks damn.
When Appetite is gone Health may depart,
But, she relieves this by her Cook'ry Art:
A Chapter for the Sick she has prepar'd,
Wherein she shews her Skill and great Regard;
Says, she meddles not in the Physick Way,
But Nurse and Cooks must her Precepts obey:
Directions proper for sick Ladies Meat,
Besides what Doctors shall prescribe to eat;
Her first Charge given to Nurse and Cook for Food,
Is Mutton and Roots be they bad or good,
To abate the Sickness or inflame the Blood.
Of Butchers Meat-gravy as strong as Glue,
To restore Health and give them Spirits new;
And when so weak as to take little Food,
Affirms the Cordial will do them most Good:
To very weak Beef-broths a hearty Drink,
Let fainting Ladies on their Matron think;
Another Cordial Draught she has in Store,

And bids the Nurse give the Sick one Draught more:
A Jill of Pork-broth in the Morning soon,
If their Stomachs will take the same at Noon:
If Nurse and Cook obey their Teacher's Will,
Sore may the Sick Mourn at her uncouth Skill.
Bad does she boil, and full as ill she roasts,
Good Meat does spoil, yet of her Cook'ry boasts.
Such Dictates might divert the whole Nation:
Had she of *Tom Thumb* made a new Translation,
So great a Property of Lady Blunder,
Might make Beaus laugh till their Sides burst asunder;
So many Criticks in Novel and Hist'ry,
Yet very few knows ought of the Cook's Myst'ry.
She must descend down from the Sapscul Race,
That such great Surfeits gives so bold a Grace;
And one likewise whose Fancies was scant,
Makes up a Book for to relieve that Want.
Here, there, and yonder Cook'ry Fragments gathers,
And dresses up her Daw in borrow'd Feathers:
Adds to her Pickings up a Cook'ry Guess,
Commits the grand Affair into the Press:
Cries, of all Books yet printed her's th' best,
Read it but Maids, and soon your Dinner's dress'd:
Be Kitchen Bustlers, learn both Trade and Trick,
Your Teacher shews to surfeit whole and sick.
Then cries, who prints her Book or any Part,
She'll prosecute for stealing Cook'ry Art:
Look at the Lady in her Title Page,
How fast it sells the Book, and gulls the Age.
A Kitchen Dairy is the Lady's Book,
And says, there's all Things fitting for the Cook.
Bids other Ladies sit and take their Ease,
She'll teach them Cooks that shall with Judgment please:
Ignorant Maids says, as they are great Sinners,
They'll buy the Book, and dress up Ladies Dinners:
And spell and put together, it will read,
And in the Art of Cook'ry shall proceed.
Famous Artist, great Kitchen Director,
Why might she not as well turn'd Architector?

Laid Plans for Houses, set forth Rules and Lines,
And bid the Ploughman build up her Designs.
Delude illit'rate Men as well as Maids,
To profess'd Builders and Masters of Trades;
And when she's fill'd the World brim full of Wonder,
To see her various Ways found out to plunder,
Vain Glory bratling forth like Blasts of Thunder.
Sole House Director of the *British* Isle,
Sounds out the Trumpet of Self-praises, while
A profess'd Cook, born in a homely Cottage,
Beholds the Surfeits of her Meat and Pottage;
Muses upon the Purport of the Book,
With God sends Meat, but who could send the Cook.
This Cottager esteems herself free-born,
That trick and bite, and all Imposters scorn.
She ne'er beheld the Splendour of a Court,
Nor has she Learning Rhetorick to support;
Had she known Grammar, might made better Rhyme,
Words more connect, and of a Style sublime.
Criticks may pick the Faults out of her Satyr,
And see the Want of Letters, not of Nature;
Or say, the Lady might expect Submission,
From one so far beneath her in Condition.
To better Birth, superior Worth and Merit,
She Homage pays with Body, Soul, and Spirit;
Yet Criticizers Sentiments may pass,
What Title can be due to **broken Glass:** [emphasis ours]
But if th' Book want Justice, Truth, and Reason,
Fair regulating can't be deem'd a Treason.
Cooks of sound Judgment may be call'd discreet,
Who use Precaution what they give to eat:
Would rather to their Breasts present a Knife,
As make known Surfeits to give Pain to Life.
Right Kitchen Cook'ry purifies the Blood,
Helps to keep Health and Constitution good;
Which to preserve requires th' purest Reason,
Who corrupts Meat with Mixtures out o' Season,
Health impairs, and guilty is of Treason:
Or teaches what they do not understand,

Grudge not them getting publick Reprimand;
Or claims an Art of which they are no Judge,
If they're detected by a labour'ng Drudge.
Who thinks the Crime on Artiface to soar,
The same to lash Imposters till they roar:
She on a Proverb oftentimes have thought,
It's best for Ladies what is dearest bought.
If so her Cook'ry does them good,
Which to refine she many a hot Fire stood;
Bought it with Health, Strength, and Resolution,
And paid for it a robust Constitution.
A Gem that far exceeds Talents of Gold,
For this superior Gem she fairly sold;
Oppress'd with Akes and Pains, 'twas her Pleasure,
What gave these Pains brought forth th' Cook'ry Treasure.
In Persecution her Soul did aspire,
To a Reward for what she lost by Fire;
Yet as the Drudge ne'er had a servile Spir't,
Nothing she asks but what's due to Merit.
She wants no Praise, if she's not best deserving,
In her slow Pace can keep herself from starving;
If Approbation is giv'n to her Myst'ry,
And she enabl'd to write out her Hist'ry:
The World will then see which Way, what Way how
Hardships was laid for her to wrestle through;
Eighteen Years Cook, and Mistress of an Inn,
During the Whole encourag'd not lude Sin;
Dukes, Lords, Ladies, many worthy Esquire,
Came to her Inn, and often did admire,
How she found Cook'ry to fit all their Palates,
Both Nobles, Gentles, to de Chamber Valets:
T' please her virtuous Guests took great Delight,
Would not connive with Vice to gain their Mite.

An Essay on The Lady's Art of Cookery

Plain Roasting and Boiling is a material Part of the Housewife, when it is done to Perfection; and this is roasting and boiling to Perfection, when every separate Order is punctually obeyed: Some love Mutton or Beef boiled very rear [rare]; some love it thoroughly roasted or boiled; but at the same Time to be sent up full of Gravy; others choose it roasted or boiled to Rags: And every Master or Mistress expects their Roast done to their Liking; and more or less roasted, requires more or less Time in Roasting. All roast Meat requires a clear brisk Fire; to be spitted level, so that the Fire plays equally round the Meat. I never salt Beef till it is spitted, laid to the Fire, and basted; then carefully strew Salt all over it, and it takes in as much as it requires. I never paper any Sort of Roasts for this Reason, the Paper is a Hindrance to the Roasting, which wastes Time and Fire; and the Pins that holds [sic] it fast to the Roast, are as many Taps after the Paper is taken off, that all the Gravy of the Meat runs out at: And here the Lady Teacher differs from me in her Charge to be sure to paper the Beef, and to baste it all the Time it is roasting: This is a hard Task to the Cook, if she obeys her Teacher's Order, she will be half roasted herself if it is a large Piece of Beef; and if she bastes it all the Time it roasts with the hot Drippings, it will burn the Beef on the Outside before it is thoroughly roasted. The Lady says, that the Loins and Necks of Mutton are to be papered, and the Fat of the Loin of Veal; and if the Fat of the Loin of Veal be papered, what will become of the Lean of the Back of the Loin? It must be burnt before the Kidney and Fillet be thoroughly roasted when it is papered: Therefore I advise none to Paper the Fat of a Loin of Veal at any Rate; the basting with Butter at laying down, and before it is drawn is right, but no papering. The Lady bids cut the Skin of a Loin of Pork a-cross with a sharp Pen-knife, but forbids cutting the Skin of the Chine: But my Advice to all my Readers, is to make checker Work of the Chine as well as the Loin of Pork, lest the Carver of it complain of the Cook. This Lady adds, that the best Way to Roast a Leg, is first to parboil it; this I call a Leg of Pork persecuted: My Way of a roasted Leg of Pork, is to salt it with common Salt and Salt-petre, and let it lie a Week in a Tray, turning it three Times; then to spit it and lay it down to the Fire, and put a Bottle of Rough Cider into a very clean Dripping-pan, and baste it with this all the Time it is roasting; and when it is enough, draw it on the Dish in which you send it to the Table, take off the Skin; for Sauce, have some boiled Apples and Sugar, and warm Vinegar and Mustard in the Dish: By this Way of roasting a Leg of Pork, it eats as delicious cold as hot; but half boiling the Leg, and then roasting, must make a sad Martyr of that venerable Part of the Swine.

To roast a Pig. Always contrive to lay the Pig down warm to the Fire that is newly killed and dressed; put Sage cut small into the Belly of it, with a Crust of Bread; then sew up the Vent, spit it, lay it down to the Fire and singe all the Hairs; then drudge it with Flour, and so let roast till it is of a light Brown; then take a Bunch of clean Feathers and whisk all the Flour clean from it; then take a little clean Beef or Mutton Drippings into a long Brass-spoon, and set it into the Dripping-pan till it is melted, into which dip the Ends of the Bunch, whisk it with the Feathers, and when it is well greased, throw all over it a handful of Salt; let the Fire be Brisk all the Time it Roasts; and when it is a dark Brown, dust off all the Salt with the Feathers, draw it before it lose any of the Gravy. This Lady Teacher bids, dust it all over with Flour, and keep Flouring it all the Time it is roasting; this wastes Abundance of Flour and Time, and hinders the Pig from roasting. She adds, as soon as the Gravy begins to run from it, the Fire is to be stirred up, Basons to be set into the Dripping-pan to receive the Gravy: Now every Bason will take Tribute of the Gravy, and there is no Gravy so preferable to its own mixed with melted Butter and the Brains, with a little of the Sage that is in the Belly of it. The illiterate Maid is by her Teacher's Order, to put a Quarter of a Pound of Butter into a coarse Cloth, to rub the Pig after its Eyes have dropt out and the Gravy run from it. Now in my Opinion this Pig must be over-roasted before this Operation is perform'd, and if the Maid rub it with this coarse Cloth till all the Butter is consumed, what Pig that ever was roasted could have a Skin to endure such a rubbing Bout? For by my Computation it would be a full half Hour, before such a Quantity of Butter could be consumed, as is in the coarse Cloth: which would not only rub off all the young Animal's Skin of its Back, but the unskilled Hand rubbing must make execution into the Flesh; so the martyr'd Pig shews this roasting to Perfection. (*HG* 3)

To roast a Hare. If the skin can be taken off clean, that there is none of the Down matted in the Flesh of the Hare; do not wash her, but keep her Blood within her; make a Pudding of her Liver, Beef-suet, Thyme, Sweet-marjoram, Parsley, Shalot, an Egg, a little grated Bread, an Anchove [anchovy] cut small; mix all together with Pepper, Nutmeg, and Salt, and put into the Belly of the Hare, and sew it up; cut some Rashers of Bacon, and with very small wooden Skewers, prick the Rashers on the Back and Buttocks of her; baste her with Butter, and when she is enough, have plain melted Butter in the Dish, which the Company mixes with the Savoury Pudding. The Lady Teacher has prescrib'd for a large Hare, two Quarts of Milk, and half a Pound of Butter, which the Hare is to soak all up, and then she will be enough, and to have a fit Sauce: A Pint of Cream, and half a Pound of Butter must, in my Opinion, take all the Taste of the Hare from her, and she must be a boil'd Hare, for I cannot think her roasted, nor can she be palatable, nor so much Cream to so little Flesh wholesome, but pernicious to Health. (*HG* 7)

To roast Venison. A large Hanch [haunch] of Venison, make Paste, and roll as thin as a Lid for a Family standing Pye; lay this all over the Venison, but put no Butter in the Paste; lay whitish brown Paper all over the Paste, and roast it at a brisk Fire: A large Hanch will take six Hours roasting, the Paste keeps the Fat of the Venison from wasting; have boil'd Bread, Water, and Cinnamon, put Half the Quantity of Red-wine, and sweeten it with Sugar; send up the Sauce in a Sauce-bason; the Venison will have Gravy sufficient for the Dish.

To roast Ducks. Be sure to pick the Ducks well, be cautious in drawing the Guts, cut not to burst them, lay them warm to the Fire with Sage and Onion within them; the Necks, Livers and Gizzards boil'd with a little Onion and Pepper will be Gravy, and Red-wine Sauce for them.

To roast Pigeons. By no Means roast them on the poor Man's Spit [see comments below] with six Hooks at the end, for this Reason; the Backs of the Pigeons will be raw when their Breasts are roasted, then they are all to be turn'd their Backs to the Fire; besides the Danger of dashing the Pigeons against the Barrs, by the Swinging of the String; as they must be untractable [sic] Rope-dancers: Lay them warm to the Fire with Parsley and Butter in their Bellies; let them have a clear Fire, and the long Spit against the Beggar's Spit, most Gravy for any Money; let the Sauce be Parsley and melted Butter. In the Chapter of *Roasts* and *Boils*, the Lady Teacher has recommended the Twining-band as the best Way to roast a Pigeon; and in her second Chapter of *Made Dishes*, is the Piece of Iron with six Hooks at the End, on which the Pigeons are to be roasted: And where she, this Teacher says, the Pigeons will swim with their own Gravy, although Reason told me the Contrary; yet I was Fool enough to believe that there might be some Magick Art in the long String tyed to the Chimney Top, by which Art the Pigeons might receive so much more Gravy than any other Pigeons ever known to have; so I fulfilled the Order, for I filled the Pigeon full of Butter and Parsley, tyed the String (according to Order) to the Chimney, and when I had perform'd all this Operation with a Pigeon, I found less Gravy in it than there would have been if it have been roasted in the common Way; besides this single Pigeon had double the Advantage of the Six, as it had all the Fire playing round it as it was turning, which Part I very diligently perform'd, as at that Time I had a proper Kitchen, which was my Bed-chamber, whose Chimney-piece was very suitable for a poor Man's Spit: Now as one Pigeon was so far from answering such a Quantity of Gravy, as to make it swim, how much worse will the Six hang on six Hooks, for the Fire can but play half Round them, for their Breasts must screen their Backs, or their Backs must screen their Breasts, so that by turning them must consume their Juice; but if the Pigeon be done by the skillfullest Cook in the Universe, still it is but a Pigeon, and cannot discharge Gravy to make it swim in the Dish; but the poor Man's Spit is a Destroyer of the Gravy, and not a Preserver of it. And as to Fowls roasting, to tell to a Minute the Time they take roasting, there should be an exact Distance from the Fire, for the Illiterate and Ignorant may very easily err in proportioning the proper Distance of the Spit from the Fire; and in Case you be so fortunate as to find it out, you may do very well in roasting a large Turkey and a small one. Likewise in roasting a Goose, the same may be observed; but if it is a clear Fire and at a proper Distance from it; the Goose will lose her Gravy; for an Hour will roast the best Goose I ever saw. By her Rules for Roasting, there is an Hour and a Quarter, and no Fowl is so insipid as a Goose serv'd up without her Gravy. I had a very worthy Guest that did practice the Law, was a Critick in one Part of Cookery but in a Goose roasting, and he would see the Fire and the Goose laid down, and never allowed more than Forty-five Minutes; he had his Watch by him, and would not let the Goose have one Minute more than the above forty-five Minutes; then there was a Dish full of the Gravy of the Goose. By these Rules a wild Duck is to have ten minutes roasting, Wood-cocks, Snipes, and Partridges, will take Twenty. Now suppose there is Woodcocks and wild Ducks for Dinner, the Ignorant and Illiterate are by these Rules of their Teacher, to lay the Woodcocks to the Fire five or ten Minutes before the Ducks; and if the Ducks are well roasted, the Woodcocks must certainly be over-much; for a Woodcock will but take half the Time of a wild Duck's roasting. (*HG* 84)

COMMENT: Roasting times seem very short for reasons unknown. An ordinary chicken takes us 4–6 hours.

As to Roots and Greens boiling. Why a wooden Vessel is not proper to wash or lay the Greens in, for Dust and Dirt may hang round a Pan as well as a Pail, and a Pail is more common to wash or lay Greens in for Kitchen Use, and may be sooner cleaned than a Pan. No Meat is to be boiled with the Greens, for that discolours; but I rather think that the Greens would discolour the Meat. Use no Iron Pan to them, for they are not proper [we tried greens in an iron pan and a brass kettle and found no color difference], but let them be Copper, Brass, or Silver. I think I durst venture a Wager, to boil Greens in an Iron Pan, as well as this Lady Teacher shall boil in a Silver one. All Sorts of young Sprouts is by this Teacher's Order to be boiled in a great deal of Water, and when the Stalks falls [sic] to the Bottom they are enough. I differ from the Teacher in boiling young Sprouts in a great deal of Water; old Sprouts or Winter Cabbage will take a great deal of boiling; but young Sprouts the less Water, and the closer they are boiled, the brighter Greener they will be but if young Sprouts are put into a great deal of Water, and boiled till the Stalks fall to the Bottom, the Sprouts will be boiled very Yellow; which will make a very bad Appearance amongst a Company of Gentlemen and Ladies at a Table. (*HG* 15)

COMMENT: We tried greens in an iron pan and a brass kettle and found no color difference. There are receipts for many more roots and greens not mentioned here.

In Parsnips boiling. They require a great deal of boiling, and you may know when they are soft by running a Fork into them; Fork may get entrance into a Parsnip before it is boiled at all, although it will not enter so easily as when it is boiled soft, which you may know as well by your Finger and Thumb pressing it, and the Fork may not be so ready; after they are boiled they are to be taken up and all the Dirt to be carefully scraped off them: But I advise you to scrape all the Dirt off them before they are put into the Pot to boil, were it but for the Sake of your Hands; for you will find it much easier scraping a cold Parsnip than a boiling hot one; besides it is more like a good Housewife to wash and scrape the Dirt off them before they are boiled. (*HG* 16)

COMMENT: We have learned that the skin slides off easily when the parsnips are hot.

The Boiling a Collyflower. Is ordered by this Teacher to be cut in four and boiled in a Sauce-pan; then taken up, and one half stewed in a Hash-pan, in a Pan full of Water, a Dust of Flour, and a Quarter of a Pound of Butter: But my Advice is to boil the Collyflower in clean Water; make Sauce of the Quarter of the Pound of Butter; and send up the Collyflower in a Dish, and the Butter in a Sauce-pan, for this Reason: The ten Minutes which is ordered to stew the one half of the Flower, will perhaps starve the other half; this is saving Trouble and likewise Butter; for if the Flower be turned and shaked according to her Order, the stewed will take up all the Butter; and there must be more Butter drawn for the boiled half of the collyflower, as the Hash-pan will take Tribute of the Butter.

COMMENT: We did not have the problems AC describes with HG's receipt (see below) when we prepared it.

To dress Cauliflowers.

TAKE your Flowers, cut off all the green Part, and then cut the Flowers into four, and lay them in Water for a Hour: Then have some Milk and Water boiling, put in the Cauliflowers, and be sure to skim the Sauce-pan well. When the Stalks are tender take them carefully up, and put them into a Cullender to drain; then put a Spoonful of Water into a clean Stew-pan with a little Dust of Flour, about a Quarter of a Pound of Butter, and shake it round till it is all finely melted, with a little Pepper and Salt; then take Half the Cauliflower and cut it as you would for Pickling, lay it into the Stew-pan, turn it, and shake the Pan round. Ten Minutes will do it. Lay the stew'd in the Middle of your Plate, and the boil'd round it: Pour the Butter you did it in over it, and send it to Table. (*HG* 17)

In dressing Artichokes. You are ordered to wring off the Stalks, and put them in cold Water with the Tops down, that all the Dust and Sand may boil out, and an Hour and a half will boil them: But my Advice is to cut the Stalks from them, and wash off all the Dust and Sand before they are put into the Pot, and not to trust to the Water boiling the Sand and Dust out of them; for instead of boiling out the Sand and Dust, and Twitchbells, which are often lodged there, the boiling may obstruct the Passage, and I am apt to think that it would rather boil them further into the Artichoke: If this Advice be reasonable, take it, if not, thy Will be done. But it is amazing to me, that the Lady should order burnt Butter, for thickening Sauces, or to boil Butter in a Pan till it is Brown, and stir Flour into it till it is thick, and to put it by and keep it for Use: She likewise makes Use of this for thickening and browning Sauces; and adds, that there are few Stomachs that they agree with, therefore it is seldom to be used: But my Advice to you is, never to use it at all, don't give thy Master or Lady a known Offender to the Stomach; for in so doing you destroy their Appetite and impair their Health; and consider what a Risk you run in giving Offence to great Ones, notwithstanding you have got your Teacher's Confirmation to use it seldom: 'Tis as much as to say, that if the Family pleases me, they shall not have burnt Sauces; but if they vex or disoblige me, they shall meet with a burnt Butter Stomach Tincture; which by standing a little Time, will be as strong as Whale Oil: So has this Lady Instructor taught her Pupils, to revenge themselves on their Superiors if offended.

COMMENT: Burnt Butter 1 stick of butter ate up about 1 cup of whole wheat flour. The reduced quantity was reflected in the amount reduced. It looked a lighter and more attractive brown. Boiling artichokes upside down is close to impossible because they insist on turning right side up unless jammed against each other.

COMMENT: From here on page numbers for *HG*'s receipts are given.

In Page 24, is a white Fricassey. To boil three Chickens tender in Milk and Water; and to throw away what they were boiled in. But my Advice is to let alone the Milk, and carefully preserve the Chicken Broth, it being a Cordial to a tender Stomach, or is a help to rich Broths; but throwing the Broth away, is doing an Injury to your Master and Mistress. And although some are of Opinion that Milk and Water boil the Chickens white, I aver the Contrary; Milk will curdle, and boil them blacker than Water alone. I have seen great want of one single Chicken for the Sake of the Broth, and could not be had for Love or Price: And does this answer the thrifty Lady Teacher's Proposals and Pretences?

COMMENT: We did chicken in both milk and water, and then in water alone. We noticed no difference in the whiteness. The milk did not curdle nor did it blacken the chicken.

In Page 29, **Is a Breast of Veal in Hodge-podge.** Cut your Breast of Veal into small Pieces, and fry it brown with Half a Pound of Butter put into a Stewpan; and fill'd up with Water, green Pease, hot Spices, sweet Herbs, Lettice, and Onions; if no Pease, three or four Cucumbers, Sellery; and if no Lettice, Cabbage Sprouts: And if you would have a very fine Dish, fill your Lettice [headed lettuce like Boston or Bib; NEVER ever iceberg lettuce] with Forcemeat, and tie the Tops close with Thread: Place your Lettice in the Middle, and the Meat all round it; then pour on your Sauce. Thus the Lady orders her delicate Dish, and says, it will serve Abundance of People: And I believe it will, and have plenty of Fragments remaining. The Lady is a little out of her Element touching her Lettice binding; for before the Meat can be done, the Bindings of her Lettice will be unloosed, in spight [sic] of all her profound Wisdom in Cookery.

COMMENT: Past Masters prepared this wonderful dish. If you are careful the binding will stay on the lettuce.

In Page 31, is to Collar a Breast of Mutton. Do it the Same Way, and take off the Skin; and it eats very well, says the Lady. And likewise prescribes another Way of cooking Mutton, by collaring it as above, and basting it with Half a Pint of Wine; and when it has drunk the Wine well up, baste it with Butter and Gravy. But in my Opinion, the Mutton will be so strongly intoxicated with the Wine, that it will be apt to lothe [sic] the Butter and Gravy.

And the Lady further adds, that the Inside of a Sirloin of Beef is very good done the above Way; and if you don't approve of Wine, a Quart of Milk, and a Quarter of a Pound of Butter, to baste the Inside of your Sirloin. Here I disagree with the celebrated Instructor; and advise you not to fuddle the Mutton with Wine; nor take out the Inside of the Sirloin of Beef, which is the most juicy Part of it; nor surfeit it with Milk; nor spoil a good roasting Piece of Beef, by robbing it of it's [sic] most delicious Part.

COMMENT: Meat doesn't drink up wine. Wine will evaporate. We added a cup of beef broth and half a stick of butter and covered a well-tinned copper saucepan to allow it to simmer for 45 minutes. The sauce was much reduced, the meat was tender and had a wonderful flavor.

In Page 34, **To force the Inside of a Sirloin of Beef.** She orders to take out all the Flesh to the Bone. But I advise you by no Means to take it from the Bone; because, after thou hast taken the Flesh, and made Force-meat with Suet and Bread, How then wilt thou get this fine Meat to stick to the Bone again? A Fillet of Beef, of a Steer, or spav'd [spay'd?] Quay, or a thorough fed Cow, will weigh eight or nine Pounds; besides the Suet, Bread, and other Ingredients, thus laid on the Bone again; the Fat skewer'd down upon it, and over that a Paper; yet, notwithstanding, the Force-meat will make Way through Fat and Paper into the Dripping-pan: Although the Teacher's Order is not to let the Paper be taken off till the Meat is in the Dish, yet the Fat and Paper will not have Strength to bear up the Force-meat; so that fall it must, if it be done as this Teacher orders. There is much Labour lost, and the Fillet is disfigured; besides the Fillet would have been better plain roasted; than by all this stupid, expensive Art of the Lady Teacher's.

I come now to shew the Extravagancy of the rolled Rump of Beef. For there is the Flesh of two Fowls, Beef-suet, cold Ham, and Abundance of other Items: But you will gain more Credit by keeping the Rump whole, and save your Master's Charges. For by *P. 35.* [sic] The rolled Beef is to boil eight or ten Hours in a Pot that can just hold it; and yet this Pot is to be fill'd with Water: But as the Bones are taken out of it, it will pack so close in the Pot, as to leave Room for very little Water; so that Reason would indicate, that eight or ten Hours is sufficient to boil the Pot dry. But the Teacher thinks that the Sauce will not be boil'd enough, as she has ordered the Beef to be taken up till it is better boil'd: And to add red Wine, Yolks of Eggs, Butter and Flour; and when it is enough, to pour it over the Meat. Though many Rumps, Sirloins, and Beef Buttocks are destroyed; yet it's much if you keep the Pot-bottom from burning.

COMMENT: We have a lot to say about HG's receipt and AC's complaints. This is really a dish for a high-style table and AC doesn't do justice to how truly extravagant it is.

The filling is supposed to contain flesh from two fowls, beef suet, boiled ham, pepper, nutmeg, thyme, parsley, mushrooms, and bread crumbs with four egg yolks. The beef is rolled around this, skewered and tied. On the bottom of the pot put a layer of bacon, a layer of thin slices of beef, a piece of carrot, a large onion, whole pepper, and sweet herbs. The beef and water to fill the pot are "to stew very softly on a slow Fire for eight or ten Hours, but not too fast" *HG* says, but AC says "boil."

For sauce, Hannah says, use reduced strained gravy from the meat, then add chopped mushrooms, morels and truffles cut small, two spoonfuls of wine, two egg yolks, and a piece of butter rolled in flour. [The latter would thicken the sauce.]

COMMENT: Ann could have done better in her comments.

In Page 37. **The Lady's Beef Collops** are made thus: They are to be ten minutes in scalding Water, with sweet Herbs; and sent to Table.

Next are **stew'd Beef-stakes.** First, stew the Stakes in Water, Wine, Butter, Flour, and Herbs; then to flour and fry them.

To Fry Beef-stakes. Take Half a Pint of Ale that is not bitter; and fry them in Rump-stakes.

Her second Way is to fry them in Butter, as much as will grease the Pan; to cut off the Fat, and fry by itself, and the Lean by itself.

Another Way to do Beef-stakes [HG calls this *rolled*]: Is to half broil them; then put them in a Stew-pan with Pepper, Salt, Gravy, and Butter rolled in Flour; and let them stew Half an Hour. But her rolled beef-stakes exceed; for four Beef-stakes there are to be Force-meat made of the Flesh of a large Fowl, a Pound of Veal, Half a Pound of cold Ham, the Kidney-fat of a Loin of Veal, Sweet-bread cut in Pieces, the Yolks of four Eggs, an Ounce of Truffles, Morels, Pepper, Salt, and half a Pint of Cream: These she pounds all together, and lays upon the Stakes: Which in my Opinion, will be about ten Pounds of Force-meat to her four Beef-stakes; and is a sufficient Quantity of Force-meat for twenty Dishes.

The Kidney-fat of a good Loin of Veal, by my Computation, must weigh three Pounds; the Flesh of a large Fowl, (I call a Turkey) three Pounds; a Pound of Beef-suet; Veal Sweet-bread, Half a Pound; a Pound of Veal; and Half a Pound of Ham; Eggs, Cream, Truffles, Morels, Herbs and Seasoning, I call a Pound; this makes up the above Computation: Of which I propose to make five very good Dishes: Three of which Substantial, with the Help of a Pound of Spice, and a Pound of Flour: There can be no less than a Pound and a Half of Beef, to roll two Pounds and a Half of Force-meat in each Stake; for the four Stakes I have six Pounds of Beef, of which I make a very good Ragoo; the Kidney Fat of the Loin of Veal, will make Stuffing for the Turkey's Crop, and Force-meat to the other Dishes; the Pound of Veal, and half a Pound of Bacon, with the Help of the Force-meat, will make a Side-dish of Scotch Collops; the Sweet-bread, with Half an Ounce of the Truffles and Morels, will make a Fricassey; the Pound of Beef-suet, Cream, and the Eggs, with the Pound of Flour, and a Pound of Fruit, will make a Hunter's Pudding; the other half Ounce of Truffles and Morels, with Force-meat Balls, Mushrooms, and the Gravy, that the Lady orders to the Beef-stakes, I thus divide; three half Jills of it I give to the Ragoo; the other half Jill to the Scotch Collops; and white Sauce to the Fricassey: So I set my Ragoo at the Head [of the dinner table]; my roast Turkey at the Foot; the Hunter's Pudding in the Middle; one Side is the Collops; the Fricassey the other: All these cram'd together would be a Surfeit; separate them in the above Manner, and they may appear before a Nobleman.

Reason is a notable Instructor in Cookery; it teaches the profess'd Cook to have Mercy on the Master's Property, and not willfully to destroy his Substance, by making such Havock, as Beef-stakes have done in all the Shapes now mentioned; for none of them are fit to appear at the Table of a Gentleman: And to see the Beef defac'd, and so shamefully wasted, would be a great Crime in any Person not to detect.

In Page 43, **Is to roast Ox Palates.** To boil them tender, and cut them in Slices two Inches long; to lard Half with Bacon; to have three Pigeons; three Chicken Peepers, to be filled with Force-meat, and nicely larded; to spit them thus; a Bird, a Sage-leaf, and a Piece of Bacon, till all is spited [sic].

To lard Cocks-combs. Parboil Oysters, and Lamb-stones with Bacon; spit and roast them with Sage-leaf and Bacon between them; baste them with Bread grated, the Yolks of Eggs, and Nutmeg, all the Time they are roasting. Now the Query is, how these tender Lamb-stones and Cocks-combs [AC doesn't mention cocks combs above], but more especially the larded Oysters, will endure the Buffets of the Bread and Eggs? the Oysters will baste to pieces, and beyond Art to keep them on the Spit; although the Task will be hard to lard a parboil'd Oyster; yet if large it may be done: But where to find a Stomach to digest these larded Oysters with Bacon, will be the greatest Hardship.

COMMENT: The whole receipt is unclear. She doesn't mention larding anything. Picture a shish-ka-bob with alternating parboiled oysters, lamb-stones, bacon, and sage inserted between each. Make a sauce with grated bread, egg yolks and nutmeg for basting. Where are the cocks-combs? Clarissa thought she was going mad because she couldn't find Hannah's receipt in any of her many editions. The receipt isn't in AC's *Professed Cookery* either. It is safe to say you can skip this!

In Page 50, **To bake Lamb and Rice.** Take a Neck and Loin of Lamb, and half roast it; boil half a Pound of Rice in a Quart of Gravy, till it is thick, and stir in a Pound of Butter the Yolks of six Eggs; butter the Dish all over; dip the Stakes into melted Butter; lay them in the Dish, and pour three Yolks of Eggs over the Rice; bake it in an Oven half an Hour. The half Pound of Rice is butter'd extravagantly; boiled in Gravy, it seems to be a Pudding: But a Gravy Rice Pudding is as uncommon as it seems to be unreasonable; for the Pound Butter being stirred into the rice; the Dish butter'd over; the Stakes dipt in melted Butter, will take another Pound, and must make a great Well of Oil upon the Rice and Lamb: For it will be far out of the Power of the Rice to keep them from swimming. To me it seems to be Surfeit to a hungry Plough-man.

COMMENT: Look for AC's uses of butter because this calls for more than a pound of butter.

In Page 52, **To stew a Lamb or Calf's Head.** She takes for Force-meat two Pounds of Veal, and two Pounds of Beef-suet, to be chopt all together;

two stale Rolls to be grated, four Yolks of Eggs, two Anchovies, with other Seasoning. But my Advice is, never to make half a Pound of Force-meat for a Calf's Head; and Half that Quantity for a Lamb's, is sufficient: Although this Lady Teacher has between five or six Pounds of Force-meats; besides a Jill of Oysters, Mushrooms Half a Pint, Truffles, Morels, and more Mushrooms; it is very great Extravagancy.

COMMENT: AC does not do justice to the extravagance of this dish which had oysters and truffles and morels and more. This is similar to *hash a calf's head* pp. 15–16 in HG's 1747 edition. It is no longer possible (unless you slaughter and butcher your own lamb or calf) to get a head to stew.

In Page 54, ***Is bombarded Veal.*** Out of a Fillet of Veal, cut five lean Pieces as Thick as your Hand; to which is ordered five Sheep Tongues to be larded; then make a well seasoned Force-meat of Veal, Bacon, Ham, Anchovy. And to make another tender Force-meat of Veal, Beef-Suet, Mushrooms, Spinage, Parsley, Thyme, Sweet-marjoram, Winter-savoury, green Onions, Pepper, and Mace: The well seasoned is to be baked for the Middle; the other is to be fill'd by Way of *Bolognia* Sausage; to boil it, and then cut and fry it: So there is Force-meat baked, boiled, and fry'd. Thus by Mismanagement, the Vulgar in this Country [England] often are Sufferers: For when their Market is made [have gone shopping], they will have roasted, boiled, baked; but in the latter End of the Week they suffer Hunger. And indeed I cannot help comparing the Lady's bombarded Veal to vulgar Extravagancy.

COMMENT: AC is not doing justice to HG's receipt. Her comment about "vulgar Extravagancy" is well taken, even though she doesn't mention the artichoke bottoms, sweetbreads and cocks combs. This dish was definitely designed to impress guests at a high-end dinner.

Scotch Collops *à la Francois.* Cut a Leg of Veal into very thin Collops, and lard them with Bacon, and pour boiling Ale over them, to take out the Blood; to pour the Ale off into a Bason; to fry the Veal in Butter; the Collops laid in a Dish with roasted Bacon round it; the Ale to be put in a Stew-pan, with a Glass of Wine, Nutmeg, Pepper, two Anchovies, and a Piece of Butter. This is monstrous Sauce, for there is neither Gravy nor Water in it: but Ale and Wine thickened with Yolks of Eggs, Butter and Anchovies.

COMMENT: So?

In Page 56, ***Are larded*** **Scotch** *Collops.* A Fillet of Veal is to be cut into thin Slices; the Skin and Fat is to be cut off; lard them with Bacon; fry them

Brown; pour out all the Butter; lay the Collops on a Dish; take a Quarter of a Pound of Butter, melt it in the Pan, and strew in a Handful of Flour; stew it till they be Brown; and put three Pints of Gravy, with Herbs and Onion; the Collops to be put in and stew'd Half a Quarter of an Hour; and the Yolks of two Eggs, Force-meat Balls, a Piece of Butter, some Mushrooms; stir all together a Minute or two till all is thick. Reason says, that the burnt Butter and a Handful of Flour might make the Gravy thick enough, without the Yolks of Eggs. When this Teacher bid put by the burnt Butter for Use; she did not tell what Quantity was to be put in to thicken and brown the Gravy for a Made-dish. But if her Readers have Penetration, they may find out the Quantity in Larded *Scotch Collops:* By which Collops, the Gentry may see the Teacher's Care of giving their Stomachs Offence.

COMMENT: This receipt requires a clock or watch. Burnt butter is like a roux. A cook would know what quantities to use.

In her *Calf Head Surprise:* The Teacher proposes a Task, that she cannot perform herself, if she do it as she has prescribed to others; which is to bone the Head, and fill it with Ragoo, as in the Form it was before; it is to be fill'd with Sweet-breads, Cocks-combs, Truffles, Morels, Mushrooms, Artichoke-bottoms, Asparagus-tops, stew'd in Gravy seasoned, Cream, Yolks of Eggs, and White-wine added to the Ragoo; to keep it stirring one Way for fear of turning; making it thick and smooth with Butter and Flour. This choice collected Ragoo, with twenty Force-meat Balls, is to be put into the Head; and then to be fastened with fine Skewers; Force-meat laid over it, and the Yolks of Eggs, Pieces of Butter over all the Head; to be bak'd two Hours in an Oven. Indeed my Opinion is, that this Calf's Head Surprise very well brooks [earns] its Name; and plainly makes manifest the Teacher's Art of Cookery: For if she had but made a Trial, she would have seen into the Error of her Imagination; Can a reasonable Person believe that this Ragoo could have the Strength of the Bones of the Calf's Head, to bear it up in the Form it was before the Bones was taken out? For if she had the true Art of Cookery, she would not have made this choice Collection of tender Rarities into a Ragoo, ready for dishing up; thickening it with Cream and Eggs; giving Orders to turn it one Way, for fear of breaking; and after it is smooth and thick, to put it into the raw Calf's Head, to bake two Hours: During which Time, what must become of the thick smooth Sauce? Would not the Yolks of Eggs break it into Tears of Envy, for the Indignity done the Ragoo? What was the Ornament of every Dish, is now become Stuffing for a Calf's Head: Which instead of raising it into its Form, makes it an Object of Infamy: The Force-meat all bedaub'd and baked upon it, must appear at the Table, as if the Head was scabbed: And the Rivers of Tears from the Ragoo, discharg'd out of the Eyes, Ears, and Mouth, must have the Symptoms of the Glanders in the Head: But when it is cut up, what a Hodge-podge will the baked Ragoo make in their various Colours. A Gentleman Critick, when he sees the scabbed Head appear at the Table, would swear it had been seized with the Plague, by the Botches, Biles, and Marks of Violence upon it.

COMMENT: Why didn't she mention the boning problem in her complaints about stewing a calf head? We wonder who would present this dish and WHY? The dish certainly appears to look disgusting.

In Page 59, A Ham à la Braise. Slices of Beef and Bacon, Herbs and Roots, are laid in the Bottom of a Kettle; upon which lies the Ham, with the fat Side uppermost; which is ordered to be covered with Slices of Beef, Bacon, Herbs, and Roots; to be covered close with a Lid, and pasted; Fire to be put under and over it; to be stewed twelve Hours with a slow Fire. A Ham indeed may be *à la Braised*; but it will take a large Quantity of Slices of Beef and Bacon to keep it gently boiling twelve Hours in the Juice of this Beef and Bacon, as there is no Water ordered: A Middling Ham will weigh fourteen Pounds; Beef and Bacon to discharge as much Juice as will stew the Ham twelve Hours, Fire under and over it: The least that I can compute is six Stone [see glossary] of Beef and Bacon; and if there is, after it has stewed twelve Hours, a Pint of Gravy, it will be surprising, when the Fat is skim'd off, if the Fat and Gravy will part; as Ham-fat is more clammy than any other Fat. The Teacher has recommended this Liquor to be Sauce for a Ragoo to the Ham; which she says will do as well as Essence of Ham. It is a strange Essence; but the pernicious Part of the Strength of the Ham is so strong, that a hungry Hound from the Field would refuse it: But since this is so plain a Demonstration, Who could believe that a Lady would prescribe a Dish so extravagant, and likewise Sauce fit to surfeit a Sow?

COMMENT: HG calls for the ragoo, with thickened gravy and red wine added, if you eat the ham hot.

The Excellency of the Teacher's Taste and Fancy is further set forth, **by various Ways of dressing a Pig:** The Pig is to be skin'd up to the Ears; and a good Plumb-pudding Batter to be made of Milk, Eggs, Flour, and Beef-fat; the Skin to be fill'd and baken [sic] in the Form of a Pig. But what would this Artist say, if the Eggs make the Pudding rise in the baking, and leap out of the Skin? had she not better have boil'd it in a Bag, than to have robbed it of its Skin, for a Bag for her Pudding. Although she has told how to dispose of the four quarters, by roasting them with Well-cresses and Mint-sauce; or to fry them with Spinage; or Ragoo it, for a Top-dish, the first Course; or a Bottom-dish, the Second; or white Fricassey it for a Top, or Side-dish, the second Course: But after all, it would have been better roasted, with the favourite Piece, even the Skin beautifully crisped.—Next it is to be skin'd, and filled with Force-meat, made of two Pounds of young Pork fat and lean, two Pounds of Veal; the same to fill it, and sew it up, and either roast or bake it, after the Skin is taken off. Query, How will this Pig's Belly hold the four Pounds of Pudding? And will not its Weight give it a fall into the Dripping-pan? Or, you may have a very good Pye of it; as you see in the *Chapter* for *Pyes*: Or you may spit, and let it roast till it is thoroughly warm; then cut it into twenty Pieces, and stew them in a Pint of White-wine, and a Pint of strong Broth: Or cut off the Head, and divide the Quarters, and lard them with Bacon, and lay a Leaf of fat Bacon at the Bottom of the Kettle; upon which lay the Pig's Head, and the four Quarters, Bay-leaves, Lemon, Currants, Parsnips, Parsley; and cover all with Bacon, stewed in strong Broth

COMMENT: The various ways of dressing a pig are described in a separate receipt in HG. The comment about eggs and pudding leaping out of the skin means that eggs might cause the pudding to swell and burst the skin. We wonder what "the favourite Piece" is? AC complains the pig stuffed with four pounds of pudding would fall off the spit into the dripping pan. Would this happen if the cook spitted it carefully?

A Pig Matelote. The Pig to be quartered; to be put into a Stew-pan, upon Slices of Bacon; to be covered with more slices of Bacon, to be stewed in a Bottle of wine: And when it is half done, put two large Eels in six Inches Lengths; stew them with a Dozen of boiled Craw-fish: Scum the Fat off the Liquor that they were stew'd in; add to it a Pint of strong Gravy, thickened with burnt Butter.

A Pig like a fat Lamb. The Pig is to be trussed up like a Lamb, when it is cut through the Middle, and skin'd, parboil it; then throw Parsley over it; roast and drudge it: Let your Sauce be a half Pound of Butter, and a Pint of Cream, stewed all together till it is smooth.

To roast a Pig with the Hair on. Cut off its Feet, and truss it, prick up the Belly, spit it; lay it to the Fire, but take Care not to scorch it, and when the Skin begins to rise up in Blisters, pull off the Skin and Hair; and also baste it with Butter and Cream; or half a Pound of Butter, and a Pint of Milk: Drudge it with Crumbs of Bread, till it is half an Inch thick: The Sauce is to be Gravy and Butter; or else half a Pound of Butter, and a Pint of Cream.

The Pig newly killed, to be roasted with the Skin on. A Hard-meat [sic] made of a Pint of Cream, Yolks of Eggs, grated Bread, and Beef-suet; with Seasoning made in a stiff Pudding; its Belly is to be stuffed; and then to be spitted and laid to the Fire: And drudge it with Flour and Lemon-peel, and a Pint of Red-wine in the Dripping-pan; and when it is enough, shake with Butter: You are to take great Care no Ashes fall into the Dripping-pan; which may be prevented by making a good Fire, which will not want any stirring. In my Opinion, the Teaching Lady has tried all the Ways of dressing a Pig, but the right one, and that she has not touched upon: And if her Stomach can digest such Food, as she prescribes in her various Ways of dressing a Pig, it will be very hard to disturb it. For the various Tortures she put the poor Pig to, might give just Suspicion, that the Teacher's Desire is to waste and consume Wealth by Extravagancy, and create good Business to the doctor. How often is the Pig robb'd of its Skin, the most delicious Morsel, and liked by every Body: Can Cream and Butter be proper Sauce for the Pig, or Eels, Craw-fish, and so much Bacon to stew with it? Who would bid roast a Pig with the Hair on; and order both Skin and Hair to be torn off together, even when it is roasting? Although it is rather more decent than to send it to the Table with the Hair on. But if I had seen the Operation made on it at the first, without reading the Orders, I would certainly have thought the Cook had broke out of *Bedlam*: for none in their Senses could perform Cookery so inconsistent with Reason.

COMMENT: AC's complaints would appear to be for the three roasted pig receipts. Her receipt for roasting a pig like a fat lamb is much more complicated, and does involve skinning the pig.

In Page 70, To dress a Turkey or Fowl to Perfection. Bone them, and make Force-meat of the Flesh of a Fowl, a Pound of Veal, half a Pound of Beef-suet, as much Crumbs of Bread, Mushrooms, Truffles and Morels cut small, sweet Herbs and Spices; all this is made into Force-meat, with Yolks of Eggs; and the Turkey to be filled with. If Extravagance will dress the Turkey to perfection, it is not wanting; but it is attended with great Hazard of being very imperfectly roasted.

COMMENT: We have found several period receipts for stuffing birds with meat. "The great Hazard of being very imperfectly roasted" would seem to refer more to taste/appearance rather than today's concern about possible illness.

Then there is *To stew a Turkey brown the nice Way*. It is to be boned, and fill'd with Force-meat, made thus; the Flesh of a Fowl, half a Pound of Veal, the Flesh of two Pigeons, a well pickled or dry'd Tongue, peal and chop it all together, and beat it in a Mortar with the Marrow of a Beef-bone, or a Pound of Kidney-fat of a Loin of Veal. I say, a Tongue is a good Dish in any Town in *England:* A pretty Side-dish may be made of a good Fowl: Two Pigeons may make another by good Management: And the true Art of Cookery, this half Pound of Veal, and the Pound of the Kidney-fat of the Loin of Veal, may make another. But if you chop all these together, it is but one; and in my Opinion, a very awkward one too. For, after all this Stuffing is put into the Turkey, it's to be put into a Pot that will just hold it; so that the Bones being taken out of it, and so much Force-meat stuffed in, and put into a Pot that just holds it; and as there is no Bones in it, it must be in the Shape of the Pot; because the Pot will be a Mould to shape it: As an additional and needless Expence, is Mushrooms, Truffles, Morels, and Oysters stewed, and put into little Loafs to surround this Turkey. Now, I think, I could make six tolerable Dishes out of this intolerable one: I would boil my well pickled Tongue with Turnips, for the Head [of the table]: Make a Side-dish of the Fowl: Paradise my Pigeons, for the Middle: Of the half Pound of Veal, and the Pound of Kidney-fat, I would make a Side-dish of Veal-olives: My Oysters, the other Side-dish: And I would plain roast my Turkey, for the Bottom [of the table].

COMMENT: HG's dish would seem to be extravagant on purpose. Has AC's frugality missed the point?

To force a Fowl. The Teacher has a particular and wonderful Method; the Skin is to be taken off the Fowl first, and then the Flesh pick'd from the Bones, which is to be minced small; a Pound of Beef-suet shred, and a Pint of large Oysters chopt, two Anchovies, a Shallot, grated Bread, and Sweet-herbs shred and mixed together, and wrought up with Yolks of Eggs; all these are to be laid on the Bones of the Fowl, the Skin to be drawn over all, and sewed up the Back. The Teacher ought to have ordered the Skin to be tann'd, to enable it to stand the Fire, and keep its Burden from falling into the Dripping-pan, before it is half roasted: The Teacher bids either boil it in a Bladder a Quarter of an Hour, or roast it: But if is to be boil'd, is not a Pint of Oysters sufficient, without stewing more which she has ordered to be made for Sauce, for this

Fowl? By which you may see the wild Extravagancy of her Cookery in every Article I mentioned, and all the Dishes spoiled into the Bargain.

COMMENT: Two cooks are required for inserting a chicken into a cow bladder. Past Master prepared chickens in bladders, a very complex dish, at Pennsbury Manor in 2010. The process was recorded for Japanese television. Compare receipts in Charles Carter, p. 55 and E. Smith, p. 62.

In Page 73, **Chicken Surprise.** It is surprisingly cook'd as any of the Rest: the Chicken is to be roasted; for a small Dish one large Fowl, the Lean to be taken from the Bone; stew'd in seven Spoonfuls of Cream, Butter and Flour; then is seven Slices of Bacon to be cut, upon which is seven Rolls made of Force-meat, with a hollow Place in each Roll, into which is the stewed Chicken to be put; covered with Force-meat, and baked in an Oven; the Rolls are to be the Height and Bigness of *French* Rolls: Each of which in my Opinion will take a Pound and a Half of Force-meat; a sufficient Quantity for twenty made Dishes: And all this for the lean Flesh of a Fowl to be baked in; and recommended by the Teacher as a pretty Side-dish for the first Course, Summer or Winter, when it can be got. I think you may have it all the Year round if you please, for Chickens or Fowls are never out of Season both at once; and it may be a large Top or Bottom-dish: For seven Force-meat Rolls in the Size, as they are ordered, will fill a large Top-dish with Gravy-sauce; and the Expence of as much Force-meat, may make four Top or Bottom-dishes.

COMMENT: It is supposed to be a surprise.

In Page 74, **Chicken roasted with Force-meat and Cucumbers:** For two Chickens, take the Flesh of a Fowl, and two Pigeons, and some Slices of Ham or Bacon, chop all well together; soak the Crumb of a Penny Loaf in Milk, boil it, and when it is cool, mix all together; and season with Herbs and Spice. This is to stuff two Chickens; and four Cucumbers, with the rich fry'd Gravy she makes the Sauce, far exceed the Price of the Chickens.

COMMENT: Price/cost was not HG's objective.

Page 79th, **Is to dress a Duck with Green Pease.** A deep Stew-pan to be put over the Fire, with fresh Butter; into which is the Duck to be put, and turned two or three minutes; then is the Fat to be put out, and half a Pint of Gravy put to it; with two Lettices cut small, a Bundle of Sweet-herbs, and a Pint of Pease: Cover your pan close, let them stew half an Hour; then put Mace and Nutmeg; thicken it with Butter and Flour; or with the Yolks of Eggs and Cream, three Spoonfuls.

Would not any reasonable Person think, that a Pint of Green Peas and two Lettices, stewed half an Hour in half a Pint of Gravy, would be thick enough, if not over thick? I should think that it would have rather wanted to be made thinner, than to have Eggs and Cream to thicken it: For to me, the Cream and Eggs would make a very odd Figure mixt with stew'd Lettices, Green Peas, and a Duck.

COMMENT: Past Master prepared HG's receipt and included it in their cookbook, The Pennsylvania Housewife. Our comment noted "excellent flavor."

*In Page 83, **Is a Goose à la Mode.*** Skin and bone the Goose; take the Fat off it: Do a Fowl the same Way; boil a dry'd Tongue; put the Fowl and Tongue into the Goose; season all with Salt, Pepper, and Mace; sew it up in the same form it was before, and put it into a little Pot that will just hold it; put two Quarts of Beef-gravy to it, a Bundle of Sweet-herbs, an Onion, Slices of Ham, or good Bacon, between it and the Fowl; let it stew an Hour, and when it begins to boil take it up: Add to the Gravy Red-wine, Sweet-bread of Veal, Mushrooms, Butter, and Flour.

Now after all this Expence, the Goose is ill used, so is the Tongue and Fowl; for it would have been much better roasted with its Skin, Bones and Fat on it; (I say this large fine Goose is very ill used) for its own Gravy is sufficient for Sauce; with Apples boil'd, a little Vinegar, and Mustard, which will not exceed Two-pence: The other Stuffing and Sauce will cost six Shillings; yet at the same Time, the Teacher would have herself thought Thrifty, by adding *N.B.* To boil the Bones of the Goose and Fowl in the Gravy.

COMMENT: What expense? Salt, pepper, mace, and wine are the imports; all the other ingredients can be found or produced locally.

*In Page 92, **Is to dress Partridges à la Braise***. Lard two Brace of Partridges with Bacon; grate Pepper, Salt, and Mace on them; lay in a few Slices of Bacon, Beef, and Veal in the Pan; upon which lay your Partridges, with Carrots, Onions, and Sweet-herbs; the Breasts of them are to be downwards; Slices of Beef and Veal laid over them; stew them eight minutes over a slow Fire, then give the Pan a shake, and put a Pint of boiling Water to them; stew them half an Hour, and then take up the Birds, and put in a Pint of thin Gravy, boil it to half a Pint; then take a Veals [sic] Sweet-bread, Truffles, Morels, Fowls-livers, and Cocks-combs, stew'd in a Pint of good Gravy half an Hour; adding Artichoke bottoms, Asparagus-tops, and Mushrooms; add the other Gravy to this; put in your Partridges to heat; and if it is not thick enough, take Butter and Flour, toss it up; or if you'll be at the Expence, take Veal, and Ham-cullis.

For Garnishing two roasted Partridges, and the Flesh of a large Fowl, a little parboil'd Bacon, some Marrow or Beef-suet cut fine, Mushrooms chopt small, Truffles, Artichoke-bottoms, Mace, Pepper, Nutmeg, Salt, and Sweet-herbs chopt fine, the Crumb of a Two-penny Loaf soak'd in hot Gravy; mix all well together with the Yolks of two Eggs; make your Pains [sic, meaning unclear] on Paper of a round Figure, and the Thickness of an Egg, form them with the Point of a Knife, which must be dipt in the Egg-yolk, in order to shape them; then neatly bake them a quarter of an Hour in a quick Oven.

Now, I think, I could make a Dinner for eight Gentlemen and Ladies, with the separate Ingredients that are perscrib'd [sic] to *Partridges à la Braise, Partridges Pains,* to garnish, *Etc.*—In the following Manner I make the Entertainment: With the Slices of Veal that are under and above the Partridges, I make a Dish of *Scotch* Collops with some of the Slices of Bacon that is under and over the Partridges, the Pint of thin Gravy, a little of the Seasoning, the Mushrooms that are first prescribed: And the Slices of Beef that are laid under and over them, I make a very good Beef-stake Pye; the Value of the over-plus Bacon will make the Crust: the Fowls Livers and Cocks-combs will be a Fricassey, that may appear at a Prince's Table: A Veal's Sweet-bread, if it be a very good one, by the Help of Truffles, Morels, and half of the Pint of strong Gravy the other: The other Half of the Cocks-combs, and Fowls Livers, boil'd Asparagus, Toast and Butter, is a Side-dish. The Crumbs of a Two-penny Loaf will make a very good Pudding: The Gravy that it is soak'd in will make a very good Soop, by the Help of the Herbs and Roots that are ordered to the Partridges: A Ragoo of Artichokes is a pretty Dish: The large Fowl and Mushroom-sauce cannot be objected to for a Top-dish: And the Best of all is three Brace of Partridges, in their Natural Shape and Taste, roasted with butter'd Crumbs.—So thus I place my Dinner: The large Fowl and Mushroom-sauce boil'd, at the Head; *Scotch* Collops at the Foot, the Soop in the Middle; one side is a Fricassey of Fowls Livers, and Cocks-combs; Toasts and Asparagus the other: The second Course is my six roasted Partridges at the Top; Beef-stake Pye at the Bottom; Pudding in Middle; one Side is the Sweet-bread; ragoo'd Artichokes the other; and has Gravy sufficient for all, besides the hot Gravy she orders the Bread to be soak'd in.—She adds, if you will be at the Expence, thicken it with Veal and Ham-cullis; but says she, it will be full as good without. In that I think her very right, for the Taste of the Partridges were so barbarously destroyed before the Veal and Ham-cullis, which was no further required, than to add to the Surfeit, and enlarge the Expence.

COMMENT: This is confusing because there are two separate receipts discussed: The first is *Partridges à la braise* on page 92. HG says "beaten mace, pepper and salt"; AC says "grate pepper, salt and mace." We question grating pepper, salt and mace. HG finishes by saying the veal and ham-cullis are not essential.

AC has omitted the title of a new receipt, *To make* Partridge *Pains*. Pains has not been defined in sources consulted; making them as directed sounds as if they could be similar to rolls. The *Scotch* collops are in the first receipt along with sweet-breads, cocks-combs, etc.

Again, did AC miss the point?

In Page 93, is a stew'd Pheasant. She bids the Pheasant be stew'd in Veal Gravy, till there is enough for Sauce; and to parboil Artichoke-bottoms; and to roast and blanch Chestnuts; and add to this Sauce, with Mace, Pepper and White-wine, and fry'd Force-meat Balls.

COMMENT: Past Master made this—"EXCELLENT, but not worth the price"; takes lots of time and needs so much processing.

Pheasant à la Braise. She bids lay a Lair [layer] of Beef all over your Pan, then a Lair of Veal, a Piece of Bacon, Carrot, Onion, six Cloves of Mace, a spoonful of Pepper, a Bundle of Sweet-herbs; then to lay the Pheasant, then a Lair of Veal, and a Lair of Beef to cover it; then to set it on the Fire six Minutes, next to pour in two Quarts of boiling Water; let it stew softly an Hour and a Half; then orders to take up the Pheasant and keep it hot, and let the Gravy boil till there is about a Pint; then strain it off, and put it in again, and put in a Veal Sweet-bread, some Truffles and Morels, some Livers of Fowls, Artichoke-bottoms, Asparagus-tops, two Spoonfuls of Catchup, two of Red-wine, Butter and Flour, shake all together; put in your Pheasant, let them stew all together, with a few Mushrooms, about five or six Minutes more; then take up your Pheasant, and pour your Ragoo all over with a few force-meat Balls: You may lard it if you chuse.

Beautiful Bird how sorry am I to see thee so toss'd up with Inconsistancies: I lived in a Family that took such Delight in their Pheasants, that neither Master nor Lady would suffer the Game-keeper to shoot any wild Fowl in the Wood, where the Pheasants inhabited, for fear of frightening them into the neighboring Woods: That Gentleman had been at some Expence in procuring a Brood of them, which he took such Care to preserve and increase, that there was never one seen at his Table, although none in the North entertained more grandly then [sic] he did: He would let his Company see his fine Birds, but at the same Time said they must not taste them. He told a Nobleman, that these Birds had been very safely protected by him, for he had let them increase and multiply these nine Years, without taking one Bird out of their Flock: And as long, said he, as I'm Master of that Wood, none shall disturb them; they are my Harmony in the Summer Mornings and Evenings. Had he ordered a Pheasant to have been dressed, how far would he have been disappointed, had it been stewed with Chestnuts, and Artichoke-bottoms; or à *la Braised* with so many strong Mixtures, which would not leave the least natural Taste; Beside the unnecessary Trouble and extravagant Expence. She says, for a roasted Pheasant, have Gravy in the Dish, and Bread-sauce in Plates; or scalded Well-cresses laid under it; or make Sellery-sauce stewed tender, strained and mixed with Cream, and poured into the Dish. She says, a *Frenchman* would order Fish-sauce to them, but then you'll quite spoil your Pheasants. But I say, that Sellery and Cream are not so proper Sauce as some Fish-sauce is: For many use plain Butter for Fish-sauce, which would be more proper Sauce than Sellery, Cream, and scalded Well-cresses to surfeit Pheasants. Her Fancy extends itself to great Lengths in wild Fowl spoiling.

COMMENT: She is just whining.

In Page 95, ***Snipes in a Sourtout, or Woodcocks.*** Take Force-meat, made with Veal, Beef-suet, an equal Quantity of Crumbs of Bread, Mace, Pepper, Salt, Parsley, and Sweet-herbs; mix them with the Yolk of an Egg; lay some of this Meat round the Dish; then lay in the Snipes, being first drawn and half roasted: Take Care of the Trail, chop it, and throw it all over the Dish. Says she, take good Gravy, according to the Bigness of your Sourtout, some Truffles, Morels, Mushrooms, a Sweet-bread cut to Pieces, Artichoke-bottoms cut small, and let all stew together. She adds, take the Yolks of two or three Eggs, according as you want them, beat them up with White-wine, stir altogether one Way; when it is thick, let it cool, and pour it into the Sourtout: Take the Yolks of a few Hard Eggs, Mace, Pepper, and Salt; and after all, cover it all over with Force-meat; rub the Yolks all over to collar, and send it to an Oven: And, she says, Half an Hour will do it. This Sourtout, to me, looks something like a Force-meat Puff-Paste Pye, dressed very Cunningly, contrived as the Force-meat is laid round the dish: And as this Teacher says, cover it with Force-meat; so Reason would think, that the Time that this Force-meat required baking, would be sufficient to bake the Snipes; for the Bread, Suet, Herbs, and other Ingredients will not roll out so thin as Puff-paste, very far from it: Then who in common Reason would order the Guts to be pulled out of Snipes, and to half roast them, and then to bake them.

I've seen a Wager on the Weight of a Snipe, that it would not weigh two Ounces, which it did not.

COMMENTS: Sourtout was a man's overcoat or great coat; in this case the snipes are in a dish, covered all over with the force-meat mixture. When the receipt says "rub the yolks all over to collar" it would appear that "collar" was a misprint for "cover".

Next, the Teacher gives Orders *to boil Snipes or Woodcocks:* Says she, boil them in good strong Broth, or Beef-gravy made thus: So summons a large Collection of Beef, Onions, Herbs, Mace, Cloves, Pepper; and while the Snipes are boiling stew the Guts and Livers, with Part of the Gravy the Snipes are boiled in. In my Opinion, this Lady Teacher pronounces double Destruction to Snipes and Woodcocks: First, in Sourtout: Secondly, in boiling them in such variety of Mixtures, to rob them of their naural [natural] Taste; the most esteemed tame Fowl may be sometimes masqueraded in Cookery, where they are more plentiful: But wild fowl are Rarities, that be very ill to catch hold of at some Seasons of the Year, and in their natural Shapes grace every Table; and a Dinner is very seldom thought elegant that has not wild Fowl plain roasted. This Teacher puts great Hardships on the ignorant Maids, by giving them very unnecessary Trouble; but far greater, the Imposition on their Masters, whose Fortunes suffer greatly by Extravagance; and if they eat those odd Mixtures and Jumbles, they will consume Health as fast as their Wealth.

COMMENT: Whine, whine, whine.

In Page 97, ***To seare a Hare.*** This Teacher bids lard your Hare, and put a Pudding in her Belly; and then put her in a Pot or Fish-kettle, with two Quarts of strong draw'd Gravy, one of Red-wine, a Lemon cut, a Faggot of Sweet-herbs, Nutmeg, Pepper, Salt, and Cloves; to stew till it be three Parts done; then it is to be taken out of the Liquor and put into a Dish, and strewed over with Crumbs of Bread, chopt Sweet-herbs, grated Lemon-peel, and half a Nutmeg; to be boiled and brown'd before the Fire: Then says she, in the mean Time take the Fat of the Gravy, and thicken it with the Yolk of an Egg; take six boil'd hard Eggs chopt small, some pickled Cucumbers cut thin; mix these with the Sauce, and pour into the Dish. But I say, that a Quart of Wine would intoxicate a Man, much more a Hare, my only Favourite: I like the Hare so well, that I am very angry to see her so much abused; for I never robb'd her of her natural Taste, but shewed the Art of Cookey in preserving it: How many Mixtures, and what various Colours, Red, White, Green, and Yellow Sauce, and Extravagance to a Degree.

She adds, that a Fillet of Mutton, or Neck of Venison, may be done the same Way. And if a Fillet of the largest Mutton weighs a Pound, it exceeds the Weight of any I ever saw. Now, I think, she should have told the Illiterate what Part of the Mutton she calls a Fillet (if she knows it herself:) The Fillet is the Collop that lies in the Inside of the Loin of Mutton, next to the Chain; and if the ignorant Maid has of herself found it out, it will not be to her Master's Profit.

Although her Mistress says, that you may do Rabbits the same Way. But instead of Beef, it must be Veal-gravy; and the Red-wine turned into White-wine, adding Cucumbers for Mushrooms.

COMMENT: HG has no such receipt. Where are those colors? We haven't been able to find the fillet of mutton or neck of venison as described in HG's book. We haven't found the rabbits either.

Page 98, She stews a Hare with as many Mixtures; but does not intoxicate her so extravagantly with Wine, prescribing only one Spoonful.

COMMENT: The seasoning is similar to that in many receipts. A spoonful of red wine and a spoonful of catchup are included.

Next is, ***A Hare Civet.*** She bids bone the Hare, and take out the Sinews; then cut one Half into thin Slices, and the other Half in Pieces an Inch thick; to flour and fry them in Butter like Collops quick, and to have ready some good Gravy made of the Hare's Bones and Beef; put a Pint of it into a Pan to the Hare, a little Mustard and Elder-vinegar; to stew it till it be as thick as Cream.

This teacher has no Connection with the true Art of Cookery: For strong Meat, as Pork, Beef, or Goose, Mustard and Vinegar, may help Digestion, and is very proper: But the harmless Hare that never gave Offence to any Stomach, except such Cookery as this Teacher has prescribed to the Hare.

COMMENTS: Hare is not available here, so use rabbit.

Her next is, ***Portuguese Rabbits.*** I have, says she, in the Beginning of my Book, given Directions for Boiled and Roasted. Get some Rabbits, truss them Chicken Fashion; their Heads must be cut off, and the Rabbits turned with their Back upwards, and two of the Legs stripped to the Claw-end, and so trussed with two Skewers: Lard and roast them with what Sauce you please. If you want Chickens, and they are to appear as such, they must be dress'd in this Manner: Or if they are to be boiled for Chickens, cut off their Heads, and cover them with white Sellery-sauce, or Rice-sauce, tossed up with Cream, says she.

When I see this Teacher's Transformation of Rabbits into Chickens, it raised me from very low to high Spirits; being but newly recovered from a long Sickness, which had sunk my Spirits very low, till *Portuguese* Rabbits raised them to their full Height: When I saw how easy it was to the Teacher to make Rabbits into Chickens, no more than cut off their Heads, turn up their Backs, and strip the two Legs to the Claw-end, and so truss'd with two Skewers. I thought myself in the Midst of an Assembly of illiterate Maids; every one had a Rabbit trying their utmost Skill to make a Chicken of the four-footed Creature; some stripped the forelegs to the Claw-end; some the Hind-legs; but none of them could make the Links of the Back ply into the Form of a Chicken Breast: And by the Strength of Imagination, I thought I heard the whole Pupil Assembly give their Teacher a general Curse for affirming her Art of Cookery easy; which by Trial they found impracticable, and her Transformation a mere Cheat on their Understandings.

COMMENT: HG has a receipt for celery sauce:

> *To make Sellery-Sauce either for roasted or boiled Fowls, Turkies, Partridges, or any other Game.*
>
> TAKE a large Bunch of Sellery, wash and pare it very clean, cut it into little Bits, and boil'd softly in a little Water till it is tender; then add a little beaten Mace, some Nutmeg, Pepper and Salt, thicken'd with a good Piece of Butter roll'd in Flour; then boil it up, and pour into your Dish.
>
> You may make it with Cream thus: Boil your Sellery as above, and add some Mace, Nutmeg, some Butter as big as a Walnut, roll'd in Flour, and Half a Pint of Cream: Boil them all together, and you may add, if you will, a Glass of White Wine, and a Spoonful of Catchup. HG, 67–68

There is no receipt for Rice Sauce in HG's book; could you use cooked rice as described in the paragraph above? AC doesn't offer a Sellery Sauce or a rice sauce receipt in her book.

Next is, *A Rabbit Surprize.* To roast two half grown Rabbits; you must cut off their Heads and first Joints; then toss the Lean of the Back-bones with Cream and Butter, till it is thick and good; and then upon the Back-bone of each Rabbit is a long Trough of Force-meat to be fix'd, and filled with the toss'd up Flesh that is taken of the roasted Rabbit's Backs, which is to be cover'd with Force-meat, rubb'd over with raw Egg; make your Troughs square at each End, and to be baked three Quarters of an Hour. Query, Whether she gave the

Force-meat a proper Foundation, to secure the Gravy or Cream-sauce from being let out by the Back-links of the Rabbits? or let it be double and treble Query'd, whether ever Troughs were built on Rabbits Backs before? If the Lady's Ingenuity enables her to metamorphize Rabbits into Chickens, and build large square ended Troughs on their Back, no doubt but through the Profoundity of her Contrivances, she'll be finding out the Mystery of transforming them to Elephants, and erecting Force-meat Castles on their Backs.

COMMENT: Typical…

In Page 100, is a Neck of Mutton, **call'd** *The hasty Dish.* This Teacher bids take a large Pewter or Silver Dish, with an Edge about an Inch deep on the Inside, on which the Lid fixes, with a Handle at Top, so fast that you may lift it up full by the Handle without falling; this dish is called a Necromancer: She bids take a Neck of Mutton of six Pounds, cut into Chops, a sliced *French* Roll, a large Onion, four Turnips, a Bundle of Sweet-herbs, three Blades of Mace; all these are to be put into this Dish, in their separate Lairs, and to fill it with boiling Water, and cover it close; to hang the Dish on the Backs of two Chairs by the Rim; to tear three Sheets of brown Paper into fifteen Pieces, which are to be drawn through your Hand; light one Piece of Paper, and hold it under the Bottom of your Dish, moving the Paper about, and as fast as one burns light another, till all is burnt, and your Meat will be enough; fifteen Minutes just does it: This Dish, says she, was first contrived by Mr. *Rich*, and is much admired by the Nobility. Very likely Mr. *Rich* might be on his Travels in a very poor Country, where there might be great Scarcity of firing and good Cooks: so Necessity, the Mother of Invention, might produce the above Contrivance to get Support on the Road: But will Reason, or the least Art of Cookery dictate, that the Flame of three Sheets of Paper will boil six Pounds of Mutton cut into Chops, with Turnips, Onions, Herbs, *Etc.* notwithstanding the boiling Water she orders at first to be poured on the Meat, *Etc.* The very Quantity of Flesh, Herbs, *Etc.* will so much abate the Heat of the Water, that to me it seems very unreasonable, that such a small Force of Heat, as can proceed from three fired Sheets, will never make her Meat and Broth to boil; and if such Cookery amounts to a tolerable scald, 'tis as much as any reasonable Person might expect, unless there be more Heat and Strength in Paper than my Imagination dictates, Trial must be allowed the best Proof: And whoever has a mind to befool'd [sic] into such a ridiculous Experiment, have my free Leave; as for my Part, I shall not make an *April* Idiot of myself, nor perswade any of my Readers thereto. If this Inventor, Mr. *Rich*, be Mr. *Rich*, the famous Harlequin and

Master-player, at the *New Theatre, Covent Garden*; it may not be altogether impossible, but that he might put such a Pun on the Lady Teacher, and such others of her Pretensions, that have laboured hard to impose on their Betters, by calling black white, sweet bitter, bitter sweet, unwholesome wholesome, *Etc.* Query, whether a Person going hastily by might not with their Cloths move one of the Chairs, or a Dog being in the Room, pushing by or through the Chairs, would not bring down this fine Invention in the Twinkling of an Eye?

COMMENT: Our thoughts too. This idea of heating with burning paper strips is not unique. See, for example *Thin Beef collups stew'd*, in Richard Bradley, *The Country Housewife and Lady's Director…Part II*, 114.

Page 102, **Another Way to make a Pellow.** Take a Leg of Veal of twelve or fourteen Pounds Weight, and an old Cock skinned; chop both to Pieces, and put into a Pot with six Blades of Mace, some whole White-pepper, and three Gallons of Water, half a Pound of Bacon, two Onions and six Cloves; cover it close, and when it boils let it do very softly, till the Meat is good for nothing, and above two Thirds wasted, then strain it; the next Day put this Soop into a Sauce-pan, with a Pound of Rice, set it over a slow Fire, take Care it don't burn; when the Rice is thick and dry, turn into a Dish. Garnish with hard Eggs cut in two; and have roasted Fowls in another Dish.

By the Rice and Eggs in one Dish, and roasted Fowls in another; in all likelihood the Teacher designs the thick dry Rice and hard Egg-sauce, for the roasted Fowls; but whoever gets the Rice in their Mouths, 'twill stick to their Teeth like Bird-lime; for the old Cock must weigh at least four Pounds, and fourteen of Veal; so that the Strength of eighteen Pounds of Meat to a Pound of Rice, will make it of so glutonous a Nature, that whoever has it in their Mouths, will find it stick so close, that they'll be thankful to have it out again; so there is wasted what would have made seven Dishes of Meat.—I divide the Veal into four Parts; five Pounds I cut to the Knockel, and boil with Greens and the half Pound of Bacon; then I cut four Pounds to the Fillet, and this I make a Ragoo of; and of three Pounds I make a Dish of *Scotch* Collops; and two Pounds I *A-la-mond*; and the Gravy of the Knockel will be Sauce for the Made Dishes; and of the Pound of Rice and Hard Eggs, I make two Rice-puddings, the one baked and the other boil'd; then, instead of the old Cock, I take a young Pout, (which may be as easily purchased in the Market as an old one) this I roast, with Egg-sauce: So far Teachers differ in their Opinions in Cookery; for as the Cock, Bacon, and Veal are to boil till the Meat be good for nothing; and as the Rice was ordered, it was good for nothing; so I make seven Dishes of Meat out of nothing, by the Lady Teacher's nothing arian Ingenuity.

> *To make Egg-Sauce, proper for roasted Chickens.* MELT your Butter thick and fine, chop two or three hard-boiled Eggs fine, put them into a Bason, pour the Butter over them, and have good Gravy in the Dish. (*HG* 35)

Next is, **Essence of Ham**, Take the Fat off the Ham, and cut the Lean in Slices; beat them well, and lay them in the Bottom of a Stew-pan, with Slices of Carrots, Parsnips, and Onions; let them stew over a gentle Fire till they begin to stick; then sprinkle a little Flour, and turn them; then moisten with Broth and Veal Gravy; season them with three or four Mushrooms, as many Truffles, a whole Leak [sic], or a Clove of Garlic; some Parsley, and half a Dozen of Cloves; put in some Crusts of Bread, and let them simmer over the Fire for a Quarter of an Hour; strain it, and set it away for Use. Any Pork or Ham does for this, that is well made.

Thus far the Lady directs, those who do not know the right Way, are apt to take the Wrong, say I: For this Teacher reminds me of the Fable of the Hen that laid the golden Eggs every Day; but the covetous Owner not being satisfied, cut up the Hen to catch all at once; but he pay'd dear for his covetous Search, losing all; even so has this Teacher done the golden Essence of Ham, by cutting it in Pieces, although she keeps the Dross for Use, which is only fit to give to Dogs. And as an Instance of her fine judicious Taste of Ham Essence; she says, any Pork Ham does for this Use; and so far I hold with her, for any Thing of that Kind is too good to waste; but that the Difference of Taste between new and old Ham Essence, is as widely different, as is the Taste of good old Beer, and New in the working Fat [vat]. Now the Difference between the Teacher's Essence, and the true Essence of Ham is this: I take a two Years old Ham, washes it in hot Water with a coarse Cloth; then lays it in warm Water four Hours, and afterwards puts it into a large Pot in cold Water, makes a brisk Fire to it, and when it is boiled enough, I take it up and run it through in several Places with an Iron Skewer, and the Gravy that runs from it, is the true Essence; and this Gravy put into Jelly-glasses hot, the Fat that issues out along with the Gravy will be as a Seal to preserve the Essence, and it will keep six Months, and the Ham will still remain very palatable; although I can't but acknowledge, that a Ham ought to go to the Table full of its Juice, if you would have it in its Perfection, but, as I above observed, it will still remain Tastable, and be a very good cold Relish.

COMMENT: Two different products, take your choice.

Next, the Teacher's ***Rules to be observed in all Made Dishes***; Are, that all White-sauces have a little Tartness, smooth, and of a fine Thickness; and that all the Time the Sauces are over the Fire, keep stirring them one Way: And that Brown-sauces are not to swim with Fat on the Top, but to be smooth, and as thick as good Cream, and not to taste of one Thing more than of another; and as to Pepper and Salt, season to your Palate; but don't put too much of either Sort, lest you take away the fine Flavour of every Thing: And as to most Made Dishes, you may put in what you think proper, to enrich or make it good, as pickel'd Mushrooms, Cocks-combs, Ox-palates, Artichoke-bottoms, Asparagus, *Etc.*

Here the Lady leaves her Pupils in a Wood, and to their own wild Imaginations; so that their Cookery may as probably be vitiated as made wholesome, by young Beginners in the Art of Cookery; and as to the judicious Cook, she might as well have remained silent; and if she bare reading these, and such like her Rules compleat the House-wife, Cookery will be very easily attained. And here I differ in my Judgment with the Lady's ordering Sauces to be stirred but one Way, all the time they are on the Fire, for the perfect experienced Cook has many various Methods in tossing and turning Sauces; and for her Brown-sauce to be as thick as good Cream, then will a Spoon stand upright in the Sauce; and as to her Seasoning to the Palate, if the illiterate Cook be void of Palate and Judgment; then she may copy after her Teacher, by heaping in all Rarities at once, without regard to Quantity, Weight, or Measure, doing all at Random, hit or miss, Luck's all.

In Page 103, This Lady Teacher bids **read this Chapter, and you will find how expensive French Cook Sauce is:** Wherein is contained two Sauces, *viz.* Essence of Ham, and five Cullisses. Partridge Sauce, she calls, an odd Jumble of Trash; and when all the Ingredients are reckoned, the Partridge will come to a fine Penny of Money.

A Cullis for all Sorts of Ragoo: This she bids compute the Expence, and see if this dish cannot be dressed full as well without this Expence.

Cullis the Italian Way: To which she says, now this *Italian*, or *French*-sauce is saucy. Concludes with, they will make as many fine Ingredients to stew a Pigeon or Fowl, as would make a very fine Dish; which is equal with boiling a Leg of Mutton in Champain [champagne]; and adds, it would be needless to name any more, though you have much more expensive Sauce than this: However, she thinks here is enough to shew the Folly of the fine *French* Cooks.

She says, in their own Country, they will make a grand Entertainment with the Expence of one of these Dishes; but here they want the little petty Profit, and by such Sort of Legerdemain, some fine Estates are jugled [sic] into *France*. By these Aspersions the Lady Teacher gives the *French* Cooks, it may be supposed, that her great Fortune has been impaired by the Extravagancy of a *French* Cook; for in this Lady's Preface, she says, if Gentlemen will have *French* Cooks, they must pay for *French* Tricks, and seems to be grieved at the blind Folly of the Age; says, they would rather be imposed on by a *French* Booby, than give Encouragement to a good *English* Cook. It appears to me, that the Lady builds her Monument of Fame upon the Ruins she makes of the *French* Cooks Characters: I don't like the Foundation she has chosen; for notwithstanding all her great Bravadoes of Thrift, she has tenfold more extravagant *French* Cookery in her book, then [sic] in the Chapter she bids you read. As to her first Charge of Partridge Sauce, it comes far short of her Partridge *à la Braise*; and as to the *French* Cook's Essence of Ham, which she has placed in that Chapter for Extravagance; that very individual Essence of Ham, she has in the very Page before; therefore I see no Reason why it should be a Mark of Infamy on the *French* Cook, and a Trophy of Honour to her.

The French Cooks Cullis for all Sorts of Ragoo: She bids, compute the Expence, and see if this Dish cannot be dressed full as well without. I have at her Request made a Computation, and cannot justly make the Charge amount to above two Shillings, and that exceeds the thrift of her Preface Cullis, which she braves them with; yet this *French* Cullis for all Sorts of Ragoo, is one Shilling cheaper than that very thrifty Preface Cullis is.

Now her second Chapter, which this Teacher calls **Made Dishes**. I have not seen a book of Cookery yet printed, that she has not plundered to make up this Chapter, which contains Two hundred and thirty Dishes and upwards. And although she seems to have been a great Traveller by the Cookery prescribed from different Nations, *viz. Turkey, Germany, Portugal,* and *India*; yet put all the Cookery she quotes from them together, she has twenty *French* Dishes in this Chapter to each one Dish of all the separate Nations.

I think she has made publick Demonstration of the Regard she pays to *French* Cooks, by engrossing so many of their Dishes of Surfeits and Inconsistencies in her Chapter; that she had not left sufficient Number to make out the eight expensive Sauces, till she broke Bulk for Essence of Ham, and was so pinched as to charge them with *Italian* Extravagance, or take more out of her own Chapter. As to all the *French* Cookery I ever see in Print, I thought it a Burlesque upon the *English,* whom they say would exceed all the World for Wisdom if they did not eat such gross Food: And as there was but little Regard taken of their Prescriptions, 'tis possible that it was generally looked on in the same Light.

Yet this Lady Teacher has artfully abused the *French* Cooks, and as cunningly recommended their Cookery for her own; so by what she collects from them and other Authors, she becomes Mistress of the Art, and says she has made it plain and easy, concluding her Preface with; she hopes her Book will answer the Ends she intended it for, which are to improve the Servants, and save the Ladies a great deal of Trouble. And begins her first Chapter by saying, that profest Cooks will find Fault with touching upon a Branch of Cookery, which they never thought worth their Notice, is what I expect, *Etc.* And adds, that she does not pretend to teach profess'd Cooks, but designs to instruct the ignorant and unlearned, (which will likewise be of great Use in all private Families) and in so plain and full a Manner, that the most illiterate and ignorant Person, who can but read, will know how to do every Thing in Cookery well.

A noble Pennyworth in Cookery, if this Teacher has performed the publick Promises of the Business of the Benefits the Ignorant and Unlearned should receive by the reading her Book: But if not, it was a Puff to help the Sale of it, as she could not give them the Knowledge she has not herself, nor ever will possess it. Therefore must be a double Imposition: First, In deluding and depriving the Ladies of their Healths. Secondly, In causing the ignorant Servants to throw away their Money, and filling them full of vain Glory. Now, if there is such a sovereign Virtue in the naked reading of her Book, without a Capacity of Understanding, which possibly cannot be in the Ignorant: Then which Way does every ignorant Maid arrive to such an exalted Pitch of Knowledge in Cookery, as to do every Thing therein well: Why might she not as well pretend to reach professed Cooks? For it is my Opinion, that the Universe cannot produce that Cook who knows how to do every Branch in Cookery well. Does not every separate Nation produce something that their Neighbours want, and differ in their various Ways of Cookery? And let a Cook search into those Arts, and be his Genius as great as possible, if he says he can do all Cookery well, I will not believe him. I have a Circumstance of Error to produce, which I can affirm for Truth, that a House-keeper to a Person of Distinction, robb'd the Sirloin of the Inside of the Fillet of Beef, the most delicious Part of the four Quarters; which she took for a Made Dish, and sent up the Sirloin to the Table with the Out-side; but no In-side was there, which is the Favorite of all Beef Eaters: Some Gentlemen being then at Dinner, and who were disappointed of their favorite Piece of roast Beef, put the Lady to the Blush; who enquired of her House-keeper, the Reason of her Sending to the Table such a naked Sirloin of Beef: She answered her Lady, that she made a fine Dish of the Fillet; but, (answers the Lady) you have spoil'd a much finer, and therefore I discharge you for ever to commit the same Fault. Yet, notwithstanding, this House-keeper prepossest in favour of, and depending upon the Infallibility of her Lady Teacher; and as her Lady Mistress was but Young, considered which of these two Ladies she owed most Duty to; and after an inward doubting, gave her Teacher the Preference, who had given her full Assurance of doing every Thing in Cookery well. So she cuts off the Fillet a second Time, and sent up a naked Sirloin to the Table; for which she got her Discharge, lost a good Place, and shed Floods of Tears for her vain Glory; for which she might thank her Lady Teacher. This plainly demonstrates, that the Age is not so blind, as that all are to be imposed upon by the Follies of this celebrated Lady Teacher: The Wisdom of the Young Lady, Mistress of her House shows, in turning off her Servant, both for wasting her Meat, and disobeying her Orders. And if these are the Teacher's promised Benefits to the Ignorant, she cheats them both of their Money and Places; and instead of saving the Ladies a great deal of Trouble, teaches their Cooks to prepare such Surfeits as may give them Pain.

COMMENT on the whole chapter: Picky, picky, picky. Cream isn't always that thick. It doesn't mean as thick as yogurt, and some are very thick, or a smooth liquid. Another example of the love/hate relationship between the English and the French. For dinners of the better sort, expense was not the primary consideration. In colonial Pennsylvania an unskilled laborer earned 2 shillings a day out of which he had to supply food, shelter, clothing, and anything else. HG objects to *French* cooks who were men rather than *English* cooks who were often women; she does not object to *French* dishes.

In Page 107, Is to force Hogs Ears: This Teacher says, the Ears are to be boiled, and a Force-meat to be made; to slit the Ears very carefully to make a Place for your Stuffing; she bids also fill and flour them, fry them; then stew them in Wine, Mustard, Pepper, Onion and Gravy: Dish them up and pour on the Sauce.

It seems very easy to the Teacher, to bid slit the Hogs Ears very carefully to make a Place for the Stuffing; yet it is out of her Power to divide the Grissel of these Ears to fill them with Force-meat; and when she has made the best of them she can, she will not make silken Purses of her Hogs Ears.

COMMENT: Does this seem appropriate for tables of the better sort? For middling and lower sorts would seem unnecessary.

Next is, **To force Cocks–combs**: Parboil your Cocks-combs, says she; then open them with the Point of a Knife at the Great-end; then take the White of a Fowl, as much Bacon and Beef-marrow, beat in a Mortar, with an Egg and Seasoning, to fill the Cocks-combs, and stew them in Gravy.

So small is the Morsel that grows on the Crown of the Cocks Heads, that the Stuffing this Teacher has ordered to be made, all the Cocks-combs in *England*, opened at the Great-end, will not have Room to hold it. The Morsel is an Ornament in Made Dishes; but where to find Room for Stuffing in that small Matter, is the Query.

COMMENT: We have also wondered. Imitation cocks combs can be made out of beef tripe and might be easier to stuff.

Next she tells, **How to preserve Cocks-combs:** To put them into a Pot with melted Bacon, and let them boil half an Hour; add Bay-salt, Pepper, Vinegar, sliced Lemon, and an Onion stuck with Cloves: When the Bacon begins to stick to the Pot, to take them up, and put them into the Pan, and pour Clarified Butter over them: These, says she, make a Pretty Plate at Supper.

This Teacher bids boil the small Morsels of Cocks-combs in melted Bacon half an Hour: A sufficient Time indeed to burn them to as many black Cinders; and after the many other Ingredients are added, *viz.* Vinegar, sliced Lemon, Onion, Cloves; and these, says she, makes [sic] a pretty Dish for Supper. The above-mentioned are the Product of this Teacher's own Cookery, but preserv'd Cocks-combs sets forth the Truth of her Art of Cookery; for, after the Cocks-combs have boiled half an Hour in Bacon; a little Vinegar, and the sliced Lemon are to be put into the boiling Fat, which would give a Crack like a Cannon; so that there would be no need of the Chimney sweeping; for the Blast would bring down the Soot at once, and destroy the pretty Supper-plate; although the Teacher had taken a Method to blast the Beauty, by the half Hour's boiling, in the Bacon-fat.

COMMENT: Preserving cocks-combs seems like a good idea because you only get one per rooster and you need a number for garnish.

In Page 112, **A forced Cabbage:** Take a White-heart Cabbage, as big as a Quarter of a Peck, half boil it, and cut out the Heart, but take Care not to break off any of the out-side Leaves; to make a Force-meat of a Pound of Veal, half a Pound of Ham, four hard Eggs, Herbs and Seasonings; Mushrooms and the Cabbage-costick chopt amongst the Rest finely, all mixt with the Yolk of an Egg, and put into the hollow Part of the Cabbage, tie it with Pack-thread; Slices of Bacon are to be laid on the Bottom of a Stew-pan, upon which is a

Pound of Beef cut thin to be laid, and the Cabbage to be laid above all close: 'Tis to be covered and set to stew over a fire till the Bacon sticks to the Pan; then, says she, shake Flour and pour in a Quart of Broth, Onion, Cloves, Mace, White-pepper, a Bundle of Sweet-herbs; close cover it, and let it stew an Hour and an Half; then put in a Glass of Red-wine, and give it a boil; then, says she, take it up and lay it in the Dish, and strain the Gravy over, untie it first. This, says she, is a fine Dish, and the next Day makes a fine Hash, with a Veal Stake nicely broiled and laid on it.

In my Opinion, this forced Cabbage would be a Hash the first Day; which would give all Stomachs that receiv'd it such a Disgust, as would make them say, from Cabbage-costick, Force-meat, *Good Lord deliver us!*

COMMENT: When thus prepared it was much enjoyed and appreciated.

*In Page 125, Is a **White Peas Soop:*** Wherein the Teacher bids, take three Pounds of thick Flank of Beef, half a Pound of Bacon, a Bundle of Sweet-herbs, and a good Quantity of dry'd Mint, a Bunch of the green Tops of Sellery, a Quart of split Peas, and three Gallons of Water, to be close covered, and set on the Fire, and let it boil till two Parts are wasted; then to be strained, and six Heads of Sellery cut small and put in it, to boil to three Quarts; then cut fat and lean Bacon, and Bread into Dices, and fry'd; to season the Soop with Salt, and rub dry'd Mint over, after it is poured into the Dish, and so send it to the Table: She says, you may add Force-meat Balls fry'd, Cocks-combs boil'd in it, an Ox's Palate stewed tender and small.

The Teacher sets forth, ***Another Way to make it:*** She says, when you boil a Leg of Pork, or a good Piece of Beef, save the Liquor: The next Day boil a Leg of Mutton, save the Liquor, when it is cold take off the Fat, and set it on the Fire with two Quarts of Peas, let them boil till they are tender; then put in the Pork and Beef Liquor, with the Ingredients as above, and let it boil till it be as thick as you would have it, allowing for the boiling. Again, says she, strain it off and add the Ingredients as above. Likewise, you may make your Soop of Veal, or Mutton-gravy, if you please, that is according to your Fancy.

None boils a Leg of Pork before it is first salted, so it is as common to salt Beef, the Broth of which very Few Gentry will let their Servants eat; but to make a Peas Soop withal. The Ingredients which this Lady has cram'd into the above, and the under Soop, scarce any Dog's Stomach, I think, is able to digest; or if it could, it would certainly throw them into some Leprosy: The first time I perused this Soop, I loathed Meat for three Days.

COMMENT: Even parboiled, an ox palate is like chewing rubber bands. We think one modern head of celery could be the equivalent of six.

In Page 127, **To make Hodge-podge:** To which she takes a Pound of Beef, a Pound of Veal, and a Pound of a Scraig of Mutton cut into little Pieces; to be set on the Fire with two Quarts of Water, an Ounce of Barley, Onion, Sweet-herbs, four Heads of Sellery, Mace, Cloves, Whole-pepper, three Turnips, one Carrot, two Lettices cut small; put all in the Pot, and let it stew softly over a slow Fire five or six Hours; take out the Spice, Herbs, and Onion, and pour all into a Soop-dish.

I think there would be no Manner of Occasion for a Soop-dish, nor any Broth to pour into it: It would be a Wonder if the three Pounds of Meat, Barley, Roots, and other Ingredients, were not burnt to the Pot-bottom, let it stew ever so slowly; for two Quarts will not stand five or six Hours Simmering without being exhausted dry, if not burnt to the Pot-bottom, as the Lady has prescribed.

COMMENT: We suggest putting the herbs, spices, and onion in a bag; cover the pot so the liquid does not evaporate. Stirring from time to time keeps things moving. With just one meat, this dish is like the many one-pot meals of the middling and lower sorts.

In Page 128, **Is a Portable Soop:** This Teacher bids, take two Legs of Beef, of fifty Pounds Weight, and take off all the Skin and Fat, and take the Meat and Sinews clean from the Bones; which Meat put into a large Pot with eight or nine Gallons of Water. She bids, add to it twelve Anchovies, Mace, and Pepper, each an Ounce, Cloves, a Quarter of an Ounce, six large Onions, a Bundle of Sweet-herbs, the Crust of a Two-penny Loaf; stir all together, cover it close, and lay a Weight on the Cover; and when it has boiled eight or nine Hours uncover it, and stir it altogether; cover it again, and let it boil till it becomes a rich good Jelly. She says, when you think it is a thick Jelly, take it off and strain it through a coarse Hair-bag, press it hard; then strain it through a Hair-sieve into a large Earthen-pan; when it is quite cold take off the Skim and Fat, and take the fine Jelly clear from the Settlings.

Now for a good Wager, I could venture to make more Glue of the Bones and Sinews, which this Teacher separates from the Meat of two fifty Pound Legs of Beef, then she shall do with the Meat and all hot Spices, Anchovies, *Etc.* which to me is poisoning any Soop. Portable Soop was contrived to support tender Travellers on the road; but what Support can reasonably be left in the Lady's Glue? for the Skin, Fat, Bones, and Sinews taken from the Meat, as the Teacher terms it; so that she leaves as much of the two Legs as she takes; to which nine Gallons of Water are to boil eight or nine Hours; a sufficient Time for all the Strength and Taste of the Meat to steam out in Smoak and Air; yet it will take sixteen Hours to bring this Meat to so thick a Jelly, by slow boiling; and the Crust of a Two-penny Loaf, boiling so long a Time in the Broth, must make it thick, after pressing the Jelly so hard through a coarse Hair-bag: Although, she bids, strain it through a Hair-sieve into a large Earthen-pan; and when cold, to take off the fine Jelly clear from the Settlings. Now, I put the Query, how this fine Jelly gets clear from the Crust of the Two-penny Loaf? because boiling so long it would become a Paste-glue, rather than a clear Jelly; which this Teacher makes manifest, in boiling it afterwards in a well tin'd Stew-pan; which, she bids, take great Care that it neither stick to the Pan or burn, as it will be Lumps about the Pan; which Lumps are to be put into China-cups set into Water and boiled; and when the Glue is cool turn it on coarse Flannel; let it lie eight or nine Hours, keep it in a warm dry Place, and turn it on fresh Flannel till it be quite dry and the glue will be quite hard. I think the Method which this Teacher prescribes to dry this Glue, must be dangerous to the Stomach; for it would pull all the Wool from off the coarse new Flannels, and by turning it on Fresh Flannel till it become quite dry, the Wool would be so interwoven with the Glue, as to make a sad Spectacle, as well as a dangerous Prescription of it: And as the Teacher has not given Orders to Strain the Gravy when the Glue was melted, it is very doubtful that those who have supp'd most of her Soop, must eat most Wool. Now, the Teacher bids, when you use it to pour boiling Water on it, and keep it stirring all the Time till it be melted: She says, a Piece as big as a large Walnut will make a Pint of Water very rich: And further the Lady directs, how to make Soops and strong Sauces of this Glue; and says, this is only in the Room of a rich good Gravy. Yet I will give any of her Adherents all this rich Glue, that she has made of her two fifty Pound Legs of Beef directed; and for a Wager will make a better Soop of five Pounds of Beef, with only the Help of Roots.

COMMENT: Portable soup is the equivalent of a modern bouillon cube and was just as portable. Past Master made both veal and beef pocket soup. The flannel did not present a problem.

In Page, 130: This Teacher bids bake an ***Oat Pudding:*** She say, of Oats decoticated [decorticated], take two Pounds, and of new Milk enough to drown it, and eight Ounces of Rasins stoned, an equal Quantity of [dried] Currans neatly pick'd, a Pound of Sweet-suet finely shred, six new-laid Eggs well beat; season with Nutmeg, Ginger, and Salt: This, says she, will make a better Pudding than Rice. But I say that Rice is far superior to half-sheel'd [shelled] Oats for Puddings, nor would I advise any to eat this Oat Pudding that has a sore Throat, for the Seeds would certainly give them great Pain.

COMMENT: Oats were home-grown; rice was purchased. Scratchy?

Her next is, *A Calf's Foot Pudding:* Take of Calves Feet a Pound minced fine, a Pound and a Half of Suet shred small, six Eggs, but half the Whites, the Crumb of a Half-penny Roll grated, a Pound of [dried] Currans, and a Handful of Flour, as much Milk as will moisten it with the Eggs, Salt, Nutmeg, and Sugar; season it to your Taste, and boil it, says she, nine Hours with your Meat.

What is there in this Pudding that can endure nine Hours boiling; the Calves Feet must be tender boil'd or they will not mince fine; the small shred Suet needs very little boiling, the Handful of Flour, the Crumbs of the Half-penny Loaf grated, Eggs, Fruit and all together, seems to me not to require above an Hour's boiling; and if it boils Nine, what will it be then, or what Limb of the Bullock can stand nine Hours boiling, and keep whole?

COMMENT: There is not a lot of meat on a calf's foot by the time you get rid of the bones, sinews, skin, and hoof. The pudding ingredients should be mixed, put in a pudding cloth and boiled with the meat. If root vegetables are cooked as well this dish is reminiscent of 17th-century one-pot meals which saved fuel, time, and energy.

In Page 136, Is Ham Pye: The Teacher bids, take some cold boil'd Ham, and slice it about half an Inch thick, to make a good Crust, and thick, over the Dish, and lay a Lair of Ham, shake Pepper over it; then lay a large young Fowl on the Ham, with Yolks of Eggs hard boil'd; and cover all with Ham, and more Pepper to be shaked on; then put on the Top-crust; bake it well, and when it comes out of the Oven, fill it with rich Beef-gravy: Adds, that a fresh Ham will not be so tender: So, says she, I always boil my Ham one Day and bring it to Table, the next Day I make a Pye of it: It does better than an unboil'd Ham.

But, I say, the Teacher might as reasonably say, that a Leg of Mutton should be first boil'd, and the next Day made into a Pye, as to boil the Ham, and then to bake it: As to her own she might order it her own Way, but when her Orders are general, her Judgment should have been better in Ham Pye making.

COMMENT: A fresh ham would be like a leg of pork. A cured ham was salted. Boiling it would have removed salt. Mutton was not salted to preserve it, so it is not a fair comparison.

In Page 193 [typo; page 139], *Is to make a Yorkshire Christmas Pye:* A Bushel of Flour is to be made into a standing Crust; which according to her Directions in *Page 145,* for *Standing Crusts* will take 24 Pounds of Butter; a Turkey, Goose, Fowl, Partridge, and a Pigeon, are to be boned, and put one within another, and all to be put into a large Turkey; Black-pepper, Nutmeg, and

Mace of each half an Ounce, Cloves a quarter of an Ounce, two Spoonfuls of Salt; this great Turkey is laid in the Crust, to look like a whole one; then is a Hare cut to Pieces, and laid on one Side; on the other Side Woodcocks, Moor-game, and what Sort of wild Fowl you can get: All to be seasoned well, and laid close; four Pounds of Butter at least is to be put into this Pye, and a very thick Lid to be laid on; and it must, says she, have a very hot Oven, and will take at least four Hours baking.

I should think that a Pye with such a Crust, and so well filled, would take fourteen Hours, if the Walls stood; which in my Opinion is impossible, for the great Quantity of Butter she orders her standing Crusts without Water, or as little as you can when you skim it off, says she; so this greasy Crust so well filled, and four Pounds of Butter put over all, must make such a Stench in the Oven, as would bring down the Pye, and if it was set whole into the Oven, it must come out in Parcels; and I think I could make a Corporation Feast of the Expence of this *Yorkshire Christmas* Pye.

COMMENT: This would have been a very large pie, to feed lots of people for several days. Such a large pie would have been trundled to the local baker and his oversized oven. Note Martha Bradley's comment, "when the pie comes home…" MB III, 357. What price tradition!

In Page 144, is Paste for Tarts. Take one Pound of Flour, three Quarters of a Pound of Butter; mixt and beat well with a Rolling-pin.

COMMENT: This is one of our favorites! Pounding any pie crust (paste) incorporates the flour smoothly and evenly.

Another Sort of *Paste for Tarts*, which is Butter, Flour, and Sugar, of each half a Pound; mixt and well beat with a Rolling-pin, and then roll it out.

But, I say, the half Pound of Flour is so far outmatch'd with the Sugar and Butter, that the ignorant Girl must exceed me in Pastry, if she can roll out a Lid for a Tart, as she is directed by her Teacher.

COMMENT: It has been made often; it is wonderful and there are never any problems with it.

In Page 145, **Is a Dripping Crust:** She orders a Pound and a Half of Beef-dripping to be boil'd up five Times in Water, and set to cool; then to work it up well in three Pounds of Flour as fine as you can, and make it up into Paste with cold Water: It makes a very fine Crust, says she, of the Sort. Say I, which Sort I would not willingly recommend to delicate Ladies Stomachs.

COMMENT: Since there isn't that much fat from roasting meat, make half the receipt from lard and it tastes just great.

Next follows *A Crust for Custards:* Take eight Ounces of Flour, to six Ounces of Butter, three Spoonfuls of Cream, mix all together, and let them stand a Quarter of an Hour; then work it up and down, and roll it thin. For my Part, I cannot find out the meaning of this up and down Custard Crust.
COMMENT: Would up and down mean back and forth with a rolling pin?

And next is, *Paste* for *Crackling Crusts.* This Crust is to be made of four Handfuls of Almonds, throw them into Water, dry them with a Cloth, and pound them in a Mortar very fine, with a little Orange-flower-water, and the White of an Egg; all to be well pounded, and put through a coarse Hair-sieve, to clear them from all the Lumps or Clods, says she; then spread it on a Dish till it is very pliable; let it stand a while, and then roll out a Piece for the Under-crust, and dry it in the Oven in the Pye-pan, while other Pastry-works are a making, as Knots, Cyphers, *Etc.* for garnishing your Pyes.

This is very odd Pastry-cookery for the Ignorant to be improv'd by, for their Teacher has left them in the Dark as to the finishing this Pye, by putting the Under-crust into the Pye-pan, and setting it in the Oven to dry; but does not tell them what this Under-crust is to be filled with, or how, or in what Manner they are to proceed with this Pye: I can see nothing she designs for it; but Knots and Cyphers for garnishing, to this Under-crust; so I call it a Cypher Pye, which in reality it must be; for if there is a Pastry-cook in *England* that can make this Paste so pliable, (as she calls it) so as to raise either Tart or Pye, or to turn either out of a Pan, I have lost my Judgment.
COMMENT: This crust is made of almond paste; it would have had a sweet filling as in the following, found in HG's first edition.

> *To make a* Sweet-meat Pudding.
>
> PUT a thin Puff-paste all over your Dish, then have candied Orange and Lemon-peel, and Citron, of each an Ounce, slice them thin, and lay them all over the Bottom of your Dish, then beat eight Yolks of Eggs, and two Whites, near half a Pound of Sugar, and half a Pound of melted Butter. Beat all well together; when the Oven is ready, pour it on your Sweetmeats; an Hour or less will bake it; the oven must not be too hot. (*HG* 110)

In Page 166, **Is to dress a Brace [pair] of Carp***.* This Teacher bids boil the Carp in Salt and Water; and for Sauce a Pint of stale Beer, and a Pint of Red-wine; she adds, Mace, Cloves, Nutmeg, Pepper, Onion, Sweet-herbs, Anchovy, Horse-raddish, Catchup, Mushroom-pickle, and a Quarter of a Pound of Butter.

Certainly the Pint of Red-wine and the Pint of stale Beer boiled with so much hot Spice, would fuddle the Brace of Carp; yet this Teacher has ordered two baked Carp to be put into a Pan, with a Bottle of White-wine, and as many Ingredients as is above prescribed.

COMMENT: Carp is a fresh water fish; think big gold fish. Neighbors with Koi ponds are not willing to share.

And, **To fry Tench***:* She gives a whole Page of such Inconsistencies of Cream, Eggs, Bread, Herbs and Spices, Gravy, Wine, *Etc. Etc.* and after all, says, you may dress them just as you do Carp.

Next is, **To roast a Cod's Head***:* The Teacher bids, after the Head is clean wash'd, to salt it and lay it in a Stew-pan before the Fire, with something behind it that the Fire may roast it; and all the Water that comes from it the first half Hour throw away; then strew on Nutmeg, Cloves, Mace, Salt, and Flour; then to be basted with Butter: When that has lain some Time, season and flour it, baste the other Side the same Way; turn it often, and baste it with Crumbs of Bread: If it is a large Head, it will take four or five Hours baking, says she; have ready melted Butter, some of the Fish Liver bruised, and an Anchovy mixt well with two Yolks of Eggs; then to be strain'd through a Sieve, and put into the Sauce-pan again; add Shrimps, pickled Cockles, Red-wine, and the Juice of a Lemon; pour it into the Pan the Head was roasted in, and stir it all together, let it boil, and pour it into a Bason; Garnish the Head with Fry'd Fish, Lemon, and Horse-raddish.

Five Hours roasting a Cod's Head would make it more fit to grind in a Mill, than to send up to a Lady's Table. The Teacher bids, at the first laying down, to turn it often: It would be a very great Wonder if the ignorant Hand did not turn it out of its natural Shape in four or five Hours; in which Time she did not consider how many Cinders the Pan it was roasted in would catch; nay, the very Crumbs it was basted with would roast to Cinders in that Space of Time; yet has this Teacher bid, pour in all her toss'd-up Sauce into this Pan and pour it into the Sauce-pan again, and boil it all together; and, I only ask, would not the Yolks of Eggs break the Sauce? But it could not spoil the Head, because that has been done already.

COMMENT: Their cod's heads were much larger than ours; we can sometimes buy them at a Asian supermarket. Roasting here does not involve a spit.

In Page 176, ***To broil Haddocks, when they are in High Perfection:*** She bids gut and wash them clean, but don't rip open their Bellies; take out the Guts and Gills [possible without ripping open the bellies], and if there be Roes or Livers take them out, and put them in again; flour them well, have a clear good Fire and clean Grate-iron, let it be hot; lay them on, and turn them quick two or three Times for fear of sticking, and let one Side be enough; then turn the other.

This Teacher is as far out of the Art of Cookery in broiling Haddocks, as in roasting a Cod's Head: First, in putting the Roes and Livers into their Bellies; Secondly, in flouring them, and turning them quick at first on the Grate-iron; for when Haddocks are at high Perfection, I will Lay a Wager to broil a Haddock as soon as any Cook in *England* will broil the Roe: Then what must the Haddock be, if it is to broil till the Roe within it be enough? And as for flouring and turning it so very soon, this would cement it to the Grateiron; but if she would broil the Fish whole, instead of Flour, lay on plenty of Salt, and don't turn it till it's half broil'd; then turn it, and broil the other Side.

COMMENT: These are just two different ways of cooking.

In Page 150, ***Is to make a Scate or Thornback Soop:*** Take two Pounds of Scate or Thornback, which is to be skin'd and boil'd in six Quarts of Water; when 'tis enough take it up, pick off the Flesh and lay it by; put in the Bones again, and take two Pounds of any other Fish, Lemon-peel, Sweet-herbs, Pepper, Mace, Horse-raddish, a Crust of Bread, and Parsley. Boil it to two Quarts; strain it off, and add an Ounce of Vermicelli, and set it to boil; and in the mean Time take a *French* Roll, cut a little Hole in the Top, fry the Crust brown in Batter; take the Flesh off the Fish you laid by, and put it into a Sauce-pan, with three Spoonfuls of the Soop, Flour and Butter, Pepper and Salt; shake them all together in a Sauce-pan till it is quite thick; then fill the Roll with it, pour your Soop into the Dish, and let the Roll swim in the Middle.

As the Roll is filled with Fish, she gives it Leave to swim, though she had robb'd the Fish of Fins, Skin and Bones, so that it could not swim, neither would it let the *French* Roll swim; therefore it must be contented to stand upon its own Bottom.

COMMENT: HG did not mean literally swim? Did she mean the roll must be surrounded by liquid? AC does the same on p. 118. (crimps and boils) AC only has only receipts for skate, not thornback.

In Page 165, She bids, **Make a Hedge-hog thus for Change:** Two Quarts of Almonds blanched, and beat in a Mortar with Canary [sweet wine] and Orange-flower-water, two Spoonfuls of the Tincture of Saffron, two Spoonfuls of Sorrel-juice; beat them into a fine Paste, put in half a Pound of melted Butter, Nutmeg, Mace, Citron, and [*Seville*] Orange, of each an Ounce, twelve Eggs, half the Whites beat up and mixed in half a Pint of Cream, a Pound of double-refined Sugar, and work it up all together; if it be not stiff enough to make into the Form you would have it, you must have a Mould for it; butter it well, then put in the Ingredients and bake it: But, says she, the Mould must be made in such a Manner as to have the Head peeping out, when it comes out of the Oven.

A Mechanical [?] Head requires well furnished Garrets [attics?], lest the Schemes run as confused as her Way to make the Hedge-hog for Change, with such an odd Jumble as sets forth the Excellency of this Teacher's Taste and Judgment: Now, I pray, what Manner of Right hath the Tincture of Saffron, Sorrel-juice, Nutmeg, Mace, Eggs, or Cream in the Hedge-hog, baked or boiled in a Mould? If it were either reasonable that the Mould should be to make after the Hog was made; or, where can you find an Artist to make the Head peep out in the Baking? Besides, she says, you may leave out the Saffron and make it up like Chickens, or in any Shape you please; or alter the Sauce to your Fancy. Butter, Sugar, and White-wine is a pretty Sauce for either baked or boiled; or you may make the Sauce of what Colour you please; or put it into a Mould with half a Pound of Currans, and boil it for a Pudding: You may use Cocheneal instead of Saffron. She adds, Roch-allum and Cocheneal boiled in Water: This, says she, is to mix Sauces with; her Orders are to make it up like Chickens, or in any Shape you please. Now, suppose it was made in the Effigy of the Lady Teacher, garnished with Cocheneal, Roch-allum, Saffron, and Sorrel, and what other Colours the Artist fancies. She must deserve garnishing that puts Roch-allum in Sauces; for Roch-allum is an excellent Ingredient in tanning Leather for Breeches; Dyers likewise set their Colours with it; and so does the Lady Teacher set Stomachs with it.

COMMENT: Skip HG's receipt and move on.

In Page 180, **To farce Eels with White-sauce:** The flesh is to be picked off the Bone of the Eel; the Head to be left whole; the Flesh is to be beat in a Mortar fine, with half the Quantity of Crumbs of Bread, Truffles, Anchovies, Pepper, Nutmeg, and Mushrooms, mix'd well with Cream with your Hand, and lay it on the Bone; but to make it in the Shape of an Eel, and bake it: For Sauce have half a Pint of Cream, and a quarter of a Pound of Butter, stir one Way till it is thick, and pour it over the Eel.

To thicken the half Pound of Butter this Teacher has ordered a Handful of Flour, and to thicken a quarter of a Pound of Butter, there is half a Pint of Cream ordered, to stir one Way till it is thick. It must not be stirred over the Fire to be made thick, for that will shortly make it thin, and the Butter will be uppermost; but in Case it is thick, where to find a Stomach that can digest Cream and a farced Eel mixed with Cream, in the above very odd Manner, I know not.

COMMENT: We have never had the roux become thin because we were stirring it over the fire. The flour and butter thicken nicely; stir in the cream. It is not thin. AC thinks this is a very rich dish, but we don't know. She is just looking for trouble.

In Page 184, **Is to make a Collar of Fish in Ragoo, to look like a Breast of Veal Collar'd:** A Force-meat made of a large Eel, a Turbutt, Scate, or Thornback is to be laid on a Dresser; take away all the Bones and Fins, the Fish to be covered with the Farce; then roll it up tight, and open the Eel Skin, and bind the Collar with it nicely, so that it may be flat Top and Bottom to stand well in the Dish; then is an Earthen-dish to be buttered, upon which set the Collar upright, flour and butter it; let it be well baked, but take great Care it is not broken.

So if the Maid by her Teacher's Order takes a Turbutt, and accordingly rolls it up tight with this Eel's Skin, which must be a long one, for such a Roll will take a Skin a Yard and half long: So she sets this Collar upright in the Oven, but as soon as the Heat does pierce the Eel skin, crack it goes; and this upright collar may stand or fall, for the Eel Skin is no longer a Bandage for it; and instead of a Collar like a roll'd Breast of Veal, she may be disappointed with a broken Dish of Fish Farce, altogether, and learn by Experience never to trust a Collar of Turbutt with an Eel Skin Bandage again.

COMMENT: Ignore AC's complaints. She did not deal with HG's receipt accurately or completely. This is an example of "fake news." There is a tin oven reference in HG's receipt.

In Page 188, is, **To Ragoo Oysters:** This Teacher bids, take a Quart of the largest Oysters you can get [theirs could be 6" long; not so today], wash them, save their Liquor and make a Batter thus; take two Yolks of Eggs, grate half a Nutmeg, Lemon-peal cut small, a good deal of Parsley, a Spoonful of Spinage-juice, two spoonfuls of Cream or Milk; beat all well up with Flour to a thick Batter; have ready some butter in a Stew-pan, and dip them one by one in the Batter; then have Crumbs of Bread, and roll them in it; fry them quick; and brown some with the Crumbs of Bread and some without; then have ready a Quart of Chestnut sheel'd [shelled], fry them, rub Butter and Flour all over the Pan; and when it is thick, then put in the Oyster Liquor, four Blades of Mace, Pistaco Nuts sheel'd; let them boil, then put in the Chestnuts, and half a Pint of Wine; have in readiness the Yolks of two Eggs beat up with four Spoonfuls of Cream, stir all together; and when it is thick lay the Oysters in the Dish, and pour the Ragoo over them.

As much as to say, smother the Oysters with Hodge-podge made of Oyster-liquor, Butter and Flour to make it thick, Yolks of Eggs and Cream to make it thicker, Chestnuts, and Pistaco Nuts, fuddled with Wine, all to smother the Quart of large Oysters; which upon their own Shells might appear at a Nobleman's Table, and create an Appetite; but as she ragoos them, creates great Trouble to the Cook, extravagant Expence to the Master, and destroys Appetite: And as to her thick Batter of Cream, Eggs, Spinage-juice, and all the rest of her various Mixtures, it may be Labour in vain; although she dips the Oysters in the Batter, and rolls them in Crumbs of Bread; yet ten to one but they make an Escape out of the Batter, and come out of the Frying a plain Oyster. If I send up Oysters in Masquerade, I put a Coat on them, and takes [sic] great Care to Button it well, lest my slippery Chaps play me the Slip, and make their Escape.

COMMENT: AC doesn't offer a Ragooed Oyster receipt; she has an oyster pie. Clearly a dish to impress on a noble's table; anyone could serve plain oysters.

In Page 201, ***Is to fry Eggs as round as Balls****:* Three Pints of clarified Butter is to be put into a deep Frying-pan, to be stirred with a Stick till it runs round like a Whirlpool; then is an Egg to be dropt into the Middle of it, and made as hard as potch'd Eggs; so whirl it on a Dish before the Fire: They keep hot, says she, half and Hour and be soft; so you may do as many as you please: Adds, you may serve those with what you please, but nothing better than stew'd Spinage; garnish with Orange, says she.

I say those Eggs will not be round as Balls are, as they are to lie on a Dish half an Hour and be soft: Now had she boiled them in this Whirlpool till they had been as hard as Stones, they might have been as round as Balls; but she has but made a Dish of fry'd Eggs and Spinage: And a Dish of Potched Eggs and Spinage would exceed them for Beauty, and moreover would save six Pound of Butter; for three Pints of clarified Butter will require six *London* Butter Pounds: In the next Place how far does she come short in Regard of the six Pounds of Butter to fry the twelve Eggs, concerning which she makes so much ado in her Preface, in exclaiming against the Extravagance of *French* Cooks; besides, when twelve Eggs are whirled out separately one by one, the clarified Boiling like a Whirlpool would become so black, as it would not make another Dish. Now, had this Teacher ordered the Eggs to be potched and spinaged, she would have saved the Servant a vast deal of Trouble, the Master Abundance of Butter, and me sufficient Laughing at the Whirlpool.

COMMENT: It took us about 45 minutes to clarify three pounds of butter [which gave us 7+ cups of clarified butter] and to twirl a dozen eggs. We don't understand how AC came up with 6 London butter pounds. It takes 2 to do this receipt: one to deal with the eggs and the other to twirl the butter. Half the eggs were prepared in a clockwise whirl and the other half in a counter clockwise whirl. They were never as round as balls. The edges kept straggling out. Some eggs were removed when softish and it really didn't make any difference. The eggs in the second batch were slightly browner than the eggs in the first batch, but the clarified butter was now a golden color and not black as AC described. The clarified butter could definitely be used for sauces, ragoos, and other such things. We ate the eggs and found them lovely. They both had a nice, but not overwhelming, buttery flavor. Very nice to serve on sippets or with spinach.

To make a grand Dish of Eggs: To break as many Eggs as the Yolks will fill a Pint-bason, the Whites by themselves, tie the Yolks by themselves in a Bladder round, boil them hard; then have a wooden Bowl that holds a Quart, made like two Butter-dishes, but in the Shape of an Egg, with a Hole in the top: a String is to be run through the Bladder, and a Quarter of a Yard is to hang out at one End: this String is to be drawn through the Hole of this Dish, and then boiled; the Yolks put in, and the two Dishes clapt together and tied close, and with a fine Tunnel [sic] pour in the Whites through the Hole, which is to be stopt close, and boiled hard an Hour; then open it and cut the String close: Then put twenty Whites into two Bladders in the Shape of Eggs, boil them hard, and cut one in two Long-ways and one Cross-ways, and with a sharp Knife cut out some of the White in the Middle; the two long Halfs on each Side, with the hollow Part uppermost, and the two round flat between. Take an Ounce of Truffles and Morels, a Pint of fresh Mushrooms, a Jill of pickled Mushrooms, all chopt small: Boil sixteen of the Yolks hard and chop them; mix them with the other Ingredients, and thicken it with a Lump of Butter rolled in Flour, shaking your Pan round till it be hot and thick; say she: Then fill the two Rounds with this, turn them down again, and fill the two long ones; and what remains keep in the Sauce-pan: Add a Pint of Cream, a quarter of a Pound of Butter, the other four Yolks beat up in a Jill of White-wine, a Jill of pickled Mushrooms, Mace and Nutmeg; put all together, and stir all one Way till it is thick and fine; then pour it all over, and garnish with notched Lemon. This, says she, is a grand Dish for a second Course; or in case you should mix it with Red-wine and Butter, it will do for a first Course.

The two Butter-dishes, by my Calculation, will take fourteen Eggs; for seven Hen Eggs I have frequently found by Experience to weigh a Pound [Eggs are characterized in six sizes; peewee, weighing 1.25 ounces; small, 1.5 ounces; medium, 1.7 ounces; large, 2 ounces; extra-large, 2.2 ounces; and jumbo, 2.5 ounces. CH 28]; then are there twenty Whites hard boiled, and some of the Middle cut out: Altho' the Teacher might have made a more natural Figure, and occasioned far less Trouble, by ordering two Goose Eggs to have been hard boiled, cut Cross and Long-ways and the Yolks would have turned out with more Ease than a Knife could cut out the Whites; and two Goose Eggs will be as big each as these ten Whites in each Bladder: Now I compute the twenty Whites of Eggs to be equal with the Bulk of ten Eggs; the Bulk of Three is cut out of the Middle of the four Halves; so there remains the Bulk of seven Eggs, which added to the other Fourteen, will make Twenty-one: To which there is for Sauce, a Quart of Mushrooms, an Ounce of Truffles and Morels, a Pint of Cream, a Jill of White-wine, sixteen Yolks of Eggs boil'd hard and cut small, which will fill a Wine-quart*, of Flour, of the Yolks, the Butter boil'd in Flour, I think at least must be a Pound, whereby the Sauce will be so thick, as that a Spoon may stand in the Middle of the Sauce-pan; and withal to add more to this thick Sauce, she bids four Yolks more be beaten up; so that these twenty Yolks make this grand Dish of Eggs extravagantly abound with Mixtures: The Quart of Mushrooms might indeed have graced twenty Dishes; the Truffles and Morels ten Dishes; the Pint of Cream with part of the Yolks, helped to have made a very good Custard-pudding; the White-wine and all the Seasoning, set by for other Uses; and part of the Butter and Eggs (by Way of butter'd Eggs,) would have saved much Cost and Trouble, and made a better Dish: For the Task is hard enough for the Disher, to make out of a Quart Wooden-bowl two Butter-dishes in the Shape of an Egg, and withal to hold a Quart of Eggs. Reason is a noble Mistress in Cookery; and where she does not bear Rule, how mean and contemptible does an Author appear in the Eyes of the World.

COMMENT: This is supposed to be a grand dish. The kitchen must be very well equipped. Although it would be fun to try this, the lack of specialized equipment and the cost of the ingredients would be prohibitive.

In Page 211, Is ***A French Barley Pudding****.* A Quart of Cream put to six Eggs well beaten, half of the Whites sweeten to your Palate; a little Orange-flower water, a Pound of melted Butter, six Handfuls of *French* Barley, that has been boiled tender in Milk, butter a Dish and pour it in; it will take as much baking as a Venison-pasty.

But a Venison-pasty will take three Hours baking, and there is nothing in that Pudding which requires above three Quarters of an Hour baking: If the Butter be left out and three more Eggs, it will become a good Pudding; but it will be out of the Power of the tender boiled Barley and Eggs to bind the Quart of Cream and Pound of Butter together; so that there will be a Well of Oil swimming upon the Barley.

COMMENT: HG says, on p. 73, two hours for a Venison-pasty, not three. We found there was no well of oil swimming on the barley which did take a very long time to cook tender in the cream.

Next is, ***An Apple Pudding****:* To boil twelve large Pippins, after pared and cored, in four Spoonfuls of Water; and when they are soft and thick, stir in a quarter of a Pound of Butter, a Pound of Loaf-sugar, the Juice of three Lemons, the Peal of two beat in a Mortar, the Yolks of eight Eggs.

Now, my own Reason tells me that twelve Pippins must certainly carry along with them Sharpness sufficient without the Juice of three Lemons: As also, that the bitter Peal of two Lemons will be too much bitter for twelve Pippins. I likewise aver that a Pound of Loaf-sugar is too sweet; so that this is, what I may justly call, a sour-bitter-sweet Pudding. A Spoonful Pudding is something odd; that is, a Spoonful of Flour, a Spoonful of Milk, and an Egg: Now, there should have been also a Cockle-shell to boil it in.

COMMENT: Why a Cockle-shell? We don't know.

Make a spoonful-pudding.

TAKE a spoonful of flour, a spoonful of cream or milk, and egg, a little nutmeg, ginger, and salt, mix all together, and boil it in a little wooden dish half an Hour. You may add Currans. (*HG 1755*, p. 220)

COMMENT: When Clarissa made it in a wooden dish, the water boiled away and the pudding was the consistency of a German pancake, which is like a cross between an omelet and a modern breakfast pancake. It was very good.

In the Pudding Chapter there are eleven different Puddings mentioned. In the Fast-dinner Chapter there are Fifty-nine. In the Sea Captains Chapter there are eight Puddings, in all Seventy-eight; many of them repeated three, four, five, or six Times over, insomuch that some of them would make one sick of Pudding; in this Fast Chapter are eighteen Pyes, and a Multitude of them very odd ones; one more particular than the rest, although Abundance of them exceeding miserable: I shall however lay open the surfeiting Quality of one, *viz. A Salt-fish Pye:* Take a Side of Salt-fish, steep and boil it, then pick it clean from the Bones and mince it small; boil a Quart of new Milk with the Crumbs of *French* rolls, and stir in a Pound of Butter, and the Salt-fish, with Parsley, Nutmeg, Pepper, and three Spoonfuls of Mustard; lay a good Crust all over your dish, and cover it up and bake it an Hour. Let the Reader consider whether this Salt-fish Pye deserves a good Crust or no?

COMMENT: Clarissa made this, and yes, it deserves a good crust. It is possible to buy salt fish [cod] in December and January because it is part of Italian Christmas culinary festivities. It will apparently keep forever.

In Page 240, This Teacher sets out ***A Chapter for Captains of Ships to make Catchup:*** Which seems to offer Indignity to these brave Gentlemen, who are the only Supports of the Nation, and Guardians from foreign Assaults and Invasions; that venture their Lives to bring Home rich Rubies, Jewels, and grand Apparel to adorn Ladies with, bringing Home all the choicest Rarities which every Nation can afford to grace their Tables with, and all choice Wines, and rich Cordials to support their Constitutions: The Ladies might all have been poor Cottagers, if the Sea Captains had not likewise brought Home Timber to build them their Palaces. To these industrious Bees, the Glory and Ornament of the Nation, she orders a Gallon of stale Beer, Anchovies, Hot-spices, Shalots, and two Quarts of large Mushroom-flaps rubbed to Pieces; which might as well have been left out, for it would not give the Gallon of Beer the least Flavour of Mushrooms; and instead of making good Fish-sauce would surfeit the Fish. This, says she, will keep twenty Years.

COMMENTS: HG has chapter 11 for "Captains of Ships." Not for the captains to don an apron and make the catchup. This receipt for catchup is not unique to HG. AC omits the anchovies used in HG's receipt. Clarissa had done extensive research into sauces for an ALHFAM presentation and had concluded that catchups and fish-sauces and others like them were more or less interchangeable, which explains why the next receipt is a fish-sauce.

Fish-*sauce to keep the whole Year:* Take twenty-four Anchovies, ten Shalots, a Handful of scraped Horse-raddish, Mace, a Quart of White-wine, sliced Lemon, Cloves, Pepper; half a Pint of Anchovy Liquor, a Pint of Red-wine, and boil them all together till it comes to a Quart; strain it off, and two Spoonfuls will be sufficient for a Pound of Butter, says she. And further adds, it is a pretty Sauce for boiled Fowl or Veal, or in the Room of Gravy, by lowering it with hot Water.

A Mess of such Gravy, in my Judgment, would be a hearty Vomit.

COMMENT: This is very similar to some catchup receipts. The "hearty Vomit" is just a nasty remark.

This Lady gives a Receipt to *Pot Dripping:* Take, says she, six Pounds of Beef-dripping; boil it eight Times; all the Gravy on the In-side must be scraped off; then it is to be tinctured with Bay-leaves, Cloves, Pepper, Salt, and strained thro' a Sieve into a Pot, when quite cold, cover it up: Thus, says she, you may do what Quantity you please. And the best Way to keep any Sort of Dripping is to turn the Pot upside down, and then the Rats cannot get at it. She says, if it will keep on Ship-board, it will make as fine Puff-paste Crust, as any Butter can do, or Crust for Puddings.

But, I say, the Difference betwixt Dripping Puff-paste and Butter Puff-paste, is as disproportionate as Pebbles are from Diamonds: Besides, I can never agree in Opinion with the Lady Teacher, for the Drippings to be shipped off, and that for two Reasons: First, I don't think it reasonable that these brave Heroes should be fed with Kitchen-stuff Pyes or Puddings: Crust made of Dripping must lie heavy upon the Stomachs of these brave Men, and cannot but disturb their active Souls. My second Reason is, that the Kitchen Of-falls are given to support the Poor by charitable Gentry; and are the Cooks Perquisites in Noblemens Families, which are purchased by the Poor at a cheaper Rate than Butter: With them Dripping may be a delicious Morsel to support Hunger; but what Lady before this Teacher ever found out such Virtue in Beef-drippings? I know not, for the Chance which they have of catching Cinders and Ashes would (I should think) set the Ladies Stomachs against it: Yet, such is the Delicacy of this Lady Teacher, as that in her Orders to bake Fish, she bids, lay it in a Dish and stick some Bits of

Butter, or fine Dripping on the Fish. And in Pea-soop, she orders salt Pork to be boiled in it. Likewise, orders for a Pudding, that a good Crust be made with Dripping; and five Pounds of salt Pork to boil four or five Hours in this good Dripping Crust. Nay, six Puddings more she has ordered, and not so much as one Egg amongst them all.

COMMENT: This was supposed to be used for shipboard use and most of the consumers would have been officers. Modern historic cooks can keep all sorts of things in metal coffee cans with plastic lids if they store them upside down as HG suggests.

In Page 251, Is to pot Pigeons or Fowls: This Teacher bids season them pretty well with Pepper and Salt, and bake them in Butter till they are tender; then drain them from the Gravy, lay them in a Cloth that will suck all the Gravy up, and season them again with Salt and Pepper, Mace and Cloves: They are to be put down close in a Pot, and cover'd with Butter near an Inch thick above the Birds: Thus, says she, you may do all Sorts of Fowl, only wild Fowl should be boned.

To season potted Fowl with so much hot Spices, and to press out the Juice or Gravy, sets forth the Teacher's Judgment in cold as well as hot Dishes; for next she pots a cold Tongue, beats it in a Mortar with melted Butter and two Anchovies till its [sic] mellow; then puts it in Pots and covers it with clarified Buter: Thus, says she, you may do wild Fowl.

How various and changeable is this Lady, when she orders so much hot Spices above! but here says not one Word of it: Two Anchovies chopt in cold Tongue or wild Fowl, would surfeit both: Can any Thing eat better than a well cured Tongue? or did any ever beat wild Fowl with Anchovies to pot? But she tells a second and third Way to pot Tongues, and to pot Beef like Venison; namely, for eight Pounds of Beef she takes four Ounces of Salt-petre, four Ounces of Peter-salt, a Pint of coarse Salt, an Ounce of Sal-prunella; the Beef is to be cut into pound Pieces and rubb'd with these Salts, to lie four Days, turning them every Day, and bake them tender as a Chicken; drain the Gravy from them, take out all the Skins and Sinews; pound it in a Morter, and mix it with an Ounce of Cloves and Mace, three quarters of an Ounce of Pepper, and a Nutmeg, all beat very fine; mix all well with the Meat, put clarified Butter to moisten it, and lay it down in Pots very hard; set it at the Oven Mouth just to settle, says she.

Indeed, so very great a Heat she has given it with Salts and hot Seasonings, might require such a settling as it would not get in the Oven's Mouth; and, says she, cover it two Inches thick with clarified Butter: To this add eight

Pounds of Beef, (there are Salts sufficient to colour a whole Beef red) and when it is baked tender, all the Sinews and Skin taken out, there will not be five Pounds; to which she puts an Ounce of Cloves and Mace; a Quantity which I would not put in five Stone of potted Beef, and would make it eat more like Venison than she has done.

COMMENT: HG does not press out the juice from the birds, so we wonder why AC complains about this.

Deb cooked 8 lbs. of beef just to see: She purchased 7.73 lbs. of chuck steak at $6.99/lb. and cooked it in a crock pot without adding any water. The steaks cooked down to 3.19 lbs. There were 13 oz. of "icky" stuff; discarded 4.37 oz. of fat. There were 407 oz. of broth.

Next, *Page 254,* she **pots** *Cheshire Cheese:* She pounds three Pounds of *Cheshire* Cheese with half a Pound of Sweet-butter, half a Pint of fine Canary, and half an Ounce of Mace beat and sifted like a fine Powder; and when all is extremely well mixed, press it hard down into a Gally-pot and set it in a cool Place, after covering it with clarified Butter; a Slice of this, she says, exceeds all the Cream Cheese that can be made: If she would have but told the Truth, she should have added, is invented for a Surfeit.

Now, I think, there are few Persons who are acquainted with Cream Cheese, but like it wondrous well; but then was ever powder'd Mace put into it? And if it be old *Cheshire* with the Mace, it would take the Skin off one's Mouth: Was ever such a Mixture in Cheese recommended by a Lady to exceed Cream Cheese, which is so mild that not one Grain of Salt is to be put into it, if it be right made? So there is Ten-pence for Mace, to powder; Nine-pence for a Jill of rich Canary; half a Pound of Butter to beat into the Mixture, and Pound to clarify, in order to cover this Surfeit of potted *Cheshire* Cheese.

COMMENT: Cheshire cheese can be found and/ordered from better cheese shops. If you can't get Cheshire you can substitute white, sharp cheddar cheese. Wouldn't this be a way of using old, hardened cheese? It makes a good spread for crackers or sippets.

Next, she **Collars a Breast of Veal or a Pig**: And amongst the rest of her Ingredients, bids, Penny-royal to be put in.

Next again, *Is to Collar Beef:* She bids take a thin Piece of flank Beef, and slip the Skin to the End, and dissolve a Quart of Petre-salt; after beating the Beef with a Rolling-pin, it is to be put into five Quarts of Pump-water, and to lie five Days; plenty of hot Spices is to be laid on the Beef, and the Skin is to be laid on again, to roll it tight; put it in a Pot, with a Pint of Claret, to bake it in the Oven with Bread.

In the first Place, the thin Piece of flank Beef is a small Piece for such a large Quantity of Petre-salt, sufficient to colour two Bacon Hogs; and what Reason can she shew for stripping the Skin to the End of the Beef, and to bid bake it, and tell us no more about it: For colour'd Beef is not finished when baked.

So she prescribes another Way to season a Collar of Beef; to which she doubles the Quantity of hot Spices, and adds a quarter of an Ounce of Coriander-seeds; a sufficient Quantity to fuddle a hundred Dares [dates]; then bakes it in the Pickle, and hangs it in a Net three Days within the Air of the Fire; then puts it in a clean Cloth, and hangs it within the Air of the Fire. A new and very odd Manner of collaring Beef.

COMMENT: HG used the skin to contain the roll of beef. Collared beef is usually baked in a pot with claret. Hanging the collared beef in the chimney was a way of drying it slowly without involving a smoke house. Dates have nothing to do with HG's receipt. Their inclusion is incomprehensible.

In Page 204, [sic, yes page 204] *is a Farce Meagre Cabbage:* This Teacher bids take a white Heart Cabbage, as big as the Bottom of a Plate, and to boil just five Minutes in Water; then to take out the Inside, leaving the outside Leaves whole; chop what you take out very fine, with the Fish [sic] of three Flounders clean pick'd from the Bone, four hard Eggs, a Handful of Parsley, chop all well together; mixt up with the Yolk of an Egg, a few Crumbs of Bread, and a quarter of a Pound of butter; all to be stuff'd into the Cabbage, and tye it together; put it into a deep Stew-pan, with half a Pint of Water, a quarter of a Pound of Butter rolled in Flour, the Yolks of four hard Eggs, Onion, Cloves, white Pepper, Mace, half an Ounce of Truffles and Morels, Catchup, and pickled Mushrooms; cover it close and let simmer an Hour; if it is not enough you must do it longer: Untye and lay it on a Dish, and pour the Sauce over, says she.

I agree with this Lady, that the white Cabbage is the poorest of all Cabbages, that is the Product of any Herd's Garth [peasant's garden patch], and the real Value cannot be above a Half-penny; to which there is half a Pound of Butter Four-pence, Eggs Three-pence, Flounders Three-pence, Truffles and Morels Nine-pence, hot Spices, Catchup and Mushrooms, I call Six-pence; which in all amounts to two Shillings and a Penny, to farce and sauce this Half-penny Cabbage; and when it is done, if Man, Woman or Child, Hog, Sow or Dog eat it, my Judgment deceives me.

COMMENT: We made this receipt and found it worthy of repeating. Even without the truffles, morels, and mushrooms, it was delicious! We don't know what the complaint is about, but AC p. 6 doesn't think much of it. See her comments on pp. 42–43.

In Page 225 [yes, page 225] ***Is a Salt-fish Pye:*** She bids boil a Side of Salt-fish tender, and let it be minced small; then take the Crumbs of two *French* Rolls cut in Slices, boil up with a Quart of new Milk, and put to it your minced Salt-fish, a Pound of melted Butter, two Spoonfuls of minced Parsley, half a Nutmeg, beaten Pepper, three Spoonfuls of Mustard; mix all well together; make a good Crust and lay all over your Dish, and cover it up; then bake it an Hour.

Will any reasonable Person say, this Salt-fish Pye deserves a good Crust? And if Remedies were not more dangerous than Diseases, why may not old left-off Shoes come in Vogue and Use.

COMMENTS: Shoes? Past Master prepared this dish and Clarissa made this with a hearth cooking class. People liked it more than they thought they would. You can buy salt cod in Italian neighborhood grocery stores before Christmas, and sometime after. Ask for *Baccala*. You can also find another receipt for this on p. 40 above.

In Page 258 [back where we belong] this Teacher sets forth ***How to make Pork Hams:*** To a Ham of fat Pork is a Pound of coarse Sugar, a Pound of common Salt, an Ounce of Salt-petre mixt together; and the Ham to be laid in a wooden Tray, bathing it every Day with the Pickle [brine] in which the Ham is to lie one Month; then to be hung up in Wood Smoak, and after put into a damp Place a Month or two to make it mouldy, that it may cut short and fine: And never lay these Hams in Water till you boil them, which must be in a Copper or the biggest Pot you have; put it in cold Water, and let it be four Hours before it boils; skim it well and often till it boils: If it be a large one, two Hours will boil it. Take it up half an Hour before Dinner, skin it and throw Raspings over it: She adds, after all to be sure to boil the Ham in as much Water as you can, and to keep it skiming [sic] all the Time it boils.

A very particular Way of the Teacher's curing Ham, as well as boiling it. For eight Pounds of Beef for Potting, she orders nine Ounces of Salts: and to 20 Pounds of Pork, (for that will be the Weight of a good Ham) she orders one Ounce of Salts, a Pound of Sugar, and a Pound of Salt well mixt, and rubb'd on the Ham; then laid in a hollow Tray for the Pickle to swell about it, and to bathing it every Day (with its own Liquor) for one Month. Now, suppose that the whole national Product of Hams in one Year, could be cured by this Teachers Orders, *viz.* with an equal Quantity of Sugar and Salt. In the first Place, the Teacher's Extravagancy would be obvious to any, though of never so weak a Capacity, the Price of Sugar and Salt Compar'd: Secondly, What would still be of worse Consequence, would be the Loss of all the Hams; for the Sugar would sweeten the Salt so much, as to entirely disable it from penetrating into the Bones of them; therefore consequently must putrify, when put into Trays, Troughs, or Tubs a Month, and all the Liquor to swell about them; the Spirits of which co-operating with the Juices of the Hams, would work like a Gile-fat, and in a Month's time stink worse than any Carrion. *Yorkshire,* says she, is famous for Hams; and the Reason is, that their Salt is much finer than ours in *London*; it being a large clear Salt, and gives the Meat a fine Flavour. And further informs you, that she used to have it from *Malden* in *Essex*; and that, the very same Salt (*viz.* of *Malden*) will make any Ham as fine as you can desire. How strangely ungrateful is *Yorkshire* with its famous Salt, in furnishing *Malden* in *Essex* therewith, and letting the greatest Metropolis of the Kingdom want so necessary a Seasoning: So that this Teacher could not get proper Salt for her Hams, except she got it from *Malden*; and by the strength of such Salt, and herself-sufficiency, by setting forth its Virtues so largely and clearly, which if it should exceed Glass itself, the Method she takes to use it would both destroy its Virtue and Beauty. The Lady further recommends, that Tongues put into the Above Pickle, and to lie for a Fortnight, they will be fine either immediately boil'd, or Wood smoked.

COMMENT: We don't see what her problem is with HG's receipt.

In her 10th *Page*, she informs you, **How to keep Hares or Venison sweet, and make them fresh, if they stink.** In *Page 259,* she says, that she has seen *potted Birds* so bad, as that no Person could bear the Smell thereof; and that by managing of them, she has made them as good as ever were eat.

The former she made sweet, first, by washing in warm Water; secondly, in Luke-warm Milk and Water; then by drying, and rubbing them all over with Ginger, and hanging them in an airy Place: The latter she made good by lying half a Minute in boiling Water; then applying Pepper, Salt, and Mace to them; scald their Pot, and cover with fresh Butter. I think the Teacher shews the ignorant Servant the Way to make Hams and Tongues stink, but gives no Directions how to make them fresh, except it be by skimming the Ham six Hours: And if a Ham require that Time, how many Cooks and Slaves would an elegant Entertainment require? Now, my own private Judgment gives me to understand, that six Hours skimming a Ham will in no Case avail to sweeten a bad one, but may be of Service to the Broth, by taking off the gross Fat, which might make the Hogs sick: And I must own, if the Hogs could shew any Gratitude to their Benefactress, they are under a far greater Obligation to the Lady, than Gentry are for her *Portable Soop* eight or nine Hours boil'd without skimming. Such monstrous prodigious Inconsistencies I am asham'd any cook any cook should recommend, especially a Lady; and had I not her Instructions lying before me I must acknowledge I should have been like St. *Thomas,* for his Unbelief. But finding her Treatise hugely abounding with such Inconsistencies and nauseous Instructions, I shall not give my Readers any further Trouble with them in my book.

COMMENT: AC doesn't bother with Chapter XIV Of *Pickling;* Chapter IV *Of Making Cakes, &c.;* Chapter XVI *Of Cheesecakes, Creams, Jellies, Whip Sylabubs, &c.;* Chapter XVII *Of Made Wines, Brewing, French Bread, Muffins, &c;.* Chapter XVIII *Jarring, Cherries, and Preserves, &c.;* Chapter XIX *To Make Anchovies, Vermichella, Catchup, Vinegar, and to keep Artichokes, French Beans, &c.;* Chapter XX, Distilling; Chapter XXI, *How to Market, and the Seasons of the Year for Butchers Meats, Poultry, Fish, Herbs, Roots, Fruit &c.;* or Chapter XXII *A certain Cure for the Bite of a Mad Dog.*

Professed Cookery

A White Fricassey of Chickens.

TAKE four Chickens and skin them, take out their Back-bones and cut them into Joints, leaving their Breasts whole; wash them very clean, and melt a Pound and a Half of sweet Butter in a small Hash-pan, on a very slow Stove, into which put your Chickens; add to them three Blades of Mace, six Cloves, half a Nutmeg bruised, and let them simmer an Hour and an Half, but not boil: In which Time wash clean the Back-bones, Necks and Gizzards of them. Add to them a Quart of Water, and put them into a Sauce-pan covered close; let them stew till they come to half a Pint, then strain it off; and when the Fricassey is tender, pour out the Butter and take out the Chickens: Clean the Pan, and skim the Butter clean from the Gravy, and strain it into the Hash-pan, into which put your Fricassey; add to it the half Pint of Gravy and set it on a Stove; boil six Eggs hard and take out the Yolks; then take a Jill of thick Cream, and add to it some Butter and Flour, and put them into the Fricassey; and when it boils, toss it up, and squeeze in the Juice of a Lemon, and set the Breasts with their Points square in the Middle of the Dish, and lay the Joints round the Yolks of Eggs, and broiled Livers all over, and pour on your Sauce: Then lay green Parsley and carved Lemon round the Dish, and strew a little cut Parsley over the Fricassey, and send it up.

Another White Fricassey of Chickens.

TAKE three well grown Chickens, blood them and pick off their Feathers, skin and cut them in Joints, and beat their Breasts flat; wash them clean in warm Water, and lay them in a Stew-pan, and put thereto as much soft Water as will cover them, a Blade of Mace and half a Nutmeg sliced: Let them stew on a slow Stove till they are tender; then take them out of the Broth they are stew'd in, let it boil to half a Pint, and strain it through a clean Hair-sieve; wash clean the Pan, into which put the Gravy, add half a Pint of Cream; or if you have not Cream, take the Quantity of Milk, adding double the Quantity of very sweet Butter, which makes it as rich as the Cream: Toss it up after it is boil'd, thicken it with the Juice of a Lemon and a Spoonful of pickled Mushrooms: Lay Sippets and Parsley round the Dish, and serve it up.

To make a White Fricassey of Rabbets.

TAKE young Rabbets and skin them, wash the Blood clean from them, dry them well with a clean coarse Towel, and cut them in Joints; season them with Mace and Nutmeg, and take a quarter of a Pound of Butter into a clean Frying-pan, set it on a very slow Stove, and keep it turning all the Time it is frying that it may not Brown; and when it is tender pour off the Butter; add half a Jill of Cream, white Veal-gravy the same Quantity, put thereto three Spoonfuls of thick melted Butter, boil'd Truffles and Morels very tender in Gravy, and make a Border of them round the Fricassey; the two Rabbets Heads in the Middle, with their Jaw-bones stuck into their Eyes: Lay Sippets round the Dish, with Parsley and Barberry-berries for Garnish.

Another White Fricassey of Rabbets.

WHEN you cannot get young rabbets, and must have a White Fricassey, old Rabbets have a strong Taste, which may be corrected by taking half a Jill of Verjuice, and after you have washed and cut the Rabbets into little Pieces, turn every one of these Pieces over in the Verjuice, and add a Pint of Water; take Care that the Water be soft, for hard Water will turn them red. Let them boil softly in the Water and Verjuice ten Minutes; then pour it all out, and add to them a Pint of White-gravy; let there be a Tea Spoonful of White-pepper and three Blades of Mace tied in a Muslin-rag, and boil on a very slow Stove till the Rabbets are tender, by which Time the better Half of the Gravy will be consum'd; then take out your Spices, add to the Fricassey a Jill of Cream, and about half a Jill of Mushrooms: Thicken your Sauce with a little Flour wrought up in Butter, *viz.* lay half a Spoonful of Flour on a Plate, take a Piece of Butter, and with the Back of a Spoon work up the Flour into the Butter; and when you put it into the Fricassey, toss it up all the Time the Butter is dissolving: So lay Sippets and Parsley round your Dish, and serve it up.

A Brown Fricassey of Rabbets.

SKIN the Rabbets, but keep the Ears on their Heads, and rub them all over with Butter, after that the Yolk of an Egg; then grate some Bread and rub over the Heads; pin the Ears upon white Paper at their full Length, or roast them in a Dripping-pan, or set them in an Oven; then cut the Rabbets into little Pieces, save the three hind Parts, and let their Tails be rubb'd with Eggs and grated Bread; broil and baste them well with Butter: Then season the Fricassey with Mace, Pepper, Nutmeg; flour and fry them a fine light brown; then take a Quart of brown Gravy into a Stew-pan, put in your Fricassey, and let it boil on a slow Stove till there is just Gravy sufficient for Sauce: To which add Force-meat Balls, a Spoonful of Walnut-pickle or Catchup; slice two or three small Girkins, and add to it: Then toss up your Fricasee with a little of thick melted Butter; lay Sippets round the Dish; set the hind Parts of the Rabbets with the Tails on the Middle of the Fricassey; take off the Papers from the Ears; and take out the Jaw-bones and put into their Eyes, then set them round the Fricassey. This serves for a Top-dish, in a first and second Course.

A Brown Fricassey of Chickens.

TAKE four Chickens, skin and cut them into Joints, only leave the Breast-bones whole, flat them with a Bill-knife, and season them with Nutmeg, Pepper, and Salt; flour and fry them Brown. Season all the Livers of the Chickens, dip them in Yolks of Eggs, and grate Bread over them; broil them before the Fire on a Tin-pan, baste them well with Butter, and turn them till they are crisp; then put them into a Stew-pan, with a Jill of strong brown Gravy; add pickled Mushrooms, Catchup, some Asparagus-tops boil'd tender in hard Water; cut in length and Breadth of your Thumb: Add them to the Gravy, with a Tea Cupful of plain melted Butter: Then put in your Fricassey, and toss it up on a clear Stove or Fire till it boils; and lay it on a Dish with the four Breasts uppermost, the Livers to be laid round the Fricassey. Garnish with sliced Lemon, and green pickled Girkin.

A White Fricassey of Veal.

TAKE the Udder of a Leg of Veal and stuff it with Force-meat, sew it up, and boil it with half a Pound of Veal put into a Sauce-pan, a Quart of Water, two Shalots, some White-pepper, and two Blades of Mace; slice half a Nutmeg, which add to it: Let it boil gently till there be three Jills consumed; then cut out of the Leg of Veal a thick Piece, about the Breadth of two of your Fingers, and the Length of one; cut it thin and season it very lightly with Nutmeg and Salt; then beat the Whites of two Eggs very well, and dip the Veal into the Eggs, flour it, and have some clarified Butter in a Frying-pan, with a clear Fire; and when the Butter is hot, be very quick and lay in the Veal: One Minute will do it. It must be crisp and white; take Care not to lose one Drop of its

Gravy. And when you have fry'd all the Veal, cover it and keep it hot before the Fire; strain off the Gravy, skim it well, take out the Udder, rub it over with the Yolk of an Egg, grate Bread over it, and crisp it before the Fire, cut some Parsley small, and throw over it; then take the Gravy and half a Jill of thick Cream, a Piece of Butter wrought up in Flour, put them into a Sauce-pan, and toss it up; and when it is smooth, squeeze it half a Lemon, or a Spoonful of Verjuice; then lay your Veal round the Dish, pour on the Sauce, set the Udder in the Middle: Garnish with Parsley and green Pickles.

A Yellow Fricassey of Chickens.

TAKE three Chickens; pick and singe them well, cut them up their Backs, wash all the Blood from their Bones, Flat them with the side of a Bill-knife; then season them with Mace and Salt, and fry them on a slow Stove a Quarter of an Hour: Then add to them a Quart of fair Water, and let them stew till they are tender, and till such Time as there's just as much Liquor as is sufficient for the Sauce: Then take a Pennyworth of Saffron, infuse it into a Glass of Rhenish-wine, and broil the Chicken Livers; add to them half a Jill of Mushrooms: And after you have extracted all the Colour from the Saffron, strain the Wine into the Fricassey; thicken it with Butter and Flour, toss it up; lay the Chickens whole on the dish, and pour the Sauce over them; lay the boiled Livers round them: Garnish with Parsley and carved Lemon.

A Red Fricassey of Chickens.

DO the Chickens as above directed; adding to them the same Quantity of Water; take some red Berries of a Lobster, bruise and boil them in a Jill of Water, and strain them through a Hair-sieve into the Fricassey; add to it some Force-meat Balls: And when it is stewed to a Gravy sufficient for Sauce, thicken it with a little drawn Butter; and broil the Livers and Gizzards, and lay them round the Fricassey: Garnish as above directed.

A Green Fricassey of Chickens.

SINGE, season and fry three Chickens as above directed; boil an hundred of the Tops of Asparagus in Water, and add to the Chickens; then melt a Quarter of a Pound in Butter; make it very Green with Sorrel beaten in a Mortar, and the Juice strained into the Butter; boil Parsley, and mix it with the Butter: Then when the Chickens are stewed till there is left about just half a Pint of Liquor, toss in the green Butter and Parsley: Toss it up, lay your Chickens in the Dish, with the Asparagus-tops round them, pour over the green Sauce: Garnish with Parsley, and serve it up.

N.B. By these above-mentioned Receipts, you may fricassey Partridge, Pigeons, Lamb or Veal.

To ragoo a Breast of Veal.

TAKE the thick Brisket-part of the Breast of Veal; cut it in thick Slices, and set on to stove in a Stew-pan; add to it two Quarts of Water and cover it close: Then bone the thin Part of it, and make a savoury Force-meat, and rub the Inside of the Veal with the Yolk of an Egg; upon which lay a thin Lair of Force-meat: Then roll up the Veal tight, and put it into a Pot, and let it stand two Hours in an Oven; the other stewing all the Time over a slow Stove: Add to it two Veal Sweet-breads cut in Pieces, Truffles and Morels: Boil two Beef-palates tender, and cut into Dices, some pickled Mushrooms; and when the Gravy is consumed to a Quantity sufficient for Sauce, thicken it up, and pour it into a Dish; set the Roll in the Middle: Garnish the Dish with Lemon.

To make Scotch Collops.

TWO Pounds of Veal will make a middling Dish of Collops. Cut them very thin and season them with Mace, Nutmeg and Pepper, and fry them of a light Brown; and as you fry them, cover them close up, and set them before the Fire: Put into the Frying-pan a little strong Broth, boil it and pour into a Porringer; so rub out your Pan exceeding clean: Put in more Butter and fry all the Collops; and put them to the other Collops: Then take Gravy into the Frying-pan and boil it up, and strain it through a clean Sieve into a Sauce-pan; take twenty Force-meat balls and fry them; add to the Sauce a Spoonful of Catchup, two Artichoke-bottoms cut in Quarters; boil up your Sauce: Dish up your Collops, pour on your Sauce, and lay over your fryed Balls with Rashers of Bacon, and so serve it up.

Stuffed Scotch Collops.

CUT your Collops out of the thick Part of the Leg of Veal; let them be thin, and rub every Collop with the Yolk of an Egg: Then have ready some savoury Force-meat, spread a thin Lair over every Collop, and lay it double; cut it square, and lay them on a flat-bottomed Earthen-dish well buttered; upon which strow over grated Bread: Then set them in an Oven of an equal Heat

Top and Bottom, till they are of a light Brown. In the mean Time take the Fragments you cut off the Collops, and fry them Brown; add two Pints of Water, two Shalots, and Anchovy, Jamaica and Black-pepper; and let it boil gently till three Jills be consum'd: Then Strain it, and add thereto a Spoonful of Mushrooms; take a Sauce-pan and a little Butter, boil it up, and pour it over the Dish, upon which lay your Stuff Collops: Garnish with green Pickles.

To make larded Scotch Collops.

TAKE a Fillet-piece of a Leg of Veal, and cut five large Collops off it; lard them all over with very clear and well cured Bacon, and cut some Collops very thin; beat and seaon them with Nutmeg, Mace, Pepper and Salt: Season the larded Collops on the Under-side, which is not the Side that is larded; fry them in clarified Butter, and after them the other Collops. Then have ready some strong brown Gravy, Catchup a Spoonful, some Mushrooms, or Truffles and Morels boiled tender in Water, and after in the Gravy: Fry Force-meat Balls, and put the plain Collops into a Hash-pan, where the Gravy and other Ingredients are, and toss them up over a clear Stove or Fire: Dish them up, and lay four of the larded Collops round the Bottom, and on the Middle: Garnish with carved Lemon and sliced Cucumber.

Veal *in Blankets.*

CUT out a Fillet of Veal six Collops, which must be five Inches long, and four broad; beat and season them with Nutmeg, Pepper and Salt; rub them all over with the Yolk of an Egg; then take Savoury-meat and lay on every Collop a thin Lair; make some cold Paste of a Quart of Flour, into which rub six Ounces of Butter very small amongst the Flour; beat up an Egg with as much Water as will make a stiff Paste; then cut it into six Sheets, and roll them into Squares, something larger than your Collops: Roll up your Collups; after that roll them in this Paste; every one must be roll'd in a clean Cloth, and to be boil'd an Hour: Then take them up, set three in the Dish with their Ends in the Middle, cut the other three down the Middle, lay the Cut-side uppermost, and two Cut-halves between each whole one: For Sauce, Gravy and Butter, send it up hot.

To make Veal *Olives.*

TAKE four Collops of the same Bigness as above-taught, and lay Yolks of Eggs, Seasoning and Force-meat, in the aforesaid Manner; then cut out of the Belly-part of the Bacon eight Rashers, every Rasher so long as to lap round the rolled Veal, two Rashers to every Roll; lay them on a flat bottom'd Earthen-plate, and set them in an Oven three Quarters of an Hour: Then have ready half a Jill of good Gravy, take out your Veal Olives, and pour out the Fat from them; lay them on the Dish, and the Gravy that they discharg'd in the Oven; pour in the other Gravy: Boil it up, and pour into the other Dish wherein the Olives are, and so serve it up.

A Breast of Veal *Ragoo'd*.

TAKE a Breast of Veal, bone and cut it with a sharp Knife on the Upper-side, by way of checker Work a-cross; make of Bacon and Lemon-skin Lardens an Inch Long, and lard the Breast all over the Upper-side with them of each an Equal Quantity, by Way of Mixture: Turn the other Side and Season it with Nutmeg, Pepper and Salt; half roast it before the Fire; then have ready a Quart of Gravy in a large Stew-pan over a slow Stove, into which put your Breast of Veal, cover the Pan close: Then take an Ox-foot, and cut the cloven Part betwixt the hoofs into very small Dices, by way of Ox-palates; it is exceeding fine, and answers to the same same Purpose: Take 20 Force-meat Balls fry'd, and when your Liquor is half wasted, add the Balls and Ox-foot; when you find the Veal very tender, have ready two Sweet-breads brown broiled, cut them in Dices, and add to the Ragoo: And when the Gravy is consumed to such a Quantity is just sufficient for Sauce, take 20 fresh Oysters bearded, and put them into the Ragoo a Minute before you send it up: Lay Sippets and carved Lemon round the Dish; then lay on the Veal and pour over the Ragoo.

To ragoo a *Fillet of* Veal.

CUT a Fillet of Veal, stuff it with savoury Force-meat, and put it into an Earthen-pot with half a Pint of Water; cover it over with two Sheets of Cap-paper, and tye it with Pack-thread; set it in an Oven three Hours: In which Time take a Pound of Beef, cut it into thin Slices, and take a Slice of Butter into a Stew-pan, and fry the Beef brown: Then put in three Pints of Water, two Shalots, and an Anchovy; let it boil very gently till one Pint is consumed, then strain it off into a Sauce-pan: Add to it half an Ounce of Truffles and Morels, and let them boil tender; likewise two Artichoke-bottoms cut in Quarters, Force-meat Balls, an Ox-palate boiled tender and cut in Pieces; add to this the Ragoo. And when the Veal is enough, take it out of the Oven, pour off the Gravy from it, skim off the Fat, and strain the Gravy into the Ragoo:

Then lay the Fillet of Veal on a Dish, pour over it the Ragoo, and lay Sippets round the Dish and carved Lemon.

A *Pokey* Tongue.

TAKE a large Loin of Lamb, make Force-meat of the Kidney and Fat; take out the Chine-bone, cut all the Lean in Slices, and lay them in the form of a boiled Tongue, a Lair of Force-meat and one of Lamb: When you have made it in the Form of a Beef's Tongue, cover it all over with Force-meat; set it in an Oven an Hour and a Half: For Sauce, have some brown Gravy and Capers: Set the Tongue on the Dish, and serve it up.

A Pallateen.

CUT out the thick Part of a Leg of Veal a Pound and a Half into round Slices; take three Quarters of a Pound of savoury Force-meat, and season the Veal with Salt, Pepper, and Nutmeg; lay the Kell of the Veal in the Bottom of a round Pot: Then lay a Slice of Veal upon the Kell, and upon the Veal a Lair of Force-meat; so Veal upon that, till all is laid in Lairs: Set it in an Oven an Hour and a Half; and for Sauce take the Gravy that it discharges, skimming off all the Fat: Add to it a Spoonful of Catchup, the Juice of half a Lemon; likewise half a Jill of good Gravy, thickened with a little melted Butter: Set the Pallateen in the Dish; and slice Girkin or pickle Cucumber, for garnishing: Then serve it up.

A Calf's Head *Hash*.

BE very careful of taking the Brains whole out of the Head; let it be very well washed, and boiled in soft Water: Take a Pound of Veal and cut it in thin Slices, fry it in a Stew-pan with Butter till it is brown; then take three Pints of the Broth that it was boiled in, and put into the Pan to the fry'd Veal; add to it Sweet-marjoram and Thyme: Let all boil till it is good; then cut One-half of the Head into thin Slices, strain off the Gravy from the Veal and Herbs; season the Head with Mace, Nutmeg, and Pepper; put it into the Hash-pan with the Gravy, and let it stew over a slow Stove: Then take the other Half of the Head, and cut off the Scull-bone and Mouth: Cut it with a sharp Knife a-cross, and rub it with the Yolk of an Egg; grate Bread over, and brown it before the Fire, basting it with Butter, and strew over it some Green Parsley cut small: Then take the Brains, and take off the red Strings they are covered with, dip them in Egg, strew over them some grated Bread, and have some boiling Fat to fry the Brains in; add 20 Force-meat Balls, half a Jill of pickled Mushrooms: and when the Hash is very tender, and there is no more Gravy than is proper for Sauce to it, pour in a little melted Butter: Lay carved Sippets round the Dish, and pour on your Hash. Set the broiled Half in the Middle, with Rashers of Bacon over it, and the fry'd Brains on each Side.

To hash a Calf's Head *White.*

BOIL the calf's Head in the above Manner, take out the Brains as aforesaid, and take two Quarts of the Liquor that the Head was boiled in: Add to it a Pound of Veal cut into little Pieces, two Blades of Mace, a Nutmeg cut into Slices, an Onion, and a little White-pepper; cut the one Side of the Head in Slices; and when the White-gravy is consumed to one Quart, strain it off, wash your Hash-pan, and put in the Hash and Gravy, and let it stew till the Gravy is half consumed; then make twenty Balls of white Force-meat and put into the Hash unfry'd: Add a Spoonful of Mushrooms; dip the Brains in Eggs and fry them: Add to the Hash half a Jill of thick Cream. Garnish the Dish with Sippets and Green Parsley; toss up your Hash and pour it into the Dish: Lay the Brains in the Middle, and some Rashers of Bacon round.

How to stew the other Side of the Head.

CUT a Pound of Veal or Beef thin, and fry it brown with Butter: Add to it two Quarts of the Broth the Head was Boiled in: Add to it likewise a Rocombal, this is a Sort of Garlic that is red, and exceeds Shalot or Onion; then take six Lamb-stones, and six Suckles, fry them brown, but season them with Nutmeg, Pepper and Salt first, and cut every Lamb-stone in two; then strain off the Gravy clean out of the Pan, and put in the half Head, Lamb-stones, and Suckles: Add some pickled Kidney-beans cut small; thicken the Gravy with Butter and Flour: Lay the half Head in the Middle, the Stones and Suckles round it fry'd. Parsley and green Pickles for Garnishing.

To stew a Lamb's Head *and* Pluck.

TAKE a Lamb's Head, take the Skin off it, and take out the Eyes, cut the Liver in two, wash the Head and Pluck very clean, and put it into a large Sauce-pan to boil; take half of the Liver, and beat it in a Marble Mortar, or shred it on a Board, grate some Bread, Thyme, Sweet-marjoram, Parsley, Nutmeg, Pepper, Salt, an Egg, and a Slice of sweet Butter, work it up with your Hand, and put it into a Piece of clean Linen Cloth, and boil it with the Head and Pluck, then cut the other half of the Liver very thin, and fry it in a Hash-pan with Butter and two Rashers of Bacon Ham; then take the Broth the Lamb's Head and Pluck were boiled in, and pour it into the Hash-pan and let it boil; boil thirty Asparagus, cut off their Tops, and add them to the Hash; then pour in a little melted Butter, and take the boiled forced Liver cut into Slices; then pour the Hash into the Dish: Set the Head in the Middle, lay over the Head and Hash the sliced forced Liver, and serve it up.

How to dress a Veal's Pluck.

TAKE one of the best Veal's Pluck you can get, take off the Liver, Heart, and Cat's-collop; and set on the Lights to boil in a large Sauce-pan that has a Cover; put Water to it, cover it close, and set it on the Fire to boil; then take half a Pound of the Veal's Liver, a quarter of a Pound of Beef-suet shred small with the Liver; season it with Parsley, Thyme, Sweet-marjoram, Nutmeg, Pepper and Salt: Add to it one Egg, and a little grated Bread, tie this in a Piece of clean Linen, and boil it with the Lights: Add to it Shalots, and Sweet-herbs; then cut the Veal's Heart into thin Slices, and fry in a Hash-pan with Butter; cut three Slices of the Liver and fry brown with the Heart; then take out the Lights, and add the Broth it was boiled in to the Heart and Liver; and when there is no more Gravy than what is sufficient for Sauce, slice Half of the Lights and add to it, and thicken the Gravy with a little of thick melted Butter, and pour all round the forced Liver. Lay Sippets round the Dish, and send it to the Table.

To make another Dish of Veal's Pluck.

TAKE the Cat's-collop, and with a sharp pointed Knife slit it open at one End down to the other; then force a Piece of the Liver as above, and stuff this Collop; sew up the End, and set it in an Oven, or broil it before the Fire; and in the mean while cut half a Pound of Veal into thin Slices, and fry in a clean Hash-pan, over a slow Stove with Butter; cut four Slices of the Liver and fry with the Veal; then put to it two Quarts of Water, an Onion stuck with four Cloves, Sweet-herbs, and a few Corns of Black-pepper; and when the Gravy is half consumed, strain it off; then take two Calf's-feet that has been boiled tender, take out their Bones, cut them in thin Slices, cut the other half of the Lights as above, and let them stew till there is no more Gravy than what is required for Sauce; then take the Cat's-collop and lay it in the Middle of the Hash; fry some Liver, and lay round all with Rashers of Bacon.

To make a *Ragoo of* Beef.

TAKE and cut four Pounds of the Rib-end of the Fore-crop next to the Chine, which is mixt like to a Neat's Tongue; season it with Mace, Nutmeg, Pepper and Salt, and put it close down into a Stew-pan or Pot, with a quarter of a Pound of Butter, a Pint of Water, a Head of Shalot, cover it close, and let it stand three Hours in an Oven; then take a Pound of the Buttock of Bullock Beef, and cut into thin Slices, and fry in a Hash-pan brown with Butter: Then add to it three Pints of Water, some Sweet-marjoram and Thyme, and let it stew over a gentle Stove; then make some savoury Force-meat into round Balls, two Ox-Palates boiled tender and cut into Dices; two Sweet-breads broiled brown and cut into square Dices, four Artichoke-bottoms boiled and cut into four each, and a Spoonful of pickled Mushrooms; when the Gravy is consumed to a Pint, strain it off and wash the Pan; then put in all as above into the Stew-pan; and when the Beef has been the full Time in the Oven, take it out and put it in the Ragoo, and skim off all the Fat from the Gravy that the Beef was stewed in; strain it and put it to the Ragoo, and let it stew till there is no more Gravy than is sufficient for Sauce: Lay Sippets round the Dish, and garnish with green Pickles. Set the Beef in the Middle, and over it pour the Ragoo.

Beef *a la Mode.*

TAKE a thin ribby Piece of Beef next to the Brisket, bone and roll it close up after seasoning it with Mace, Cloves, Nutmeg, and Salt; then put it into a Stew-pot that will just hold it, and let it stand in an Oven all Night; then take Bones of the Beef and boil in three Quarts of Water, with a Bundle of Sweet-herbs and an Onion; then take a Pound of Veal and cut into thin Collops, and fry brown; and when one Half of the Broth the Beef-bones was boiled in is consumed, strain it into the Stew-pan to the fry'd Veal, and let it stew to a Pint, then boil a Hundred of large Asparagus, strain off the Gravy from the Veal, and cut the green Tops of the Grass into Inch Lengths, and let them stew in the Gravy five Minutes: To keep the Beef hot you must keep it before a hot Fire, and pour the Gravy from it, and skim off all the Fat; then add the Beef-gravy to the Asparagus, and boil it up: Toast some Bread and lay round the Dish. Set the Beef in the Middle, pour over the stew'd Asparagus, and send it up.

Dov'd Beef.

TAKE four or five Pounds of the Part of the Buttock of Beef, that has Fat at the Top, Some calls it the Steek, stick ten Cloves all over, and set it into the

Oven in a Stew-pot, with a Quarter of a Pound of Butter, and half a Pint of Water; then take two Pounds of the Buttock of Beef, and fry it in thin Slices with Butter in a Stew-pan brown, then add to it three Quarts of Water, and let it stew over the Stove; then take a Pound of Carrots, boil and cut them in Dices, and a Pound of Turnips half boil them, and cut one of them in the Form of carved Sippets and lay round the Dish; cut the rest of the Turnips in Dices, and strain the Gravy when it is consumed to a Pint, wash the Pan clean and put the Turnips and Carrots with the Gravy into it; and when the Beef is tender take it out, skim off all the Fat, and strain the Gravy to the Roots and let it boil: Then set the Beef on the Middle of the Dish, your carved Sippets round, pour over your Roots and Gravy, and serve it up.

A stew'd Rump *of* Beef.

TAKE a Rump of Beef and bone it, put it into a broad Stewing-pot: add to it a Quart of Water, Shalot, a Bundle of Sweet-herbs; then cover it, and paste the Cover close, so that no Steam can get out, and let it stand in a moderate Oven eight Hours; boil two Ox-palates six Hours of that Time, an Ounce of Truffles and Morels boiled tender, cut the Palates into small Dices; then take the Beef out of the Stewing-pot, and skim off all the Fat from the Gravy, and set the Beef on a Soup-dish, and strain the Gravy into a Hash-pan: Add the Palates, Truffles and Morels, and boil them one Minute; toast Bread and cut into Dices, and put it into the Dish: Pour in the Soup and serve it up. By this Receipt you may see what Strength is in Beef, and what it is able to do without Hot-spices: If the Beef be good, the Beef and Soup will have one Taste, and by this Method any Part of the Beef may be done.

To Stew an Ox Head.

TAKE a sharp Knife and take off the Flesh from the Bones, and wash it through many warm Waters; season it with Nutmeg, Pepper and Salt, and put it into a Stewing-pot: Add to it a Pint of stale Beer, two Heads of Shalot, a Bundle of Sweet-herbs; then break the Jaw-bones, lay over the Head, cover it close, paste it, and set it in the Oven all Night; and when you take it out, if it is very tender, put the Head into a Pot, and press it down with a Cover, strain the Gravy into another Pot, and so cut some of the Head in Slices, to warm in a Hash-pan with Part of the Gravy: Lay Sippets round the Dish and send it up.

A made Dish of Lamb.

TAKE a hind Quarter of Lamb and cut off the Leg, bone it, and cut some of the Lean out of the Leg; take the Fat of the Loin and some of the Lean, and shred very fine, and season it with Nutmeg, Pepper and Salt; cut some green Thyme and Sweet-marjoram small, and add to it grated Bread and two Eggs, stuff the Leg with this, and set it into an Oven in an Earthen-pot; then cut the Loin into Collops, and season it with Nutmeg, Mace, Pepper and Salt; set on the Bones of the Leg and Loin to boil in a Quart of Water, stick an Onion with three Cloves, and boil it with the Sweet-herbs; then fry your Collops a light Brown, put them in a Hash-pan, and when the Gravy is consumed to a Jill, strain it on the Collops, and add a Spoonful of Pickled Mushrooms: When the Leg of Lamb is enough take it out, pour off the Gravy, skim off the Fat, and put the Gravy into the Collops; toss them up, pour them on the Dish, and set the forced Leg in the Middle. Garnish the Dish with green Pickles and serve it up.

Stew'd Lambs Heads.

TAKE two Lamb's Heads and split them, take out the Brains and Tongues whole, and wash them very clean, boil them in a Stew-pan till tender; then take out the Heads, and cut a Pound of Veal into Collops, and fry them in a Stew-pan on a slow Fire with Butter till they are Brown, pour in the Broth the Heads were boil'd in; then take two half Heads, and with a Knife cut each a-cross by way of Checker-work, and rub them over with the Yolk of an Egg; then strew over grated Bread and Parsley cut small, and set them on a Tin-pan before the Fire, baste them with Butter and crisp them: Strain off the Gravy, and wash the Stew-pan, and put the Gravy and the two other Halfs into it; and while it is stewing, you may take out of the Brains all the red Strings that is on them; dip them in Egg, and strew over them some grated Bread, and have some boiling Fat and fry them in; then make up half a Pound of savoury Force-meat into Balls, and fry them; then add to the stewed Head a Spoonful of Catchup, four Artichoke-bottoms cut in Quarters; and thicken the Sauce with Flour and Butter: Then set your broiled Halfs opposite to each other in the Dish, the stewed Halfs the same Way; and pour your Sauce in, and lay the Brains round the Dish with the Force-meat Balls, and serve it up.

To stew a Calf's Head.

CLEAVE the Head, and take out the Brains and Eyes; cut the Skull off and the Grisley Part with the Mouth, and put it into a Stew-pot; season with Mace, Nutmeg, and Pepper; add to it a Pint of Water, a Quarter of a Pound of Butter, some Shalot, and Sweet-herbs; cover it close, paste the Cover that no Steam can get out; and three Hours will do in a moderate Oven: And in the mean Time fry a Pound of Buttock Beef cut into Collops with Butter brown; then add to it a Quart or three Pints of Water, and let it stew into a Pint; then strain it off, and clean your Pan; boil Half a Hundred of Asparagus, and cut the Tops in half Inches long, and stew them in this Gravy; then dip the Brains in Egg, and boil them in the above Manner: Fry some Rashers of the Flank Part of the Bacon; take out the Head and lay it in the Dish; skim off all the Fat of the Gravy the Head was stew'd in; add as much as you need to the Gravy and Asparagus, and pour it over the Head; then lay the Brain and Rashers of Bacon round the Dish, and serve it up.

A rolled Breast *of* Veal.

TAKE a Breast of Veal and bone it, lay it out its Length on the Table; season it with Nutmeg, Pepper and Salt, green Thyme, Sweet-marjoram, and Parsley cut very small, rub the Yolk of Egg over the Inside of it; then strew on the Herbs, and lay Force-meat over the Roll of Veal the long way, and bind it with Pack-thread; boil it in a Stew-pan in as much Water as will cover it; and when it boils down, turn it, so that it may boil equally; when it is boiled thoroughly, pour off its Gravy, and skim off all the Fat; clean wash your Pan, and strain in the Gravy: Add to it a Jill of brown drawn Gravy, with two Veal Sweet-breads broiled and cut each into six Parts, some Force-meat Balls, and a few Mushrooms: Cut the Breast in Three, let each Part stand upright; lay carv'd Sippets and Lemon round the Dish; pour on the Gravy, and serve it up.

To dress Sheep Rumps.

TAKE eight Sheep Rumps and boil them tender; and take in the mean Time six Lamb-stones, and as many Suckles, and fry them Brown; then take some Puff-paste, and with a Jager-iron, or what is commonly term'd Runners, cut this Puff-paste into Strings as small as Tape of three Yards a Penny; then rub each Rump with Yolk of Egg, and throw over some Parsley cut small; and take the Puff-paste and lay on each Rump in the long-way, and cross them with the Paste, so as to make them a small Diamond Figure, and set them in the Oven, which is to be a sharp one; then take half a Pint of Gravy, fry 20 Force-meat Balls, and toss up with the Lamb-stones and Suckles, adding a little thick drawn Butter: Toss all together and pour on the Dish, and lay the Rumps all round it.

To dress Hog's Feet *and* Ears.

TAKE a Gang of Hog's Feet and Ears and boil them tender; then cut off all the Flesh from the Bones of the Feet, and cut it into Slices as for a Hash; then season it with Mace, Cloves, Nutmeg, Salt, and Pepper, and put it into a Stew-pan; add to it a Pint of brown Veal-gravy; and cut a Calf's Foot boil'd tender into thin Slices, and cut them in Pieces, and add to the Gravy and Feet: Then cut one Ear into thin Slices, and add to it the other cut in the same Form, dip them in Egg, and fry'd brown with Fat: Then cut pickled Cucumbers and lay round the Dish; pour in the Stew, and lay the fry'd Ear all over it, and serve it up.

To Ragoo a Beef's Heart.

TAKE a Beef's Heart, and cut out the Inside of the Meat, and lard it all over with Bacon; take a Pound of Beef-suet with a Quarter of a Pound of Meat you cut out of the Heart, shred it very fine, or beat it in a Mortar, and grate into it the Crumbs of a *French* Roll: Season it with Nutmeg, Pepper, and Salt; cut small some Cloves, Thyme, Parsley, and Sweet-marjoram; break into it two Eggs, and work it up with your Hand, and stuff the Heart with this Force-meat; set it with the Point of the Heart up in a Pot into an Oven, and cover the Pot; it will take two Hours and a Half baking: In which Time cut the Remainder of the Meat you took out of the Heart as thin as *Scotch* Collops; season them with Nutmeg, Pepper, and Salt, and fry them in a Stew-pan with Butter; then add to them a Quart of strong Broth, and let it stew, cut a Neat's Foot into thin Pieces, and add to it: When there is Gravy sufficient for Sauce, and the Heart is the Oven the above Time, take it out, set it in the Middle of the Dish, and pour over the Ragoo; throw Mushrooms over, and lay Sippets round.

To a la mode a Calf's Head.

YOUR Calf's Head must have the Skin on, the Hair singed off with a hot Poker, and after scraped clean with a Knife; then with a very sharp Pen-knife take the Head from the Bone, the Tongue taken out and boiled, the Head larded all over with Bacon, and fill'd with Force-meat made very stiff, and skewer'd in the full Height and Form it was in before, and put it into a long Pot that will hold it with Ease; cover and set it into an Oven three Hours; then take the Tongue and cut it into thin Slices, with two Sweet-breads fryed brown: And take three Jills of Beef-gravy and put into a Stew-pan, into which put the sliced Tongue and Sweet-bread, each cut into eight Pieces; add to them some Mushrooms, Truffles, and Morels, being first boiled tender in Water; and when the Gravy is consumed by gentle stewing on a slow Fire, to as much as is sufficient for Sauce, and the Head enough, take it out: Garnish your Dish with carved Lemon and green Pickles, pour on the Stew; set the Head in the Middle, and serve it up.

Lamb *in Blankets.*

TAKE a Loin of Lamb, and take the Kidney and Fat for Force-meat; cut the Flesh the long Way from the Chine, and make the Collop half a Quarter square, beat it, and make eight Collops of the above Size, and rub them over with Yolk of Egg: Season them with Nutmeg and Salt, and lay a thin Lair of Force-meat, and roll it up: In the same Manner do all the Eight. Then break six Ounces of Butter into three Pints of Flour very small, work the Butter in the Flour, then beat up two Eggs with a Jill of fair Water; make a Paste of this Flour and Butter, and roll out eight Sheets, into each one roll up a Roll of Lamb, and tye a Cloth over every one at each End; and have a Stew-pan of boiling Water ready, into which put your Lamb, let them boil a full Hour: For Sauce, have Gravy and Butter: Take them out of the Clothes; lay them round the Dish, and pour over the Sauce. Garnish with Puff-paste baked, and Sippets.

To Ragoo a Shoulder *of* Lamb.

TAKE a well grown Fore-quarter of Lamb, and cut off the Shoulder close to the Breast; with a Knife cut open the Shoulder at the broad End, take out the Shull and Shank-bones, but take Care not to break through on either Side; then stuff the Pieces where the Bones were taken out with Force-meat; lay the Shoulder on an Earthen-dish, and set it in an Oven an Hour: Then take six Lamb-stones and eight Suckles, split the Stones, season them with Nutmeg, Pepper and Salt; fry them brown, and put them in a Stew-pan; adding a Pint of Gravy, some Mushrooms, a Quarter of a Hundred of Asparagus boiled tended; cut off the green Tops, and add to the Suckles and Stones: When the Shoulder is enough take it out, pour off all the Fat; put the Gravy into the

Stew-pan, and let it boil with the Ragoo one Minute; then lay the Shoulder in the Middle of the Dish, and pour over it the Ragoo: Lay green Pickles round the Dish, and serve it up.

Minced Beef Collops.

CUT a Pound and a Half out of the Fillet; the Part of the Sirloin that lies next the Chine under the Suet, mince this as small as minced Veal; take the Marrow of two Beef-bones, cut small, and mix it with the minced Collops: Then fry them in a Pan over a slow Fire; season them with a little Pepper and Salt, keep them stirring all the Time: Lay toasted Bread round the Dish, and have no Sauce but the Marrow and themselves.

Broiled Beef Collops.

CUT Stakes off the Rump of Buttock-beef half an Inch thick; have a very clear Fire and a clean hot Grate-iron, lay two Stakes on at a Time, and keep them frequently turning; when the Stakes are rather hard, they will be enough: Then lay them on a hot Dish, with scraped Horse-raddish. If you observe the Directions, the Beef-stakes will discharge more Gravy than needful for Sauce.

To make Veal Cutlets.

TAKE a Neck of fine Veal, cut a Rib to Every Cutlet, and flat them with the side of a Bill-knife; then season them with Mace, Nutmeg, Pepper and Salt; rub each Cutlet with the Yolk of Eggs, grate some Bread, and roll each Cutlet in it; have some clean Beef-fat boiling hot in a Hash-pan on a Stove, and fry them very quickly on it: For Sauce, have some Butter, Gravy, and Mushrooms; pour it into a hot Dish, lay the Cutlets crisp and hot on the Sauce, with Lemon round the Dish, and serve it up.

To make a Pellow.

IF you boil a Knockle of Veal, take care your Pot be very clean; put no more Water than will cover it, with a little White-pepper, and three Blades of Mace; when the Veal is enough boiled, strain off the Broth into an Earthen-pot, and let it stand all Night; then skim off all the Top, and take two Quarts of this Broth into a large Sauce-pan, set it on the Fire, and when it boils, put in a large Fowl; be sure to skim it very well when it boils: Then add to it three Quarters of a Pound of Rice, let it boil till the Fowl is tender, and the Rice seems thick; then take up the Fowl, and add a Jill of thick Cream to the

Rice; when it boils, cover the Fowl with Rice, and pour the Remainder into the Dish: Lay boiled Spinnage round the Dish-edge, by Way of Garnishing.

Turkey *a la Royal.*

TAKE a Turkey after it is well pick'd and sing'd, cut it down the Back, and bone it, only leave the Pinions on, and lard it all over with Bacon; make savoury Force-meat, and fill the Places where you took out the Bones; put into the Body and Crop a Pound and a Half of Force-meat, sew the Back up again with strong Thread, leaving a Piece of the Thread to pull out the Rest by, when it is ready to send to Table: Skewer it in the same Form as for roasting: Then set it on a deep Earthen-dish, and set it two Hours in an Oven; cover it over with a sheet of Cap-paper well butter'd: For Sauce, take a Jill of brown Veal-gravy, and take off the Beards of 30 Oysters, after you have plumpt them; then add a Spoonful of pickled Mushrooms. When you take out your Turkey, skim all the Fat off the Gravy, that is in the Dish it was baked in; add this Gravy to your Sauce: Lay carved Lemon and Sippets round the Dish, pour on your Sauce, and set on your Turkey. Remember to pull out the Thread you sewed up the Back.

To a la mode a Goose.

AFTER your Goose is well picked and singed, cut it down the Back, and bone it in the above Manner; make two Pounds of Force-meat, and stuff it with; sew up the Back as aforesaid, and with a sharp Knife make checkered Work on the Breast of it; lay it on a flat-bottom'd Dish, and rub it all over with the Yolk of Egg; then strew on grated Bread and some Butter; set three Hours in the Oven: For Sauce, have a Jill of Gravy, and a Jill of scalded Goose-berries, which pour into the Dish; set the Goose on the Middle, and serve it up.

To a la mode Fowls.

TAKE three young Pouts and bone them, put a Quarter of a Pound of Force-met into every Fowl, but they are not to be cut down the Backs, the Bones are to be taken out at the Neck-end of them; when they are equally stuffed, put every Fowl into a Bladder, and boil them an Hour: Lay Puff-paste, Sippets, and carved Lemon round the Dish: For Sauce, have some white Veal-gravy and Mushrooms, six Yolks of Eggs hard boil'd whole; thicken it with Flour and Butter. Take out the Fowls, set them on the Dish, pour on the Sauce, and serve them up.

Chickens *a la Royal.*

TAKE four large Chickens, pick, singe, and clean them well, cut them down the Back, and bone them; take half a Pound of Marrow, half a Pound of Beef-suet, and half a Pound of the Flesh of a Fowl, with grated Bread, Eggs, and Seasoning into a Force-meat, stuff them, lard them with Bacon, sew up their Backs, and skewer them as if for roasting, leave on their Pinions; lay them on a flat-bottomed Earthen-dish, and set them in an Oven: Boil half a hundred of Asparagus-tops tender, and cut into half Inch Lengths; take a Jill of brown Veal-gravy, and boil the Grass up in it, thicken it with Butter and Flour; then take out your Chickens, and set on the Dish. Garnish with carved Lemon, and pickled Kidney-beans.

A Ragoo of young Ducks.

KILL three young Ducks, pick, singe, and bone them well; stuff them with savoury Force-meat, let the Feet be kept on, and take off their Stockings; put in each three small Skewers at an equal Distance from each other, to keep them as in the Form for roasting: Then take a Stew-pan, and set it on a slow Stove, with four Ounces of Butter, and melt it; then flour your Ducks, and fry them brown; adding a Quart of Veal-broth, and let them stew with their Livers, Gizzards, and Pinions, an Onion, and Sweet-herbs; and when half of the Gravy is consumed, take out the Ducks, strain it, and skim off the Fat; boil a Pint of green Peas in Water, and drain them through a Hair-sieve; then put them to the Gravy that the Ducks were stewed in, and keep it on the Stove till it boils, then put in the Ducks; squeeze in the Juice of a Lemon, pour in half a Jill of thick melted Butter, toss all well together, and serve them up.

A jugg'd Hare.

SKIN your Hare and cut it into Joints, season it with Mace, Nutmeg, Pepper and Salt; clap it close in an Earthen-mug, and lay over it half a Pound of sweet Butter; then cover it close, paste it down, and set it three Hours in an Oven: Take its Liver, with a Quarter of a Pound of Beef-suet shred very fine, or beat in a Marble Mortar; add Shalot, green Thyme, Parsley, Sweet-marjoram, Nutmeg, Pepper and Salt, the Crumb of a Half-penny Roll steep'd in Milk; then squeeze out the Milk, and take the Bread and an Egg, mix all together; flour a Piece of Linen Cloth, and put this Pudding into it, tye it up, and boil it: Then take the Head of the Hare, and rub it over with the Yolk of

Egg, baste it with melted Butter, then grate Bread over it, and set it into the Oven: When the Hare is enough, that is, when it has been in the Oven the above Time, take it out, and pour from it all the Gravy; add to it half a Jill of Beef-gravy, and thicken it with Butter and Flour: Then lay Sippets round the Dish, into which lay the Hare; pour over the Gravy, cut the Pudding in Slices, and lay all over; set the Head in the Middle, and send it up to Table.

Cocks-combed Tripes.

TO cocks-combed Tripes, you must have an Iron made in the Shape of a Cocks-comb, and take the lean Part of the finest Tripe you can get; cut out a Pound of Cocks-combs, and have three Jills of Beef-gravy, into which put your Cocks-combs, and let them stew; then cut the thick Part of a Bullock's-foot into thin Dices, and add to them; cut a Piece of the Double-round, and dip it in Batter; cut some of the thin Tripe, in the Shape of half a Crown, and ten of these fry Brown: Then toss up the Cock's-combs, with a little Vinegar and Mustard, and pour them on to the Dish: Lay the Double-tripe in the Middle, and the other round it. Garnish with pickled Onions and Barberry-berries.

To fry Tripes.

WASH and dry your Tripes well, make a Batter of an Egg, a Spoonful of Flour, and three Spoonfuls of Milk beat very smooth; then dip in your Tripe, and have ready some fine Beef-fat boiling, and fry the Tripe a fine crisp light brown: For Sauce, melted Butter and Mustard.

To fry Neat's Feet.

TAKE all the Bones out of the Bullock's Feet, and cut in Pieces the Length of your Finger, and the Breadth of Two; make the aforesaid Batter, and dip each Piece, frying it in Fat as for Tripes: For Sauce, Mustard, melted Butter and Vinegar.

Cased Veal Cutlets.

CUT out of a leg of Veal twelve thin Collops, let them be a direct Square; season them with Mace, Nutmeg, and Salt; rub them over with Yolk of Egg, grate some Bread and throw on each Side of them, and make for each a Sheet of Puff-Paste no thicker than Wafer, paper close round the Sides of the Cutlets, and set them in a Tin-pan into a hot Oven: If the Oven is equally hot Top and Bottom, they will be done in ten Minutes, and will be savoury and crisp, and is sent up without Sauce. This Way is very much liked by Ladies and Gentlemen of weak Constitutions and tender Stomachs.

To dress a Calf's Head.

TAKE out the Eyes and split the Head, take out the Brains, wash the Head in warm Water, and afterwards in cold Water, till it is very clean, and then boil it; when it is enough, take it up and cut it a-cross with a sharp Knife till you make Dice-work of each Side; then rub it over with Yolk of Egg, throw on some grated Bread, and set it in a Tin-pan before the Fire; but if you have an Oven rather use it, only you must baste with melted Butter before you put it in, and let it stand till it is brown: For Sauce, boil the Brains and mix with melted Butter, and a Spoonful of Vinegar. Set on the two Halfs upright in the Dish, lay broiled Rashers of Bacon all over the Skull, and round the Dish; then serve it up.

To roast a Pig *like* Lamb.

TAKE a fat Pig and kill it, take off the Hair and skin it, cut into Quarters and draw it with Parsley: Take the Skin and Head of it; take the Bones out of Two Rabbets, rub the Inside of the Pig with Yolk of Eggs, and join the Rabbets close to the Skin of the Pig; take the Bottom of a long *French* Roll, take out the Crumb, put a clean Rag within the Roll to keep it up, fix the Roll to the Pig's Head, and lay it in the Inside of the Pig; then turn them over into a Tin-pan, and set it into an Oven, with Flour drudged over it; when it is near done, take it out, and wipe off the Flour with a clean Wing of a Goose, rub it all over with clean Feathers dipt in melted Butter, throw Salt over it, and set it into an Oven till it is enough; then have in readiness a Jill of Gravy, with a little boiled Sage in it; draw the Pig, and with a clean Wing dust all the Salt off it; take the Cloth out of the Roll, send it up Whole to the Table; let the Roll stay within it, and pour the Gravy into the Dish. So you have four Quarters of a Pig and a whole one, out of one Pig, by the Art of Cookery and a little Help.

A Made-Dish of Sheep Heads *and* Tongues.

TAKE two good Weather Heads and eight Tongues, wash your Heads well after you have split them and taken their Eyes out; put them into a Pot with just as much Water as will cover them, and take Care of all the Brains; wash all the Tongues, and boil them with the Heads: Take a Pound of Veal and cut into thin Collops, fry them brown on a slow Stove, in a Hash-pan; then take up the Heads and Tongues, strain three Pints of the Broth into the Hash-pan, and let it boil; then take the eight Tongues, lard and blanch them with Bacon, pick the Flesh clean from the Bone of the Heads, and take great Care to keep it whole, *viz.* not to break through, and disfigure the half Face of the Sheep: Then season the Heads with Mace, Nutmeg, Pepper, and Herbs cut very small; roll out a Sheet of Puff-paste as thin as Wafer-paste, cover each Side of the Sheep's Face with it, and set it in the Oven: Take out the larded Tongues and strain off the Gravy, wash your Pan clean, put in your Gravy and Tongues; add to them some Mushrooms, Truffles and Morels stew'd tender, 20 Force-meat Balls, dip the Brains in Egg and fry them in hot Fat: Toss all up, lay the Tongues round the Dish, pour on the Gravy, Balls, and Mushrooms; set the Heads in the Middle, the Brains all over, so serve it up. This is a Head-dish for a first Course.

A Made-dish of Sweet-breads.

TAKE four Sweet-breads, and season with Nutmeg and Salt; one of the Largest rub over with Yolk of Egg, grate Bread, roll it on, and broil it before the Fire; season the other Three, and fry them brown with Butter; take a Pint of brown Veal-gravy, cut the three Sweetbreads into Dices, and put them into the Gravy to stew; boil eight Eggs hard, and take out the Yolks whole: When the Gravy is consumed to what is sufficient for Sauce, add to it a little melted Butter, and toss it up. Lay Sippets and carved Lemon round the Dish, pour on the stew'd Sweet-breads, lay the broiled one in the Middle, with Yolk of Eggs all over, and serve it up.

A boiled Turkey.

BOIL your Turkey in Oat-meal and Water; take Sellery and cut in Pieces no larger than the Breadth of your Finger; take a Pint of White-gravy of Veal, and put to it a Pint of cut Sellery, let it stew till the Sellery is tender, then grate in a little Nutmeg and Salt, add to it some plain melted Butter: And when the Turkey is enough, take it up and set it on a Dish; pour over your Sauce, and garnish your Dish with carved Lemon.

A boiled Turkey *with* Rice.

SKEWER your Turkey for boiling, and take a Quarter of a Pound of Beef-suet, and the Crumbs of a Halfpenny Roll grated, a little Nutmeg and Egg work'd up together with your Hand, put it into the Turkey's Crop, sew it up, and put it into a Pot and boil it; then take half a Pound of Rice and boil tender in Water, and when it begins to thicken, take a Quarter of a Pound of Butter and toss it up with, adding a little Nutmeg and Salt to it: Set the Turkey on a Dish, and smother it with Rice; pour the Remainder on the Dish and serve it up.

A boiled Turkey *and* Oyster *Sauce.*

PUT your Turkey up for boiling, and grate the Crumb of a Penny *French* Roll; take a Slice of sweet Butter and work up in the Crumbs, grate Nutmeg and Salt: Add an Egg, and stuff a little Thyme, Parsley, and Sweet-marjoram cut very small; work all well together, and stuff the Crop of the Turkey, sew it up, and boil it; then take half a Hundred of good fresh Oysters, and put them a Minute or two on the Fire to plump, and take one by one out of their Liquor; then melt a Quarter of a Pound of Butter, into which put your Oysters with a little of their Liquor: Add a little White-wine, Nutmeg, a very little Bread boiled in Water, toss up all very well; take up your Turkey, and lay it in your Dish, and pour on your Oyster-sauce: Lay Sippets round Dish and carved Lemon, so send it up.

A boiled Fowl *smother'd with* Onions.

PUT up your Fowl for boiling, and let it be well singed; after rub it very well, wash and dry it; then dust a little Flour over it, boil it in soft Water, it will be white if you do not over-boil it; and boil six large Onions very soft, beat them to Pulp, and mix them with melted Butter: Lay the Fowl on a Dish, and pour over the Onion-sauce. The same Sauce is made for boiled Rabbets.

To make a Venison Pasty.

BONE your Venison and season it with Black-pepper and Salt, put it in a Pot and cover it close; set it two Hours in an Oven, put into the Pot over it, half a Pound of sweet Butter, and accord-to the Size of your Pasty-pan make a Quantity of Paste; break two Pounds of Butter into four Pounds of Flour, mix it with cold Water to a Paste; cut a Pound of Butter into Slices and lay over the Paste, drudge Flour over the Butter, and roll it out three Times, drudging Flour each time, cover the Inside and Edges of the Pan; take the Venison out of the Oven, and put into it, and if it wants Fat, take the Fat Laps of a good Shoulder of Weather Mutton and lay over it; then lay over all a Sheet of Paste, and cut out Leaves and Flowers on the Top of the Pasty: Two Hours will bake it; have a Pint of rich Gravy in Readiness to pour into the Pasty as soon as it comes out of the Oven, and send it up.

A Mutton Pasty.

TAKE a hind Quarter of little *Scotch* Mutton, bone and skin it, and bake it in an Oven in the aforesaid Manner; put it in a Pasty-pan, as is directed; and give it the same Time to bake in: It will not be much inferior to a Venison Pasty.

A Florentine.

TAKE two Bullock's Feet and take out all the Bones, shred the Meat very small, as if for minced Pyes; blanch a Pound of *Jourdon* Almonds, and mince small with the Feet, stone half a Pound of Rasins and cut small, a Pound and a Half of Currants well picked and washed, a Pound of Apples cut small, and half a Pound of Sugar; season with Mace, Cinnamon, and Nutmeg; make Pasty-paste and lay round the Dish-edge, and put in your minced Meat, mixing it well; then cover it with a Sheet of Paste, and cut out your Florentine: Bake it two Hours, and serve it up.

A Sweet Veal Pye.

CUT a Loin of Veal into Chops, and season it with Nutmeg, *Jamaica* Pepper, and Salt; take half a Pound of Currants, half a Pound of Rasins stoned, and a Quarter of a Pound of Almonds; take Part of the Kidney-fat, shred it small or beat in a Mortar, and some grated Bread; season it with Nutmeg and Salt, add Currants and an Egg, and mix all up into round Balls; then lay a Lair of Veal, and upon that strew Fruit and Almonds, then another Lair of Veal, and upon that strew Fruit and Almonds, lay over that the Force-meat Balls, cover up your Pye, and bake it an Hour and a half in an Oven; make a Caudle of a Jill of Cream, with a little Butter, half a Jill of White-wine, and a little Sugar. You may make a sweet Lamb Pye after the same Manner.

A Mutton Pye.

TAKE a Neck of Mutton and cut into Chops, scrape some small Potatoes, and season your Chops with Pepper and Salt, and lay a Rim of Paste round a Soup-dish; then lay a Lair of Mutton, and on that Potatoes, cover the Potatoes with the rest of the Mutton, and fill up the Dish with the rest of the Potatoes, put a Pint of Water into the Dish and cover it up: It will take two Hours Baking.

A Hare Pye.

BONE a Hare, and make a Pudding for her of the Liver, a Quarter of a Pound of Beef-suet, some grated Bread, and an Egg; season with Nutmeg, Pepper, and Salt; cut Thyme, Parsley, Sweet-marjoram very small, and a little Shalot; mix these with the Pudding, and put it into the Hare; raise a standing Crust for it, and model your Paste into the shape of a Hare, set the Hare on her Belly as she is in her natural Seat: When you take off the Skin, skin the Ears, and set her with her Head down, and her Ears between her Shoulders; if you are an expert Pastry-cook make the Figure of the Hare on the Lid of the Pye: Let her have two Hours and a half baking; pour into your Pye as soon as taken out of the Oven, a Pint of Veal Gravy that Spices have been boiled in, and send it up.

An Alio *of small* Birds.

TAKE two Dozen of small Birds and pick clean, make a Force-meat of the Marrow of a Beef-bone, and the Breast of a Fowl, beat in a Marble Mortar, or shred very fine on a Board; season with Mace, Nutmeg, and Salt; take the Crumbs of a Half-penny Roll and soak in the Cream, and an Egg, mix all well together; boil two Beef-palates tender, and cut into small Squares; then season the Birds and Palates with Nutmeg and Salt; lay the Birds into a raised Crust not above three Inches high, lay the Palates between the Birds, and spread the Force-meat all over: An Hour will bake it; have in Readiness half a Pint of Veal-gravy, and pour into it as soon as it is taken out of the Oven.

A Chicken Pye.

TAKE five young Chickens and skin them very clean, grate a Nutmeg and mix with Salt; take a Quarter of a Pound of Butter and mix with the Nutmeg and Salt, and divide it into five Parts; take out the Breast-bones of the Chickens, put them up as for boiling, cut off their Legs, put into each Chicken a Part of the Butter, lay them into a Dish or a Baker that just holds them, turn their Breasts down, lay Puff-paste round the Sides of the Dish or Baker, cover it with Puff-paste, and bake it in an Oven an Hour; then boil half a hundred of Asparagus in Water, cut them into half Inch Lengths, have some Veal-gravy ready, and stew them in the Gravy a Quarter of an Hour; then take the Lid off the Chickens, and turn the Breasts up, and pour on the stewed Asparagus and Gravy.

A Beef-stake Pye.

TAKE two Pounds of Beef out of the Fore-chine, that lies next to the Ribby-end, cut it very thin; season with Mace, Nutmeg, Pepper, and Salt; boil three Ox-palates tender, and cut small; make Pasty-paste, roll it out, and lay a Paste round the Rim of the Dish; lay in your Beef-stakes, and the Palates between the Stakes, add three Slices of Butter, and cover them with the Paste: Bake the Pye two Hours, and when you take it out of the Oven, pour into it half a Pint of strong Broth, and send it up.

A Mutton-stake Pye.

CUT out the Part of a Leg of Mutton where the Pope's Eye is, and cut it round, so that the Pope's Eye may appear in the Middle, the Mutton round it as a Border, and cut the Slices thin; take a Pound of very small Kidney-potatoes and scrape them; season the Mutton with Pepper and Salt; lay a Lair of Mutton, and a Lair of Potatoes till your Dish is full, cover it with thin Slices of Butter, and make the aforesaid Paste in the above Manner: Bake it, and when it is enough pour in a Pint of Mutton-gravy, and send it up.

A Duck Pye.

BONE a Couple of Ducks, and after you have picked and singed them well, wash them clean, and dry them with clean Towels; take a Pound of white Force-meat made of the Breasts of Fowls, Beef-suet, and grated Bread; season it with Nutmeg, Pepper and Salt, Thyme, Sweet-marjoram, and Parsley cut small, and work it up with an Egg; rub the Inside of the Ducks with the Yolk of an Egg, and lay a thin Lair of Force-meat upon it; put the Ducks in their natural Form, and raise an ovel Crust, into which lay the Ducks, and lid the Pye: Bake it two Hour, in which Time make some brown Gravy: Add to it a Veal's-suckle cut into eight Parts, two Artichoke-bottoms cut into Quarters;

when the Pye is baked cut up the Lid, boil up the Gravy and pour over the Ducks, and send it up.

A Ham Pye.

TAKE a two Years old well cured Ham, and lay it in cold Water all Night, or twelve Hours; then take it out, take off all the Skin, cut off the rusty Part of the under Side of it with a sharp Knife; then put it into a long Earthen-pot that will just hold it, and lay it with the fat Side uppermost; then put to it two Bottles of rough Cider; cover it close, and set it in an Oven an Hour and a half; raise a Crust in the Shape of a Ham, as thick as the Walls of a Goose Pye, into which put the whole Ham; lid the Pye, and set it in an Oven two Hours and a half; in which Time make a Ragoo of strong Gravy, two Veal-suckles broil'd and cut in Dices, six Artichoke-bottoms cut in Quarters, Force-meat Balls, Truffles and Morels boiled tender, and Mushrooms, and toss up the Ragoo; when you take out the Pye cut up the Lid, and pour it over the Ham; ornament it with various Shapes of Paste cut out, as wild Beasts, and Flowers: Send it up without the Lid.

A Christmas Goose Pye.

TAKE a Stone of Flour, and boil up four Pounds of Butter in three Quarts of Water, and mix the Flour with the Butter first; then take as much of the Water as will mix the other Part of the Flour, work it well together, and when it is cool raise an ovel Crust; then take a fat Goose and a Turkey, pick off all the Feathers, clean and cut up their Backs, and take out all their Bones; take a Bullock's Tongue, blanch and split it; season the Turkey and Goose with Nutmeg, *Jamaica* and Black-pepper: Lay the Turkey on the Bottom of the Pye, and upon it the split Tongue, cover it with the Goose; lay over the Goose all the Seam, that is the Fat you took out of her; and make a thick Lid, cover the Pye, and paper it well: It will take six Hours baking; when you take it out of the Oven, pour into it a Pound of melted Butter, and set upon a cold Stone till it is cool.

An Ox Cheek Pye.

BONE an Ox Cheek and wash it in many Waters, dry it with a clean Cloth, and season it with Black and *Jamaica* Pepper, and Salt; put it into a Pot, and put a Jill of Claret to it, cover it close, pasting it so that no Steam can get out, and set it four Hours in an Oven; then make Pasty-paste, and lay a Sheet round the Edge of a Soup-dish; take the Ox Cheek whole out of the Pot it was baked in, and put it into the Soup-dish: Add to it a Quarter of a Pound of Butter, lay on it a thick Sheet of Paste, and bake it two Hours in an Oven; make a Pint of strong Beef-gravy, with a Jill of the Liquor the Head was first stewed in, and when it is taken out of the Oven, pour this into the Pye, shake it well and send it up: This eats very much like Venison, and has been taken for Venison by tolerable Judges.

A *Sweet* Mutton Pye.

TAKE a Loin of Mutton and take off the Skin, cut the thin Flank Part off it, and cut the Chine Part into Chops; season it with *Jamaica* and Black-pepper, and Nutmeg; take half a Pound of Currants, and half a Pound of Rasins, stone the Rasins, pick the Currants, wash them and dry them with a Cloth; take a Quarter of a Pound of Sugar; then lay a Lair of Mutton, upon which lay Fruit and Sugar, cover the Fruit with Mutton, and strow over the Remainder of the Fruit and Sugar; then put in a Pint of Water, so cover the Dish with Paste, and bake it two Hours.

A *Savoury* Turbot Pye.

TAKE two Pounds of Turbot and cut a Pound and a half into thick Slices; season it with Nutmeg, Pepper and Salt; make a raised Crust very thin, lay in your Turbot, lay on it a Quarter of a Pound of Butter, lid the Pye, and bake it an Hour and a half; in which Time cut the other Half into thin Slices, and fry brown with Butter in a little Hash-pan, and add to it a Quart of Water; then take half a Hundred of Oysters, heat them in a Sauce-pan, take off their Beards, and when the Fish-gravy is two Parts consumed, strain it into a Sauce-pan: Add to it the Oysters with a little of the Liquor, a Spoonful of Catchup, and a Spoonful of Walnut Liquor; work a Piece of Butter and Flour, and thicken it up, set it on the Fire till it boils, and toss it up; when the Pye has been the above Time in the Oven, take it out, cut up the Lid, pour in the Oysters and Gravy, lay on the Lid, and serve it up.

A *Sweet* Turbot Pye.

TAKE a Pound and a half of Turbot and cut into thin Slices; season with Nutmeg, Mace and Salt; take half a Pound of Currants, wash and pick them, and half a Pound of Rasins, stone them; make a Puff-paste Crust, lay Paste round the Sides of the Dish, lay a Lair of Turbot, and cover it with Fruit; then cover the Fruit with Turbot, and on it strew the Remainder of the Fruit, and lay over all a Quarter of a Pound of Butter, then fix on the Lid; one Hour will bake it: And when it comes out of the Oven, make a Caudle of melted Butter and Sugar, and half a Jill of White-wine, and pour into the Pye after you have cut up the Lid, and send it up.

A Salmon Pye.

TAKE a Joul of Salmon and cut into thin Slices, take half a Jill of Verjuice, and rub over each Piece of Salmon; season it with *Jamaica* and Black-pepper, Nutmeg and Salt; roll each Piece, and set round the Bottom of a raised Crust, lay on the Lid, and bake it two Hours; boil the Bones of the Salmon, and fry four Slices in Butter; and when it is fried brown, pour in the Fish Broth, and boil it with the fried Salmon till it is something strong; then take a Jill of Gooseberries, pick and scald them in Water, add them to the Gravy, and some melted Butter; and when you have taken the Pye out of the Oven, cut the Lid up and take it off, and pour over all the Salmon the Gravy and Gooseberries; cut the Lid in eight Parts, and set round the Inside of the Pye, and send to Table.

A Eel Pye.

TAKE eight large Eels, skin and wash them clean, open and split them down the Middle, and take out their Back-bones; season them with Nutmeg, Pepper and Salt, and put them into an Earthen-pot, put three Spoonfuls of Butter over them, cover them close, and set them in an Oven four Hours, in which time the Bones of the Eels will dissolve; then lay a Sheet of Puff-paste all over the Dish that will just hold them, and put them close; observe to roll them as if for collaring, before you put them in the Pot; then lay a very thin Cover of Paste over them, and let them bake an Hour: In which Time set their Heads and Back-bones on the Fire with a Pint of Water, and let it boil to a Jill; then add to it a Spoonful of Catchup, thicken it with Butter and Flour; take out the Pye, pour in the Gravy, and set it upon the Table.

An Oyster Pye.

TAKE a Rock Codling and cut out the Back-bone, lay it in an Earthen-pan, pour upon it a Pint of White-wine or Gooseberry-vinegar, and let it lie an Hour; then make a Pasty-paste Crust, and lay it very thin round the Dish; cut the Skin off the Fish, take out all the Bones, and cut it in Pieces no larger than your Finger; then season it with Mace, Nutmeg, Pepper and Salt, and lay it into your Dish, with a Quarter of a Pound of Butter over it and a thin Paste, and bake it an Hour in an Oven: Then take a Haddock and cut down the Middle, after it is cleaned, fry it brown in Butter, with the Tail of the Codling, in a Hash-pan; adding to it a Quart of Water and the Bones of the Codling; when it is consumed to little above a Jill, strain through a Hair-sieve: Take 100 of Oysters, scald them, take off all their Beards, and put them into a Sauce-pan with the Fish-gravy, and let them just boil: Then take the Pye out of the Oven, cut up the Lid and take it off, pour all the Oysters over the Pye; cut the Lid into six Pieces, set them round, and send it up.

An Apple Custard Pye.

LAY a Puff-paste Crust all over a Baker, peel and core as many Apples as will fill it, put in Sugar and cover it, and bake it an Hour and a Half in an Oven; then take a Pint of Cream and boil it on the Fire with a Stick of Cinnamon, and set it to cool; then beat the Yolks of six Eggs very well, mix with the Cream, and sweeten to your Taste: Take out the Pye, cut up the Lid and take it off, and with the Back of your Spoon put down the Apples, and make it Smooth; then pour over the Cream and Yolks of Eggs, and set it in five Minutes; then take it out, cut the Lid into Sippets and set round the Custard; send it up to the Table cold. In all Apple Pyes be sure to put in Lemon-skin cut small.

A Cherry Pye.

LAY Puff-paste all over a Baker, fill it with stoned Cherries, and sweeten it to your Taste; then roll out the Remainder of your Paste, and cut it in lengths to reach over the Pye; make each Piece into half Inch-breadths, and lay them cross and cross, to make them into Diamonds: Then set it into the Oven, take great Care to bake it beautiful, and send it up cold.

N.B. All Sweet-meat Pyes are to have open Lids, such as Damsens, Plumbs, *&c.* and to be sent up cold; or, red, white or black Currants in the same Manner; likewise Rasps and Strawberries.

A French Bean Pye.

TAKE a Quart of *French* blanched Beans, lay Puff-paste over a Dish-edge, boil eight Eggs hard, take out their Yolks whole, and lay all over the Top of the Beans, likewise a Quarter of a Pound of Sugar and the same of Butter, cover it up and bake it an Hour; Then take a Jill of melted Butter and half a Jill of Rhenish, sweeten it to your Taste, and pour it on.

To dress a Cod's Head.

CUT three Inches of the Cod's Shoulder towards the Head, then rub the Head all over with very strong Vinegar, and cover it with Salt an Hour before you put it in to boil, and have hard Water to boil it, let the Fire be very good, for it must boil very fast an Hour; skin eight Whitings and dip in Batter, and fry in clarified Butter; drain the Head over the Water it was boiled in, and while it is draining, take off all the black Skin; when the Fish is boiling, break a Lobster and take out all the Meat, cut it small, and boil it up in melted Butter, grate on some Nutmeg, add Catchup, Red-wine, of each a Spoonful; cut some of the Liver and dip into Batter, fry it; then take the long small Bones out of the Jaw Fins of the Head, and stick on each End Mushrooms, Oysters, Barberryberry; set the Head on a Dish, and let it be hot, lay your forced Fish round it, and the Liver all over the Head, stick the Jaw-bones between, lay fried Parsley and Horseradish and Barberryberries round the Dish-edge, and send it to Table.

To dress the Cod's Tail.

THE thick End of the Cod cut into Slices an Inch thick, and lay them into an Earthen-dish, pour over them a Jill of Beer-vinegar, and strew over some Salt; then take out the Bones, and cut the Remainder into thin Slices for frying; season with Nutmeg, Pepper and Salt; then set on some Water in a broad Hash-pan, and when it boils put in the Cod that is in the Vinegar; have no more Water then will cover it, and put in the Vinegar that it lay in; then dip the Cod cut for frying, in Batter, made of half a Jill of stale Beer and Flour; if the Fish be for those that abstain from Flesh, fry it in Clarified Butter, if not, clean Fat; then take half a Hundred of Oysters, and jut plumb them; melt half a Pound of Butter, and put in the Oysters, with a little of their Pickle, some Catchup, and a Spoonful of Mushrooms; if you have a Double-dish, fill it with hot Water; then take out your boiled Fish with a Fish-slice, and lay on the hot Dish, pour over the Oyster-sauce, and lay the fry'd Fish all over: Lay Sippets, Barberry-berries, and Horse-radish round, and send it up.

A Ragoo of Ling.

TAKE a Side of a Ling and cut a Quarter and a Half off the broad End, and cut a thick Slice off it, and a Piece of its Liver, and boil in Vinegar and Water; then take it up, and beat it in a Marble Mortar; add to it the Crumb of a *French* Roll; season it with Nutmeg, Pepper and Salt, Thyme, Sweet-marjoram, and Parsley cut small, a Glass of Rhenish and an Egg, mix all well together with a Piece of Butter; take the Fish and cut off that Part next the Back, to make it of the same Thickness of the thinner Side, and take out the small Bones; season with Nutmeg, Pepper and Salt; beat two Yolks of Eggs in a Spoonful of Verjuice, and rub all over the Fish; then lay a thin Lair of the forced Fish on the Ling, and roll it tight up; roll a broad Tape round, butter an Earthen-dish and lay it in, and set it into an Oven an Hour: Then fry a Pound of the Ling, cut thin into Collops, brown in Butter, and set on the Bones and Fins to boil in a Sauce-pan, with an Anchovy, Horse-radish, Shalot, Thyme, and Marjoram; when the Strength is boiled out, strain out the Broth into the Hash-pan to the fry'd Ling, and when it is strong strain it through a Hair-sieve; add to it half a Jill of pickled Mushrooms, a Spoonful of Cockles, twenty fresh Oysters, make twenty Balls of the forced Fish, and fry in clarified Butter; then take the Fish out of the Oven, pour off all its Gravy, strain off the Fat and add to the Ragoo, thicken it with Butter-sauce; set the Collar in the Middle of the Dish, and pour over the Ragoo: Lay Sippets and fry'd Parsley round the Dish, and serve it up.

Scotch Collops *of* **Ling.**

CUT two Pound of Ling into Collops, and season with *Jamaica* and Black-pepper, Nutmeg and Salt; boil a Quarter of a Pound of Ling, and take the Crumb of a *French* Roll, with a Slice of very sweet Butter and mix with it; add Thyme, Sweet-marjoram, and Parsley cut small, Nutmeg, Pepper and Salt; work it all up together with an Egg, and make them up into little Balls; then make a Batter of half a Jill of Verjuice, the Yolks of two Eggs, and a little Flour; dip each Collop into the Batter, and fry them brown in clarified Butter; take them into a Dish, set them before the Fire, and fry the Balls and lay by them; fry a Pound of the Fish cut into thin Slices in Butter, put to it a Pint of Fish-broth, an Anchovy, some Catchup, and a Spoonful of Claret; when one Half is consumed, strain it off, and put it into a Sauce-pan, with a little Butter and Flour, and boil it up; add to it some Mushrooms, and pickled Cockles: Lay the fry'd Collops on a clean hot Dish, the Balls all over them, and pour over the Sauce; lay Sippets round the Dish, and garnish with scraped Horse-radish and Barberry-berries, so serve it up

A Brown Fricassey of Ling.

CUT out of the thick Part of the Ling a Pound and a Half, and cut into Collops as long as your Finger, as broad as Two, and the Thickness of a Beefstake; season them with Mace, Cloves, Pepper and Salt; make a Batter of two Spoonfuls of White-wine Vinegar, two Yolks of Eggs, and a little Flour; dip the Fish in the Batter, and fry it in clarified Butter; cut the Liver after it is boil'd and cold into thin Slices, and make a Batter of Vinegar and Flour, and dip each Slice in it, and fry it crisp; then have some strong Fish-gravy, made as before directed, and thicken it with Butter and Flour; add to the Gravy half a Jill of pickled Mushrooms, some Catchup and Claret, and boil it up: Lay the fried Fish in the Middle of the Dish, the fry'd Liver round by Way of Sippets, fry'd Parsley round the Dish-edge and some Barberry-berries; pour over the Sauce, and send it up hot.

A boiled Codling.

TAKE a Codling when it is in Perfection, which you may know by the ribby Shades on the Sides, and the Crease down the Back of the Head, or Sirkle more properly termed; rip it up and take out its Liver; turn the Tail of the Fish to its Head, and lay Salt all over it an Hour; have a Kettle or Pan a boiling, that will just hold it, so as to cover it with Water; take half of the Liver and shred it very small, boil it in a Sauce-pan in a Pint of Water with an Anchovy, let it boil to a Jill, strain it thro' a Hair-sieve into a Sauce-pan, and thicken it with Butter and Flour; take up your Fish, drain it, take off the Skin, and set it on a Dish: Garnish with green Parsley and Horse-radish, and send up your Sauce in a Bason.

A boiled Ling.

TAKE a Share of Ling, and boil it with the Liver, and put in some Salt with it into the Pan, take two Crabs, beat the Claws, and take out all the Meat; take some of the Body of the Crab, melt half a Pound of Butter, add to it the Meat of the Crabs, a little Black-Pepper, and boil it; take up the Fish, laying it on a hot Dish, and send it up with the Skin on; slice the Liver and lay over it: Garnish with green Parsley, Horse-radish, and Barberry-berries.

To boil a Cod.

IF you can get a Cod hot out of the Sea, cut off the Head and Shoulders, and cut the Cod into Inch thick Slices, as much as will serve your Family, five Slices will make a Substantial Dish; cut it as above directed, put it into an Earthen-pot, pour upon it a Pint of strong Beer Vinegar, and let it lie an Hour in the Vinegar, turning it over several Times; then have a Pan of Water boiling on a very good Fire, put in a Handful of Salt, and wash the Fish out of the Vinegar, pour it into the boiling Water and Salt, and let it boil fast half an Hour: For Sauce take thirty Oysters, and half a Pound of sweet Butter, melt it as Sauce; when the Oysters are clean washed, put them into the Butter and boil them up; add a Spoonful of Catchup and Spoonful of Mushrooms; take up the Fish and drain it over a hot Stove or Chafing-dish of hot Cinders a Minute or two; lay it on a hot Water-dish if you have one, otherwise let the Dish you lay it on be very hot, and pour over your Sauce: Garnish with Horse-radish, Parsley and Barberry-berries.

To boil Haddocks.

TAKE Haddocks when they are in Perfection, take out their Livers and Roes, and boil the Livers with the Haddocks, four will make a very good Dish; take off their Heads, and skin them, cut them thro' the Middle, boil them, and broil their Roes before the Fire very well, they will take as much broiling as the Fish will boiling, *viz.* half an Hour; take them up, and place the Tails in the Middle of the Dish, lay the other Halves between them, and lay their Livers and Roes all round the Dish: Garnish with green Parsley and Barberry-berries; and have for Sauce very sweet Butter plain melted.

To boil Whitings.

WASH the Whitings clean, and with a sharp Knife cut off all their Fins, skin them, take out their Eyes, and put each Tail through the Bone of the Head; boil as many as will do for your Purpose, for a Head-dish or a Side-dish: Garnish with green Parsley; lay the Fish on a warm Dish, and have plain melted Butter for Sauce.

To fry Whitings.

EITHER put them up as above directed, or cut off their Heads, rub them over with Yolks of Eggs, drudge Flour over them, and fry them in hot melted Fat, or clarified Butter; fry Parsley, set up their Tails in the Middle of the Dish, and lay the fry'd Parsley round for garnishing; lay some Barberry-berries over the Fish.

To Fry Flounders.

TAKE Flounders or any Sort of Flat-fish, that is not over thick for frying, cut them on the Side of their Belly, and gut them, wash them clean, and dry them with a coarse Cloth; take a sharp Case-knife and cut them cross and cross by Way of Diamond Cut; then rub them over with Yolks of Eggs, flour them, and fry them as above directed: Garnish with fry'd parsley, and plain Butter-sauce; set up their Tails in the Middle of the Dish, and send them up to Table.

To stew Soles.

TAKE a Pair of Soles and skin them, fry them brown in Butter, take a Pint of strong Fish-gravy and put to them, add a little Mace, Nutmeg and Salt, let them stew over a slow Stove till there is no more Gravy than what is sufficient for Sauce; then add some pickled Mushrooms and a little melted Butter, lay Sippets round the Dish; then lay in your Soles, pour over your Sauce: Garnish with carved Lemon, and send them up.

To crimp Skate.

TAKE a Maiden Skate, and cut off all the bony Part, cut the two Wings into Pieces an Inch broad, and the Length of the Skate, wash it clean in Water, and let it lie in Vinegar and Salt an Hour; then have some Pump Water boiling on a hot Stove in a broad Hash-pan, into which put your Skate and a little of the Vinegar, and let it boil six Minutes; then take it up into a hot Dish, lay green Parsley round it; and have plain melted Butter-sauce, and send it up.

To boil Skate.

TAKE the broad Wing of a Maiden Skate and wash clean, hang it up on a Crook in the Air one Day; then boil it in Pump Water with Salt in it eight Minutes, take it up and take off the Skin, and lay the two Wings on a Dish whole: Garnish with green Parsley and Horse-radish; have some plain Butter-sauce.

To stew Butts.

TAKE four Butts and wash them clean, set them on a Stove in a broad Hash-pan, cover them with Water, and put to them some Blades of Mace and White-pepper tied up in a Muslin-rag; then take 30 fresh Oysters, scald and beard them; when the Fish is stewed and the Gravy consumed to no more then what is required for Sauce, thicken it with Butter and Flour; then put in your Oysters, and add a Spoonful of Rhenish; lay Sippets and Barberry-berries round the Dish, set your Fish Tails in the Middle, and send it up to the Table.

To boil Mackarel.

CUT your Mackarel in two, and if you have three make a Star, set the Heads in the Middle, and a Tail between each Head; boil them in a broad Hash-pan on a Stove in Salt and Water; have Herbs, Parsley, and Fennel, boiled tender, and cut very small, and mix up with plain Butter melted: Garnish with green Parsley.

To ragoo Salmon.

TAKE a fore Jowl of Salmon, cut off the Head, take out the Bone, and rub it all over with Verjuice, or White-wine Vinegar; then boil the Head, and take the Fish off it; grate Bread, with a Slice of sweet Butter, an Egg, green Thyme, Parsley, Sweet-marjoram cut very small, Nutmeg, Pepper, and Salt mix'd all together, and make Force-meat; season your Salmon with Nutmeg, Pepper, and Salt, and put over the Inside of it the Yolk of an Egg; then lay on your Force-meat, roll it up, put it into a Pot, and set it into an Oven an Hour and a half; if it is not a Fast-day, have half a Pint of good Gravy, a Quarter of a Pound of sweet Butter, made for Sauce, and a Jill of scalded Gooseberries; lay Sippets round the Dish, and lay on your Salmon: Garnish with carved Lemon.

Scotch Collops *of* Salmon.

CUT out a fore Jowl of Salmon collops, rub each Collop with Verjuice, and season with *Jamaica* and Black-pepper, Nutmeg, and Salt; make Force-meat and put it into a little round Bason, and bake it in an Oven; then flour and fry the Collops; fry a Codling cut into Pieces, brown in Butter; add a Pint of Fish-broth, when it is strong enough strain it off, and thicken it with Butter and Flour; add to it a Jill of scalded Gooseberries: Set the Force-meat in the

Middle, lay the Collops round it, pour the Sauce all over it, and lay crisp Parsley round.

Olives *of* Salmon.

TAKE a hind Jowl of Salmon, skin and split it, cut the first two half a Quarter in Length, and the Breadth of the Fish, and make the other End to the same Size; boil what Cuttings you leave for Force-meat, in the same Manner as is before directed; rub Yolks of Eggs all round each Piece of Fish, and season it with Nutmeg, Pepper, and Salt; spread over each Collop a thin Lair of Force-meat, roll them up tight, lay them on a little long Tin-pan close, and set them in an Oven half an Hour: For Sauce boil the Fish-bones, with an Anchovy, and Horse-radish, and strain it off; then add two Spoonfuls of Catchup, half a Jill of pickled Mushrooms, thicken it with Butter and Flour, and lay the Olives: Garnish with crisp Parsley.

To dress a Turbot.

BOIL the Head of a Turbot, save the Broth, and take off all the Fish; make Force-meat beat in a Mortar, adding Nutmeg, Pepper and Salt, two Eggs, grated Bread, and the Juice of a Lemon, mix a little of the Liver with the Force-meat, mix it all together, make it into Force-meat Balls, fry them in clarified Butter, and they will keep three Days; a Turbot of a moderate Size will be four very good Dishes, one boiled, and the Fins fry'd and laid round it, plain Butter-sauce, green Parsley, and scraped Horse-radish for garnishing; another Part ragoo'd, and the Fish-broth made Gravy by frying two or three Slices, and boiling it; Force-meat Balls and Oysters made for the Ragoo, and the Turbot seasoned and broiled before the Fire, and set in the Middle of the Dish, and the Ragoo turn'd over it; Scotch Collops cut out of the thickest Part of the Turbot, dipp'd in Eggs and fry'd brown, after seasoning them with Nutmeg, Pepper and Salt; put on a Dish the Fish-gravy, Forced-balls, and pickled Mushrooms boiled, and pour over them Sippets and carved Lemon; a white Fricassey is, to cut out of the Turbot as many Pieces half Inch thick, and in Length two Inches, dip them in Whites of Eggs well beat, and fry them in clarified Butter; boil eight Yolks of Eggs, and take off the Beards of thirty Oyster, have white Fish-gravy, boil up the Oysters and thicken with melted Butter: Lay the Fricassey on the Dish, the Yolks round it, and pour over the Oysters and the Sauce.

To boil Salmon.

SCALE a Jowl of Salmon, make the Water very Salt, when it boils put in the Fish, and let it boil quickly; take Parsley, Fennel, and a little Mint boil'd and cut very small, and lay round the Dish-edge; pick and scald a Jill of Gooseberries, and melt Butter: Lay your Salmon on a Dish, and the Gooseberries all over it, and send up the Butter in a Sauce-boat.

To bake a Salmon.

TAKE a whole Salmon, take off its Skin, take out its Liver and Roe, and turn the Tail of the Fish to the Head, fasten it with Tape, cut the Fish a-cross Diamond Shape, and rub it all over with Mace, Nutmeg, Pepper and Salt, Yolks of Eggs, and grated Bread; laying thin Slices of Butter all over the Back of the Salmon; then bake it two Hours in an Earthen-dish; the Liver and Roe beat in a Mortar, add Nutmeg, Mace, Pepper, Salt, Thyme, Parsley, and Sweet-marjoram cut small, and as much grated Bread as an Egg will make stiff enough to roll into Balls, and fry them; have Gravy made of Flesh of Fish, into which put half a Jill of pickled Mushrooms and the Force-balls: Set your Fish on a Dish, lay Sippets and Lemon round, and pour on the Sauce.

To stew Tench.

PUT them alive into a Stew-pan, set them over a Stove till they are dead, let them be close covered; then take out the Tench, scale them, and take out their Guts, and let their Blood be in the Hash-pan; then put in the Tench with a Pint of Water, a Jill of Claret, and let them stew till there is Sauce left to eat them, add nothing but Salt to it; lay Sippets and carved Lemon round the Dish, and send it up.

To dress Pike.

TAKE a large Pike and scale him, take out his Guts and Liver, boil and beat the Liver in a Mortar; add to it a Slice of Butter, grated Bread, Nutmeg, an Egg, Mace, Pepper, Salt, Thyme, Sweet-marjoram, Parsley, and Chives cut small; then mix them well together, and put it into the Belly of the Pike; then turn the Tail of the Pike to its Head, and rub him all over with Yolk of Egg, and strew grated Bread upon the Egg; set him on a Tin Dripping-pan before a clear Fire, and baste it with Butter, but take Care to turn it as it browns;

when it is thoroughly done, lay it on a warm Dish: Garnish with crisp Parsley, and plain melted Butter for Sauce, and send it to Table.

To stew Burn Trouts.

WASH as many Trouts as will make a substantial Dish, season them with Pepper, Salt and Nutmeg; lay them into a Pot that just holds them, which must be of a longish Shape, and put to them Butter and Shalot, and set them in an Oven two Hours; then take them into a Stew-pan, and add to them a Spoonful of Verjuice or the Juice of a Lemon, and half a Jill of melted Butter; lay them with their Tails in the Middle of your Dish, and their Heads round it: Garnish with green Parsley.

To fry Trouts.

WASH and dry them with a Cloth, and dip them in Vinegar and Flour, and fry them in Butter to crisp, that they will stand round the Sauce-bason in the Dish, with crisped Parsley round the Dish-edge, and send them up.

To fry Sparlings.

DON'T wash them but dry them with a clean Cloth, and draw a small Gut out of their Neck: Make Batter of Egg, Flour and Water, dip them in and fry them in clarified Butter, Hog's Lare, or Beef-fat; let it boil when you put in your Sparlings: For Sauce, plain melted Butter: Garnish with dry'd Parsley and Barberry-berries.

Instructions for Potting Fish or Fowl

To pot Salmon.

CUT a Salmon down the Middle, cut off the Head, scale and wash it clean, take out the Chine-bone, and cut the Salmon to the Shape of your Pot or Pots; season with Black-pepper and Salt; let your Pots be deep enough to contain a Double of the Salmon, and put into your Pot with it a Pound of Butter; bake it two Hours and take it out, pour off all the Gravy and Butter, and press it hard so as all may drain out of it; then set it into the Oven, and put the Butter into the Pot, but none of the Gravy, and let it stand four Hours longer in the Oven, in which Time all the Bones of the Salmon will be dissolved to Fish; then take it out and drain off all the Butter, set a Press on the Salmon and lay on a Weight to squeeze it well; when it is cold cover it with the Butter it was baked in, and some more Butter clarified.

To make Trouts *like potted* Jars.

TAKE black back'd Trouts that cuts Red, and wash very clean, and dry them with a Cloth; season them with Mace, Nutmeg, *Jamaica* and Black-pepper and Salt; put them into a Pot with Butter sufficient to boil them in, and set them in an Oven close covered; when they have been an Hour and a Half in the Oven, take them out, lay them on a flat Board, let all the Gravy drain from them, and take off all the Butter, but none of the Gravy: Then lay your Trouts into the Pot, and to every Lair add a little more of your Seasoning, according to what your Judgment supposes may be washed off in their boiling; put the Butter to them, and set them in an Oven three Hours and a Half, in which Time their Fins and Bones will become Fish; then take out your Pot, pour off the Butter they were baked in, and lay a small Weight on the Trouts; when they are cold, cover them with the Butter they were baked in; but if you have not enough to cover them with, clarify more Butter, and to have better than half an Inch Thickness above your Trouts.

To pot Lobsters.

TAKE large Lobsters when they are in their Prime, boil them, and take off their Claws and Tails; split the Tails, but keep the Claws as whole as you can, and take the Bone out of the Claws; season them with Black-pepper and Salt, and pot them, with plenty of Butter over them, and set them in an Oven an Hour; then take them out and drain all the Butter and Gravy off the Lobsters, take the Butter from the Gravy, and add as much clarified Butter as will cover the Lobsters: You must not press the Lobsters, but let the Butter run through them, and when they are cut it will be a fine Mixture representing of Marble.

To pot Lampar Eels.

TAKE Lampar Eels and cut off a Grissel that lies down their Backs, skin and season them with Mace, Nutmeg, Pepper and Salt, and put them close into a Pot, with Butter over them and a Paper tied very close, put them into an Oven two Hours; then draw off their Gravy and the Butter, squeeze out all the Gravy, and put the Butter into the Eels, and let them have four Hours more baking, in which time their Bones will dissolve; then take them out of the Oven, pour the Butter from them, and press the Eels close down in the Pot; when they are cold cover them with the Butter they were baked in, adding more clarified Butter if wanted.—These potted Eels are by most Judges thought to exceed all Sort of potted Fish.

To pot Woodcocks.

PICK your Woodcocks clean, take out the Trail, and take off the Gizzard; work up some Pepper and Salt into half a Pound of Butter, and put the Size of a small Chicken Egg into each Woodcock, put them into a Pot with their Breasts turned down, lay as much Butter over as will cover them when it is melted, and set them two Hours in an Oven; then take out the Cocks, put out all the Butter and take it off the Gravy, put the Trails of the Woodcock into their Gravy, set them into the Oven, and let them stew till it is thick; then put it all over the Cocks, put them close down into the Pots, and cover them with the Butter they were baked in, adding more clarified Butter to them; let their Breasts lie uppermost.

To pot Moor-fowl *or* Gore.

IF you have plenty of Gore take out their Backbones, and season them with Black-pepper and Salt, cover them with Butter, lay their Breasts down in the

Pot, and set them two Hours and a Half in the Oven; when they are taken out have in Readiness the Pots you design to pot them in, and take them out of the Pot they were baked in, turn their Breasts up in the Pots, press them close down, and cover them with clarified Butter.—Partridges and Pigeons much the same, only you are not to take the Back-bone off the Partridges or Pigeons, but let them be Pye Fashion.

To pot a Hare.

SKIN it, and if not mangled, you need not wash it, cut it into Joints, and season with Mace, Nutmeg, *Jamaica* and Black-pepper, Salt, dried Thyme, Sweet-marjoram rubb'd small and sifted through a Hair-sieve; put each Joint close down into a Stewing-pot, with the Liver, Heart, and three Shalots, bake it till it is very tender: A young Hare will be tender in Two Hours, an old one will take four Hours baking; when it is enough take it out, pour out all the Gravy and Butter into another Pot, strip off all the Flesh from the Bones, beat the Meat in a Wooden Bowl or Marble Mortar, and beat all the Butter that was taken from the Hare with the Meat, put it into Pots, and cover it with clarified Butter.

To pot Beef.

TAKE six Pounds of a Buttock of Beef and cut into Collops an Inch thick, beat an Ounce of Salt-petre to Powder, mix with four Ounces of Salt and a little Sugar; lay a little of this on each Collop, and one Collop upon another, and put them into a Pot that just holds them; twenty-four Hours will make them red; then take them out and season with *Jamaica* and Black-pepper, dried Thyme and Sweet-marjoram; put into it a Rocambole, and put it into a Stew-pan with the Marrow of three Beef-bones, or a Pound and a Half of Butter; when it is tender, take it out and beat it fine, and beat up with it the Marrow or Butter that it was baked with, or half of the Butter; put it into the Pots, cover with clarified Butter.

Potted Veal.

TAKE out of the Thick of a Leg of Veal with the Udder and Kell, and cut into Collops; season with Mace, Nutmeg, Pepper and Salt, cover them close into a Pot, and bake them two Hours; then take them out, and beat them with the Udder and Kell in a Mortar; when it is well mixed, put them into Pots, and cover with clarified Butter.

Potted Herrings.

WHEN Herrings are in Perfection, cut off their Heads, and take out their Roes and Back-bones, season them with Black-pepper and Salt; roll each Herring up like a Collar round the Bottom of the Pot you are to bake them in, and set one Row upon another till your Pot is full; then tie a Paper close about the Top of the Pot, and set them three Hours in an Oven; cover them over with Bay-leaves as soon as you draw them out, and fill the Pot as high as the Fish with White-wine Vinegar: Then put the Livers and Roes into a Pot by themselves, and let them stand an Hour in the Oven, and then put the Roes into the Herrings: When they are dish'd up, lay the Livers round the Herrings, and send up some of the Liquor: Have Fennel for garnishing.

To collar Beef.

TAKE twenty Pounds of the Belly-end of the Flank of an Ox, and lay it in Salt and Water two Hours; then beat two Ounces of Salt-petre, mix it with a Pint of white Salt, and rub it all over the Beef, let it lie Five Days, and turn it every Day; then wash off all the Pickle, and dry it, spread it on a Board, cut it straight, and lay the Cuttings a-cross; season with Nutmeg, Mace, *Jamaica* and Black-pepper, green Thyme, Sweet-marjoram, and Parsley cut small; then lay your Cuttings cross the Collar, roll it tight up with Tape, put it into a long Pot or Pan, and set it into an Oven all Night after the scorching Heat is off; in the Morning take it out, uncover it, take it out of the Pot, lay the Collar on a Tin, roll it round and press it; when cold take off the Tin, and keep it for Use.

To collar a Pig.

TAKE a good fat Pig, and after you have kill'd and dress'd it clean, wash it well from the Blood, cut off the Head and split it even in two, bone it, and wash the Blood clean away; then dry the Flesh well with Rubbers, laying it out at its full Length, and rubbing on it Yolk of Egg on the Inside of each Half; season with Nutmeg, Pepper, Salt, green Thyme, Sweet-marjoram, Parsley shred small and strew'd on, rolling each Side very tight, and tie a Cloth round each Side, and Tape upon the Cloth, and let it be tied close at each End, and boil it two Hours; then take it up, undo the Sides, and tie it up again very tight: Make a Sauce of Bran-water and Salt, and a Jill of Vinegar, when it boils strain it off, and when it is cold, put in the Pig, and keep for use.

To collar Ling.

TAKE the largest Ling you can get, cut it down the Middle, cut off all the Fins, and cut off the thick Part of it, to make it of an equal Thickness, cut it into three half Quarter lengths, and roll it up in as many Collars as will be of the Ling; make a strong Brine of a Pound of Bay-salt and as much common Salt as will make an Egg swim to the Top; then set it on to boil, and boil the Liver of the Ling in the Brine; tie all the Collars firm with Tape, and boil them an Hour and a half; then take up the Collars, and strain the Liquor into a deep Earthen-pot, and when it is cold, put in the Collars: It eats like Sturgeon, and is eaten with Mustard, Vinegar, Oil and Sugar.

To marble a Calf's Head.

TAKE a large fat Calf's Head, wash it through many Waters, take out the Eyes, and boil it till all the Bones will come out from the Flesh; then have for Seasoning, Mace, Nutmeg, Pepper, Salt, green Thyme, Sweet-marjoram and Parsley cut small; take out all the Bones and the Skin of the Palate, cut the Head on a Shreading-board, and put it into a Cloth when it is very hot, and tie it up close: It will cut out like Marble, and is a pretty Dish for a second Course.

To collar Calves Feet.

TAKE a Gang of good Feet, and boil them in soft Water as for Gelly, take out the Feet, and make great Haste to take out all the Bones while the Feet is hot; then cut and throw a little Salt over them, and put them close down in a Pint Water-glass, and carve it in cutting like Brawn, in thin Slices; when you take it out of the Glass, lay the carved Slices round, and set the Collar in the Middle of the Dish: Garnish with green Parsley.

To make a Veal Soop.

TAKE a Leg of Veal, cut off the Flesh, break the Bones, and put Bones and Meat into a Stewing-pan, add to it two Quarts of Water, stick six Cloves in a large Onion, two Carrots, two Turnips and a little Salt; cover it very close, paste down the Lid, and set it all Night in an Oven; take it out in the Morning, pour off all your Soop, skim off the Fat, and put the Soop into a clean Flannel-bag, used for nothing but straining Gravy, and put it into a very clean Hash-pan; add to it an Ounce of Vermicelli, and let it boil gently; grate half an Ounce of Loaf-sugar all over the Bottom of the Hash-pan, and set it on some clear Cinders till the Sugar boils and turns to the Colour of Treacle; then put to it a little of the Soop, and boil till all the Colour is mixt with the Soop; then mix it with the other Soop; toast two thin slices of Bread cut into Dices, and put into the Soop-dish, lay boiled Rice round the Dish-edge, and pour in the Soop; or send it up a Canteen. The Veal will be very good to eat cold, minced or potted, with adding Seasoning to it, as directed for Potted Veal.

A Sellery Soop.

IF you would go to the thrifty Way of Soop making, boil a Leg of Mutton for a Family Dish, strain your Broth into an Earthen-pot, and let it stand all Night; take off the Top, pour off the Clear, and strain the Bottom through your Flannel-bag; take four Pounds of the Buttock of an Ox, and put your Broth into a small Boiler; put in your Beef, and be careful to skim it when it begins to boil; when you have skimm'd it well, wash as much Sellery and cut it, as will fill a Pint-bason; after the Sellery has stewed with the Beef three Hours, add a Pint-basin of diced Turnips and Carrots of an equal Quantity, and let it stew an Hour; then boil Spinage and lay round the Dish-edge, toast Bread and cut into Sippets: Set the Beef in the Middle of the Dish, pour in the Soop, lay the Sippets round, and send it up.

A Cabbage Soop.

TAKE four Quarts of Beef, Mutton, or Veal broth, and put into a small Boiler, and six Pounds of the best Part of the Beef without Bones, put the Beef into the Pot, let it boil, and skim it well; then take a White-cabbage and cut it into four Quarters, cut out the Core, and put it to the Beef; let it stew four Hours, keeping it close covered, and be sure to let it stew very gently; then set the Beef in the Middle of the Dish, lay the Cabbage round it, and pour over the Soop: The Beef and Cabbage is as good as the Soop.

To make a Soop *without* Water.

TAKE a Stone of Beef, a Stone of Mutton, a Stone of Veal, and cut all into Inch thick Collops; then take a large Earthen-pot, lay in a Lair of Collops and a Lair of sliced Turnips, then Collops and sliced Carrots, cover that with Flesh; then have Sellery, and intermix the Meat with the Roots and Sellery; when all is put into the Pot cover it close, set it into a hot Oven, and let it stand two Hours; then take it out, pour off all your Gravy, and strain it through a

Flannel-bag, and set it another Hour into the Oven; then drain off all your Gravy, and filter it through a Flannel-bag into your other Soop: Put it into a clean Hash-pan, and add to it an Ounce of Vermicelli, boil it ten Minutes; then cut some Bread and toast brown, and put a little into the Soop-dish, pour in the Soop, and send it up.

To make a white Soop.

BOIL a Neck of Veal to Rags, stick six Cloves in an Onion, and boil it all the time the Meat boils; then strain it off, and skim off all the Fat, filter it through a Flannel-bag, and put it into a clean Hash-pan; add to it half a Pound of Rice, and let it boil softly Half an Hour; take a Quarter of a Pound of Rice, and let it boil a Quarter of an Hour in fair Water, and put it into a Hair-sieve to let the Water run from it; then take a Pennyworth of Saffron, infuse it in two Spoonfuls of Water, put the Rice into it, and it will make it yellow; then put a Rim of Paste round the Brim of the Dish, lay the Rice round the Edge of the Dish; then boil up the Soop, and take the Crumb of a *French* Roll, rasp it, and set it in the Middle of the Dish; pour on the Soop, and send it up.

To make a Hodge-podge.

TAKE a Neck of Mutton, cut it into Chops, and put a Gallon of Water to it, and as it begins to boil skim it well; add to it two Ounces of Pearl-barley, two Turnips, two Carrots, cut into Dices, a Pint of green Pease, green Thyme, Sweet-marjoram, Parsley, and two Cabbage Lettices cut small, some Chives, and let all boil together, till there is as much as will fill a good Dish, and so send it up.

To make a Portable Soop.

TAKE a Buttock of Ox Beef and cut into Inch thick Collops; take three Carrots and cut into Slices, and slice four Turnips, and cut as much Sellery as will fill a Quart; then lay into your Pot a Lair of Beef, lay Roots and Sellery upon it, and so intermix the Beef, Roots, Sellery and all close together down in an Earthen-pot that just holds it; then cover and paste the Pot, and set it in an Oven three Hours; then take it out, strain off all the Fat and let the Gravy run through a Flannel-bag; then put it into a Stew-pan, set it on a clear Stove, let it boil till it is thick, and stirring it with a Spoon; when it begins to stick take it off, put it into Tea-cups, let it stand till it is cold, turn it into a clean Linen-cloth, turn them once a Day into a dry Part, and set it in the Sun now and then till it is perfectly dry. This is for a Traveling Soop; an Ounce of this when it is dry will make a Porringer of Soop, cut it and put it into a Sauce-pan, and add Water to it, set it on the Fire and it will dissolve; toast some Bread, cut it into Dices, and pour in the Soop.

A Pease Soop.

TAKE two Quarts of Marrow Pease, put to them two Gallons of Water, let them boil till one Half is consumed and the Pease burst; take a Sieve and strain your Pease, putting some of the Pulp through the Sieve; then set it on a Stove in a Hash-pan, cut some Sellery and boil with it, rub dry Mint and sift it through a Sieve; mix with the Soop some *Jamaica* Pepper powder'd, and two Anchovies; cut some Bread into Dices and fry brown, and put into your Soop-dish; when the Soop is boiled to two Quarts, put to it a Slice of Butter and half a Jill of thick sweet Cream; just as it boils put it into your Soop-dish, and send it up.

A green Pease *Soop.*

TAKE two Quarts of old green Pease, put them into a Gallon of Water, and let them boil till they are consumed to two Quarts; then strain them through a Hair-sieve, and put through all the Pulp you can get into a Hash-pan; dry some green Mint, put it through a Sieve, and add to it, with some powdered *Jamaica* Pepper, an Anchovy, and a Jill of young green Pease; set the Soop on a Stove, and let it boil gently half an Hour: Then take some of the Husks of the Pease and some young Spinage, beat them in a Mortar, squeeze the Juice into the Soop, and let it boil up; add a Slice of sweet Butter, half a Jill of Cream, and fry'd Bread cut into Dices, put them into the Dish, pour in the Soop, and send it up.

To make a Cheshire Cheese Soup.

PUT the Crumb of a Penny-loaf into three Pints of Water, boil it, and grate half a Pound of old *Cheshire*, put it into the Bread and boil it.

To make an Onion Soop.

TAKE a Quart of green Pease, put three Quarts of Water to it, and let it boil to two Quarts; then take six Onions, two Cabbage Lettices, green Thyme, Sweet-marjoram, Parsley, green Mint and Chives all cut small; take a Quarter of a Pound of Butter into a Frying-pan, make it hot, put in the Onions and Herbs, fry them, and put into the Soop; add a little Black-pepper and Salt to your Taste, cut a large Slice of Bread, and toast it brown; pour the Soop into the Dish, and cut the Bread into Dices, pour over the Soop, and send it up.

To make a Turnip Soop.

BOIL a Pennyworth of Turnips and Carrots in six Quarts of Water and a Pennyworth of Sellery, let them boil into three Quarts and strain it off; then cut the Turnips and one Carrot into Dices, and cut the Tops of half a Hundred of Asparagus very small; take a Piece of Butter into a Frying-pan, and make it hot, fry the Carrots, Turnips, and Asparagus, and put them into the Soop; add a Quarter of a Pound of Pearl-barley, and salt it to your Taste, dust in a little Pepper, and send it up.

To make a Fish Soop.

BOIL a large Tail of Cod or Ling with a good Quantity of Haddocks Heads, fry some split Haddocks brown in Butter, and when the Fish-broth is strong strain it into the fry'd Haddocks; then let it boil, and strain it off when you judge it strong enough, skim off all the Fat, and put the Broth into a clean Hash-pan; add to it two Ounces of Sagoe, and let it boil, stick eight Cloves into two large Onions and add to the Soop; skin a Whiting and put its Tail through its Head, rub it with the Yolk of Egg, fry it in clarified Butter, and set it in the Middle of the Soop-dish; scald half a Hundred of Oysters in their own Liquor, take off all their Beards, and put them into your Soop-dish: Lay Shrimps round the Dish-edge, pour your Soop upon the Oysters, set the Whiting in the Middle, and send it up.

To make a Craw Fish Soop.

TAKE four Codlings and cut into Slices, season them with Pepper and Salt, and put them into an Earthen-pot; add to them a Bundle of sweet-Herbs, some Shalots, and two Quarts of Water, cover the Pot close, paste it down, and let it stand three Hours in an Oven; in the mean Time take a hundred Craw-fish out of their Shells after they are boiled, beat ten of them and as many Shrimps in a Mortar, grate the Crumb of a *French* Roll, a Slice of Butter, an Egg, green Thyme, Sweet-marjoram, Parsley, Chives, Nutmeg, Pepper and Salt; mix all these well together, make up into little Balls, and brown them before the Fire, or set them in an Earthen-Plate into an Oven; when your Fish has been the above time in the Oven, take it out, and pour it into a Flannel-bag, let it run into a Hash-pan, and set it on a Stove; cut the Craw-fish small and add to it, pick the Meat out of the Claws of the Crabs and lay round the Edge of the Soop-dish: Toast Bread and cut it into Dices, pour the Soop into the Dish, put the forced Balls and toasted Bread all over it, and send it up.

A Calf Foot Soop.

TAKE the Stock that is boiled of a Gang of Calf's Feet, as if for Gellies, and when it is cold take off the Top and Bottom, put the other into a Hash-pan, set it on a slow Stove, and put to it a Stick of Cinnamon; take a Quarter of a Pound of Rice, boil it in Water a Quarter of an Hour, and put it into a Sieve to let the Water run from it; then take the Yolks of six Eggs and the Whites of two, and beat them well in a Bason; then put three Jills of thick Cream to the Soop, and sweeten it to your Taste, lay Rice round the Edge of the Soop-dish, and put what remains into the Soop; then take a Pint of White-wine and mix with the Eggs, grate in a little Nutmeg and mix all with the Soop, tossing it up with a Whisk, and stir it on the Stove till it is very near boiling, but by no Means let it boil, for that will break it; it must be smooth and thick, pour it into the Dish, and send it up.—The Receipt of this Soop was desired of me by three Baronets Ladies: It is a very good Supper Soop.

An Orange Pudding.

BOIL two *Seville* Oranges in several Waters till they are tender, take out all the In-meat, and beat the Skins to a Paste in a Mortar; add to it half a Pound of fine Powder-sugar, half a Pound of Butter beat to Cream in a Mortar; then take out the Seed and the Strings, and add the Pulp of the Oranges to it, and the Yolks of ten Eggs, beat all together till it is smooth; then lay a Sheet of Puff-paste all over your Dish, pour in your Pudding and bake it three Quarters of an Hour.

A boiled Orange Pudding.

GRATE the Rind of two *Seville* Oranges, and beat it in a Mortar to a Paste; put a Quarter of a Pound of Naple Biscuits into a Pint of thick Cream, mix this with the Paste of Orange, and sweeten it to your Taste; beat up five Eggs, mix all well together, flour a Pudding-cloth, put in your Pudding, and put it into a Pot of boiling Water, an Hour will boil it: Take White-wine, a little Sugar and sweet melted Butter for Sauce.

A Lemon Pudding.

PARE the Skin off three Lemons, and boil them in several Waters till they are tender; then beat them in a Mortar till they become Paste; add half a Pound of Butter and half a Pound of Sugar, beat all smooth; take eight Eggs, leave out the Whites of four, and add a Glass of Rhenish-wine; lay a very thin Sheet of Puff-paste over the Dish, and pour on the Pudding: Three Quarters of an Hour will bake it.

A boiled Lemon Pudding.

GRATE off the yellow Rind of three Lemons, and beat it into a Paste in a marble Mortar; take the Crumb of a three Half-penny *French* Roll, boil a Pint of thick Cream and pour upon it, sweeten it to your Taste, beat five Eggs and mix with it; flour a Cloth well and put in your Pudding: After all is well mixt, an Hour will boil it, and have for Sauce Plain melted Butter, Sugar, the Juice of a Lemon, a little White-wine, and grate Loaf-sugar all over the Dish.

A Sego Pudding.

BOIL three Ounces of Sego in a Quart of Water a Quarter of an Hour, put it into a Hair-sieve, and drain out all the Water; take a Quart of Cream and boil the Sego in it till it is thick, set it to cool, and sweeten it to your Taste; then beat eight Eggs, the Whites of four leave out, let them be well beat, and mix with the Pudding, grate into it a little Nutmeg, and lay a Sheet of Puff-paste over a Dish, and pour in your Pudding; an Hour will bake it.

A Carrot Pudding.

TAKE half a Pound of boiled Carrots and beat to Paste in a Mortar, add a Quarter of a Pound of Sugar, grate a little Nutmeg, melt a Quarter of a Pound of Butter, beat five Eggs and mix all well together; lay Puff-paste over the Dish, pour in the Pudding, and bake it half an Hour.

A boiled Carrot Pudding.

TAKE half a Pound of boiled Carrots and beat them in a Mortar to Paste; take the Crumb of a *French* Roll and soak in thick Cream, beat eight Eggs, and leave the Whites of four out; mix all well with the Carrots, and grate in a little Nutmeg, rub a Piece of Butter on your Pudding-cloth, and pour on the Pudding, tie it fast and boil it an Hour; grate Sugar all over the Dish, and let your Sauce be plain Butter, Sugar, and a little White-wine; turn the Pudding into the Dish, and pour on your Sauce.

An Apple Pudding.

TAKE half a Pound of pared and cored Apples, boil them ten Minutes in Water, beat them in a Mortar to Pulp, and sweeten to your Taste; then melt a good Slice of Butter and mix with the Pulp; take the Yolks of eight Eggs beat well, and a little grated Lemon-peal; mix all well together, and lay Puff-paste over a Dish, pour in the Pudding, and bake it half an Hour.

A Rice Pudding.

TAKE three Ounces of the Flour of Rice and three Jills of new Milk, and put it into a Brass-pan over a clear Fire, stirring it with a Spoon all the Time; when it boils take it off, and stir in a Slice of Butter, grate in some Nutmeg, and sweeten to your Taste, beat up six Eggs and leave out three Whites; mix all well together, and lay Puff-paste over the Dish, pour in your Pudding, and bake it half an Hour.

A *boiled* Rice Pudding.

TAKE half a Pound of Rice and boil it half an Hour in Water, put it into a Hair-sieve, and let the Water drain from it; then beat up the Yolks of eight Eggs, with a Jill of sweet Cream, grate some Nutmeg, and mix all with the boiled Rice, butter a Cloth, put in the Pudding and boil it an Hour; grate Sugar all over the Edge of the Dish, and for Sauce have Butter, Sugar and White-wine; set the Pudding on its Dish, and send up your Sauce in a Bason.

A Hunter's Pudding.

TAKE a Pound of Flour, a Pound of Currants, and a Pound of Beef-suet, pick and wash the Currants clean, shred the Suet very small, and mix all together; beat up six Eggs with a Jill of Cream, grate in some Nutmeg, and mix all well together; flour a Cloth, and boil it two Hours and a Half: For Sauce, Butter and Sugar.

A Bread *and* Butter Pudding.

TAKE a Penny *French* Roll two Days old, cut off all the Crust, and cut the Crumb into thin Slices, spreading it as you cut it very thin with Butter on each Slice; then take a Quarter of a Pound of Rasins stoned, half a Pound of Currants well washed and pick'd; then lay a Lair of Bread and Butter, and upon that Fruit in a Pudding-dish, so cover the Fruit with the buttered Bread, and when it is disposed of into your Dish, beat up five Eggs with a Quart of new Milk, sweeten it to your Taste, and put to it a Glass of Rose-water, pour it into the Dish upon the Bread and Fruit, and bake it an Hour.

A boiled Bread Pudding.

TAKE a Pound of the Crumbs of *French* Rolls, boil a Pint of new Milk and pour upon it; take the Yolks of seven Eggs, and the Whites of Three, beat very well, and mix with the Milk and Bread; grate in a little Nutmeg, butter your Cloth, pour in your Pudding, tie it up tight, and boil it an Hour: For Sauce plain Butter.

A boiled Custard Pudding.

TAKE a Quart of Cream and boil with six Laurel-leaves; set it to cool and break fourteen Eggs, leave out the Whites of five, and beat them very well; sweeten to your Taste, put in your Sugar when the Cream is on the Fire that it may dissolve and mix with the Cream; then when it is cold mix the Eggs with it, have a very fine Cloth to boil it in, rub some Butter on your Cloth, put on your Pudding, tie it tight, put it into boiling Water, and let it boil an Hour; grate Sugar all over the Dish, turn in the Pudding, and send it up.

To make a Calf's Feet Pudding.

TAKE half a Pound of Calf's Feet-meat after it is boiled tender, and all the Bones separated from the Meat, blanch half a Pound of *Jourdon* Almonds, and shred the Calf's Feet and Almonds as small as possible; pick and wash half a Pound of Currants, and mix with the Feet; add a little Sugar, and a little grated Nutmeg; beat up the Yolks of eight Eggs in a Jill of thick Cream, mix all well together, lay Puff-paste all over a Dish, put on the Pudding, and send it to the Oven: Half an Hour will bake it.

A boiled Calf's Feet Pudding.

TAKE half a Pound of Calf's Feet, and half a Pound of Beef-suet and shred very small; half a Pound of pick'd Currants, a Quarter of a Pound of Rasins, and mix all together; soak the Crumb of a Penny Loaf in new Milk, break five Eggs and beat and mix all well together; butter a Cloth, put on your Pudding, boil it an Hour and a half, grate Sugar all over the Dish, and turn on your Pudding: Have for Sauce Butter and Sugar, pour it over the Pudding, and send it up.

To make an Almond Pudding.

BLANCH half a Pound of *Jourdon* Almonds, and beat them in a Marble Mortar to Paste; take three Jills of thick sweet Cream, and sweeten to your Taste; add to it two Pennyworth of Orange Flower-water; take seven Eggs leaving out the Whites of four, and mix all together; laying Puff-paste over the Dish, pour on your Pudding, and bake it in an Oven three Quarters of an Hour.

A Gooseberry Pudding.

TAKE half a Pound of Butter, break into it a Pound of Flour, and rub it small; beat two Yolks of Eggs in a Jill of Water, take as much of this as you need to work the Butter and Flour into a Paste, roll it into a Sheet, let it be thin round the Edge, put in a Quart of Gooseberries, and near a Quarter of a Pound of Powder-sugar; then rub it round the Edge of the Paste with Water, gather it up together close, put it into a Pudding-cloth, tie and boil it an Hour: For Sauce plain Butter and Sugar.

A Prune Pudding.

TAKE a Pound and a half of Flour, and a Pint of new Milk and mix it with; beat six Eggs and mix with the Milk and Flour, then take a Pound of Prunes, half a Pound of stoned Rasins, and half a Pound of Currants, mix all with the Flour and Milk, and let it boil three Hours: For Sauce have plain melted Butter and Sugar, and a little Rose-water; grate Sugar all over the Dish, turn on the Pudding, and so send it to Table.

A Marrow Pudding.

TAKE half a Pound of Marrow and cut very small, three Quarters of a Pound of Flour, half a Pound of stoned Rasins, and half a Pound of well-picked Currants, mix all well together, with five Eggs, a Jill of Cream, and grate in some Nutmeg; put the Pudding in a Cloth, and boil it two Hours, grate Sugar over the Dish, and have Sweet-sauce.

A French Bean Pudding.

TAKE a Quart of young *French* Beans, boil and blanch them, and beat them in a Mortar to a fine Paste; add to it a Glass of Verjuice, a Quarter of a Pound of Powder-sugar, half a Pound of Butter, and seven Eggs, the Whites of Three left out, beat all well together; lay a Puff-paste on the Dish, pour on the Pudding, and bake it three Quarters of an Hour: For Sauce have melted Butter, White-wine and Sugar.

A Ratafia Pudding.

TAKE a Quart of sweet Cream, and boil six Laurel-leaves two Minutes, take them out, and let the Cream stand till it be cold; then take half a Pound of Flour and mix with the Cream, and beat six Eggs and mix all together; add a little Salt, butter your Pudding-cloth, pour in the Pudding, tie it tight, and boil it an Hour and a half; grate Sugar all over the Dish, have Sweet-sauce, turn in your Pudding, and send it up.

A Tansy Pudding.

GRATE the Crumbs of two Penny *French* Rolls, beat up eight Eggs with a Pint of Cream, and mix the Bread with it; then take a Handful of Tansy, and a Handful of Spinage, and beat in a Mortar, squeeze the Juice through a Sieve into the Pudding, and sweeten to your Taste; take a Quarter of a Pound of Butter into a Frying-pan, pour your Tansy into the Pan, set it over a clear Fire or Stove, and stir it all the Time till it is thick; then put it into a Dish and let it stand half an Hour in an Oven; then cut a *Seville* Orange into eight Parts, and set round the Dish: Have for Sauce White-wine and Sugar.

A Gelly Tansey.

TAKE a Quart of sweet Cream, and the Yolks of twelve Eggs, and sweeten to your Taste; take a Handful of Tansy, and a Handful of green Wheat and beat in a Mortar, squeeze the Juice through a Hair-sieve, put it to the Cream and Yolks of Eggs, mix it well together, and set it ten Minutes in a slow Oven: Garnish with Orange.

An Herby Pudding.

TAKE a Pint of Groats and boil half an Hour in Water, and put them into a Sieve to drain the Water from them; then take green Thyme, Parsley,

Sweet-marjoram, Pot-marjoram, Dates and young Onions of each an equal Quantity, cut them very small and mix with the Groats; then take a Jill of thick Cream, and the Yolks of ten Eggs, and mix all well together with a little Salt; then butter a Cloth and tie it in, and boil it an Hour: Have plain Butter for Sauce.

A Liver Pudding.

TAKE the Liver of a good Calf and cut one half into Inch thick Slices; take a Quart of Water into a broad Hash-pan, set it on a hot Stove, when it boils put in the sliced Liver, and let it boil five Minutes; then take it up and cut it very small on a Shreding-board; take half the Weight of the Liver of Beef-suet and mix with it; add green Thyme, Parsley, Sweet-marjoram, Chives cut small, Nutmeg, Pepper and Salt, and beat six Eggs and mix with it; put it into a Pudding-cloth, and boil it three Quarters of a Hour: For Sauce have Gravy and Butter.

Apple Dumplins.

TAKE large Apples pare and core them, make a cold Paste, and roll out a Sheet for each Apple; cut a Lemon-skin very small, and put a little into the Middle of each four Quarters of the Apple, but no Sugar, it may be sweetened at the Table as People like; roll up one Apple in every Sheet of Paste, take Care to leave no Room for the Water to enter in, and boil them three Quarters of an Hour; have Butter and Sugar to eat the Dumplins with.

To make Spice Dumplins.

TAKE a Quarter of a Pound of Butter and a Jill of Cream, and boil together, work it up with Flour; add to it some Cinnamon beat fine, and grate in some Nutmeg, a Quarter of a Pound of ston'd Rasins, and some Currants, make them into little Dumplins and fry them; then grate Sugar over them: For Sauce, have plain melted Butter and Sugar.

An Amalet *of* Eggs.

TAKE twelve Eggs and beat well, boil half a Hundred of Asparagus, and cut the green Ends small, and mix with the Eggs; then make some clarified Butter hot in a Frying-pan on a Stove or clear Fire, into which put the Eggs and Grass cast over them, a little Pepper and Salt, and fry them a nice brown; the Amalet will be an Inch thick; lay it on a Dish, and garnish with Parsley: Have Vinegar and Butter for Sauce.

Clary Pancakes.

MAKE a Batter of a Jill of Cream, four Eggs, and four Spoonfuls of Flour, a Glass of Sack, grate a little Nutmeg, and beat all well together; take a large Leaf of Clary and wash it clean, take some clarified Butter into a Frying-pan, and pour in Half of your Batter, and lay on your Clary leaf, cover it with the other Half of your Batter, and fry it very crisp on both Sides: Have Sugar and hot White-wine for Sauce, and grate Sugar round the Dish.

Wafer Pancakes.

TAKE a Pint of Cream, three Spoonfuls of Flour, and five Eggs; then put a Slice of Butter into a Piece of thin Linen-cloth; take a Girdle and set on a clear Fire, rub the butter'd Cloth over the Bottom of it, and pour on a large Spoonful of Batter, so fry them very quick and crisp.

Ratafia Pancakes.

BOIL six Laurel-leaves in a Pint of Milk, take them out and set the Milk to cool; then beat up four Eggs with a little of the Milk and Flour, and add the Remainder of the Milk, let the Batter be thin, and take a Frying-pan, put into it a Slice of Butter and let it be hot, and pour in your Batter, but not to make your Pancakes thick; fry them crisp, and send them single to the Table hot.

Apple Fritters.

MAKE a Batter of a Jill of Cream, Flour, and four Eggs, let it be thick and beat it half an Hour; add to it a Glass of Orange-flower Water; grate in a little Nutmeg, and Cinnamon finely beat and sifted, and sweeten it with Loaf-sugar; cut off the Skins of some large Pippins, and cut round Slices off them, taking out the Seeds; then take a Pint of clarified Butter or Hog's Lare into a little Hash-pan, and set it over a clear Stove; when it is hot dip each sliced Apple into the Batter, and boil it up, turning each Fritter, and they will be as round as Balls; grate Sugar over them, and send them up.

To fry Cream.

TAKE a Pint of Cream and sweeten it to your Taste, grate in some Nutmeg and mix with it; cut a large Slice round a six-penny Loaf an Inch thick and square, lay it on a clean Board and pour on the Cream by degrees, so as to let the Bread soak most of it up, and have some clarified Butter in a Frying-pan upon a clear Stove or Fire; let the Butter be hot, and with a Knife cut the Bread into Inch square Dices; fry them crisp in the clarified Butter, and put them on a Dish, grate Sugar all over them, and send them up.

A Calf Foot Gelly.

FIRST scald a Gang of Calf Feet, scrape off all the Hair very clean, and take off the Hoofs; have a very clean Pot with two Gallons of soft Water, put in your Feet, and let them boil softly till there is three Quarts; then strain it into an Earthen-pot, let it stand till it is cold and take all the Fat off the Top, put the Stock into a clean Pan, beat the Whites of eight Eggs to a Froth and add to it, with the Juice of three Lemons and the Skin of one, three Quarters of a Pound of single refin'd Sugar, and mix all well together with a Pint of Rhenish-wine; set the Pan on a Stove or clear Fire, and have a clean Flannel-bag ready to run it through; when it boils pour it into the Bag, and let it run into a Bason, put it into the Bag again till it runs off very clear, then you may glass it or put it in Basons; when it is cold you may get three Laurel-leaves, lay them upon the Top of the Bason, and with your Finger loosen the Gelly from the Side, whelm a Dish on the Bason, turn the Gelly upside down, and it makes a pretty Globe.

To make Hartshorn Gelly.

TAKE half a Pound of Hartshorn Shavings and put into a Pan with two Quarts of Water, and let it boil till one half is consumed; then strain it off and take the Whites of five Eggs beat to a Froth, a Quarter of a Pound of Sugar, a Jill of Rhenish, the Juice of a Lemon, and a Stick of Cinnamon, mix all well together and set on the Fire; when it boils strain it through a Flannel-bag as above directed.

To make Calf Foot Flummery.

TAKE the Stock of a Gang of Calf's Feet, after they are boiled and cool'd, and the Top taken off and the Bottom left; let your Pan be clean, and put in this Stock into a clean Pan, beat a Quarter of a Pound of bitter Almonds and put to it, and sweeten to your Taste, and let it boil half an Hour; then take a Pint of Cream and add to it, and strain it through a clean Linen-cloth into a Delf-bowl, and keep it stirring till it is almost cold; then put it into Shapes of various Forms, such as Scallops, Shells, Harts, *Etc.* After you have set them to Gelly, when you want them for Use, you must press them round with your Fingers which will loosen them, and make them turn out smooth and easy on your Dishes.

To make Hartshorn Flummery.

TAKE Half a Pound of the Shavings of Hartshorn, two Ounces of Ising-glass, and three Quarts of Water boiled to three Pints over a slow Fire, strain it through a Gelly-bag, and put it into a clean Pan again, and set it on a clear Fire; add to it a Stick of Cinnamon, and let it boil to a Quart, and sweeten to your Taste; then put to it a little Orange-flower Water and a Jill of Cream, and strain it off through a Linen-cloth, and stir it till it is almost cold: Then put it into sundry Shapes as above directed.

To make Leach.

BOIL the Stock of Calf's Feet as strong as for Flummery, and clear them with the Whites of Eggs, Lemon-juice, White-wine, Sugar, and powder two Penny-worth of Cocheneal, and boil with it; strain it through a Gelly-bag, and put it into Flummery Shapes.

Steeple Cream.

BEAT and sift through a Hair-sieve a Pound of double refin'd Sugar; and take a Quarter of a Pound of Currant-gelly, and the Whites of two Eggs into a China or Delf-bowl, and beat it an Hour with a Silver-spoon: It is a pretty Side-dish.

Rasp Cream.

TAKE a Quart of Cream, a Quarter of a Pound of Rasp-juice, mix the Cream with the Rasp-juice, and put it into a China-bowl; take a Chocolate-stick and mill up the Cream as you do Chocolate; turn up the Bottom of a clean Hair-sieve, and as the Froth rises on your Cream take if off with a Spoon and lay it on your Sieve, and when it will cast no more Froth, pour it into the Dish, and heap it up with the Froth.

To make Currant Cream.

TAKE a Quart of Cream and put into a China-bowl, and mill it up in the above Manner, laying the Froth on the Bottom of a Hair-sieve; and when you have Froth sufficient to make a large Heap, take a Quarter of a Pound of Currant-gelly and mix with the Cream; put it into the Dish, and heap it up with the Froth.

Lemon Cream.

TAKE a Quart of Cream and sweeten to your Taste, squeeze into it the Juice of a Lemon, and put it into a China or Delf-bowl, and mull as aforesaid, putting the Froth upon it; cut the Lemon into small Shreds, and lay the Froth over and round the Dish.

A Whip Posset.

TAKE a Quart of Cream and sweeten to your Taste, add a Glass of Orange-flower Water to it; then put a Pint of Sack into a Quart Glass-bowl, and mill up the Cream, lay the Froth on a Hair-sieve to drain the Milk from it, and let it lie on it Half an Hour before you lay it on the Sack; be careful to keep a steady Hand as you drop it from the Spoon, and heap the Glass-bowl with Froth.

A Crow Crant.

TAKE wet or dry Sweet-meats, and fill a Dish as full as for a Pye; then take a deep Dish of the same Breadth of the other that your Sweet-meats are in, turn it upside down, and cover it with a Sheet of Paste of Milk and Sugar boil'd, wrought with Flour; then roll it out thin, and cut it out in various Shapes and Forms, bake it on the Dish, and take great Care not to have any burnt Spots on it; when it is enough take it out of the Dish, and set it upon the Sweet-meats.

Sweet-meat Tarts.

TURN up the Bottom of a Tart-pan, and cut out of a Sheet of common raised Paste with your Jager-irons into Strings, no broader than Tape three Yards a Penny, rub the Outside of your Tart-pan with a little Butter, and lay over your Paste, cross it into Diamond Figures, and bake it in as many as will make a Dish; put preserv'd Plumbs, Cherries, or Gooseberries into Saucers, and set the Diamond-paste Covers over your Preserves.

To make Glazed Tarts.

FILL your Tart-pans with Sweet-meats, make a Paste of double-refin'd Sugar beat and sifted, take the Whites of three Eggs and a little Orange-flower Water, and beat an Hour to an Icing; then lay round the Edge of your Tart-pan a little of this Icing, and cover it with Wafer-paper, and with a Pair of Scissors clip the Wafer-paper close to the Edge of the Tart-pan; then lay over a thin Icing and set it in a slow Oven five Minutes: Do as many as your Icing will make. You are not to put any Syrup in with your preserv'd Plumbs, Gooseberries, or Cherries, or any other Thing.

To make Tart Puff-paste.

MIX Flour and fair Water into Paste, take the same Weight of Butter and divide it into three Parts, roll out the Paste three Times, and lay on one Part of the Butter each Time, dashing on a little Flour over the Butter every Time: This Paste is for fine Puddings and Tarts, but is too rich for Pyes.

Crisp Paste *for* Tarts.

TAKE three Pints of Flour, and five Ounces of Butter, rub the Butter into the Flour as small as possible, so that the least Piece of Butter cannot be seen, so that all the Flour be as if no Butter was in it by being so mealy; then take six Eggs, leaving out the Whites of Two, and put three Spoonfuls of Water, mix this Paste, and roll it out almost as thin as Wafers; bake it crisp, and if it be kept till it softens, setting it a while before the Fire crispens it again.

To make Light Wigs.

RUB six Ounces of Butter into three Pounds of fine Flour, and take a Quart of Milk, beat up three Eggs, and half a Pound of Powder-sugar; warm the Milk and mix with the Sugar, Flour, and Eggs well together; add two Spoonfuls of fresh Yest, mix all well together, and set it an Hour before the Fire to rise; then put half an Ounce of Carroway [sic]-seeds, and roll out your Wigs; let them stand on a Board before the Fire to rise, before you set them into the Oven.

Bath Cakes.

TAKE a Pound of Flour and a Pint of Milk, beat up three Eggs with a Spoonful of Yest, mix all together and set in a Bowl before the Fire; when it is risen very high, take half a Pound of Butter and half a Pound of Sugar, and work into it with your Hands; add a little Rose-water, grate a Nutmeg, beat a little Cinnamon and mix thereto; then bake them in Queen-cake Pans, some plain, and some you may put Currants into.

A Pound Cake.

TAKE a Pound of Loaf-sugar beat and sift it through a Sieve, add to it a Pound of Eggs and a little Rose-water, beat it till it turns very thick and white; then take a Pound of Butter and beat up with your Hand to a Cream, the Eggs and Sugar beat with a Whisk; then take a Pound of very fine Flour, dry it before the Fire, and mix all with your Hand half an Hour; add to it an Ounce of Carroway-seeds, put it into a Pan and bake it an Hour and a Half.

A Fruit Cake.

TAKE eight Pounds of Currants and pick them clean, stone three Pounds of Raisins and cut them small, beat Cinnamon, Mace, and Nutmeg of each half an Ounce, Cloves a Quarter of an Ounce, a Pound and a Half of *Jourdon* Almonds blanched and cut very small, and the hot Spice to be powdered; then take three Pounds of Butter and beat to Cream, mix it with fourteen Eggs, and take four Pounds of Flour and mix with the Butter and Eggs; add a Jill of Brandy, a Jill of Sack, and a little new Yest, beat it till it is light; then put in the hot Spices and cut Almonds, mix them well together, and then put in the Fruit, beat and mix all well together; then cut a Pound of Orange and Lemon-peal, half a Pound of Citron cut into thin Slices, and grease your Pan with Butter; lay in your Cake at three Lairs, on each lay the Lemon and Orange-peal, and Citron intermix'd; when it is all in and your Cake pack'd close in the Cake-pan, set it into an Oven: It will take four Hours baking.

To make Queen Cakes.

TAKE half a Pound of Butter and beat up to Cream, beat and sift half a Pound of Loaf-sugar, beat four Eggs and mix with the Sugar, and beat the Eggs and Sugar a Quarter of an Hour before you mix your Butter; then weigh half a Pound of Flour, setting it before the Fire on a Dish ten Minutes before you mix your Butter, and so mix all together; add to it a Glass of Orange-flower Water, and beat it half an Hour longer with your Hand; then put them into Pans and bake them in a slow Oven, which is better for these Cakes than any other.

To preserve Plumbs.

TAKE large Magnum Plumbs and let their Stalks be kept on, and to every Pound of Plumbs take a Pound and a half of double-refined Sugar; then to every Pound of Sugar put a Jill of Water, and put it into a clean Preserving-pan, boil it near to candy Height, and with a Penknife make a very little Slit at the End of each Plumb and take off the Skin, set them upon their Ends with the Stalk-end uppermost in an Earthen-pot, and pour on your Syrup to the Plumbs, cover them up and let them stand three Days, by which Time the Syrup will be thin, you must put it into your Pan and boil it up till it will rope, pour it upon the Plumbs, and let them stand a Week; if your Syrup be thin, boil it up again to a ropy Thickness, and pour upon your Plumbs, and let them stand a Fortnight; if the Syrup keeps Substance, put up your Plumbs in Pots, cover them with Papers and Bladders, and keep them for your Use.

To candy the above Plumbs.

TAKE Magnum Plumbs, cut off all the Plumb, but leave the Stone and Stalk together; the Plumbs must not be ripe, but at their full Growth; take great Care to have a sharp Knife, and not to separate the Stone from the Stalk; take the Weight of the Plumbs of double-refined Sugar, put the Plumbs and Sugar into a Pot, and set them into a slow Oven two Hours; set the Plumb-stones and Stalks into the Sun to dry; then take out the Plumbs and mix them with their Syrup, put them through a Hair-sieve and press through all their Pulp, and put into your Preserving-pan, and boil it to a Plumb-paste; make on the Stalk the Form of a Plumb with this Paste, and dry them in cool Ovens or in the Sun; when they are thoroughly dried boil up double-refined Sugar, candy Height, and dip in each Plumb one by one, set them on their Ends on a flat-bottomed Delft-dish, and when the Candy is dry, take up each Plumbs with a thin sharp Knife.

To preserve green Gages.

TAKE to every Pound of green Gages a Pound and a half of Sugar; take the Plumbs and set on a slow Fire to scald, when they are ready take off all their Skins, and put the Plumbs into the Water they were scalded in; add to them a little Piece of Allum beat to a Powder, cover the Plumbs with Plumb Tree-leaves, and set them a great Distance from the Fire till they be green; then take them out, set them on a flat-bottomed Dish with their Stalks up, and when they are drained put them into a broad Pot in the same Way; boil up your Sugar to a thick Syrup, pour it over your Plumbs, cover them up, and let them stand two Days; boil up the Syrup again till it will rope, and pour it on your Plumbs, and let them stand a Week; boil the Syrup as strong up as before, pour it over the Plumbs; when they have stood a Fortnight, if the Syrup be any thinner boil it up again; then you may put them into Pots for Use, and tie them close with White-paper and Bladders.

Currant Gelly.

STRIP the Currants of their Stalks, when they are thoroughly ripe, put them into a Jar, and set them into an Oven or a Pot of hot Water; when the Berries are thoroughly hot, so as to discharge their Juice, strain it through a Flannel-bag, and to every Jill of this Juice put a Pound of double-refined Sugar; put it into a Brass-pan clean scoured, and boil it over a Stove till it becomes a thick Gelly, scuming it all the Time; then put it into Glasses or Pots for Use. If you have any Rasps you may put a Quart into the Currants; the Currants after the Juice is run from them, will make a small Wine.

To make Rasp Jam.

AFTER you have picked all the Worms and Greens out of the Rasps, take their Weight of Loaf-sugar, and put into a Preserving-pan; set it over a clear Stove, let it boil till you see it stiff, and take great Care to keep stirring it; when it begins to fly in Sparks, take it off, and put it in Pots or Glasses; cover it with White-paper dipp'd in Brandy, and put Bladders over it.

To preserve Rasps *whole.*

TAKE a Pint of the Juice of Currants; add to it three Pound of double-refined Sugar, put into a Preserving-pan upon a clear Stove, and boil it to a very strong Gelly; then have a Quart of fine Pick'd Rasps, put them into the Gelly, let them boil five Minutes, and put them into Glasses.

To preserve Gooseberries.

TAKE Gooseberries when at their full Growth, cut a Nick on each Side, and with a Pin pick out the Seeds; to every Pound of Berries, take a Pound and a Half of double-refined Sugar; put a Jill of Water to every Pound, and boil your Sugar to a thick Syrup; put your Gooseberries into a Pot, pour upon them this Syrup, and let them stand two Days; if the Syrup be thin, boil it up again till it be ropy, and then pour it on them, and let them stand a Week; then boil it up, and put in the Berries, let them boil three Minutes; put them into your Glasses, and keep them for Use.

To preserve Currants *in* Strops.

TAKE red Currants, and with a Pin make a Hole at the End of each Currant, pick out all the Seeds, and make a Syrup of double-refin'd Sugar and pour upon the Berries, and let it stand two Days; then strip as many Currants as will make a Jill of Juice, pour the Syrup from the Berries in Strops, and boil up with this Currant-juice, till it becomes a weak Gelly; then take it off the Fire, put in your Currants in Strops, and put them into Glasses, and keep them for Use.

To preserve Peaches.

TAKE green Peaches when a Pin will run through the Stone, put them into a Pan with Water, set them on a slow Fire, and let them stand till they are scalding hot; when they are so done, take them out of the Water, take off the Skins, and put them into the Water you took them out of, cover them with Peach-leaves, put a little Allum into the Pan, and cover it very close; set it on a very slow Fire, and let it stand till the Peaches are green; then take them out of the Water, to every Pound of Peaches take a Pound and a half of double-refined Sugar; add Water to the Sugar, and boil in a clear Brass-pan till it is a rich Syrup; put your Peaches into a Pot, pour this Syrup upon them, cover them close, and let them stand a Week; take the Syrup into the Pan again, and boil it till it will rope; then put in your Peaches and give them a boil, not exceeding three Minutes; then put the Peaches into Pots, covering them with Syrup, and paper them up; if the Syrup turns thin, boil it up till it is rich, and pour upon them again: Keep them for Deserts, Sweet-meat Tarts, or send them up in Sweet-meat Glasses. You do Apricots, and Nectars in the same Manner.

To make Gooseberry Wine.

TAKE Crystal Gooseberries, pick and bruise them in a Wooden-bowl or Mortar, and to every Gallon of bruised Berries put two Quarts of Water, and let them stand in a clean Tub twenty-four Hours; then strain them through a Hair-sieve, take out the Skins and Seeds, but be sure to press through all the Pulp you possibly can; to every Gallon of Liquor add four Pounds of double-refined Sugar; tun it up into a Brandy-cask if you have one of the Size, and bung it down, but leave the Spile-hole open; when it has done fomenting, put in the Spile, and let it stand six Months; then bottle it.

To make red Currant Wine.

GATHER your Currants when they are full ripe, pick off their Stalks, and bruize them with a Wooden-pestle; to every Gallon of bruised Berries put a Gallon of Spring-water, and let it stand two Days, stirring it every six Hours; then strain it through a Hair-sieve, take out the Skins and Seeds and press the Pulp through the Sieve; to every Gallon of Liquor put in three Pound and a half of double-refined Sugar, and to every twenty Quarts add a Pint of the best *French* Brandy; then tun it and bung it down, leaving open your Spile-hole; when it has done fomenting close it up, and in four Months you may bottle if off. Black Currants are done after the same Manner.

To make Cowslip Wine.

PICK your Cowslips, to every Pound of Flowers take a Gallon of Water, and beat the Flowers in a Marble Mortar; then mix them with the Water, to every six Gallons of Water add a Dozen of *Seville* Oranges; squeeze in their Juice, let six of their Skins be put in with the Juice, and let it stand all Night in the Tub, then strain them through a Sieve; to every Gallon of Liquor add four Pounds of double-refined Sugar, and stir all well together; add two Spoonfuls of Gile-yeast, and let it stand all Night in the Tub; tun it up into a Cask, adding a Pint of Brandy to every six Gallons of Wine, bung it down close, leaving the Spile-hold open till it be done working; then close it up, and in six Months Time you may bottle it.

To make Baum Wine.

TAKE Baum at full Growth, the first Cutting, and beat in a Mortar or Wooden-bowl; to every Pound of Baum put a Gallon of Water, and let the Water and Baum stand twenty-four Hours; then strain it through a Flannel-bag, and squeeze its Juice out of it; to every Gallon of Liquor add three Pounds of double-refined Sugar, and stir it till all the Sugar is mix'd well with the Liquor; then add to it a Jill of Ale-yeast, very fresh off the Fats, and tun it up, leaving the Spile-hole open, till it be done fomenting; then close it up, and it will be ready in four Months for bottling.

To make Raisin Wine.

TAKE *Malaga* Raisins, and to every Stone of Raisins put six Quarts of Water in an open headed Cask, and let them stand twelve Days, stirring them every Day; then strain the Raisins all out of the Tub, squeeze them well in your Hands as you take them out, and then take a clean Hair-cloth, put as many Raisins into it as will press without letting any of the Skins out, and the Pulp thereof put into your Liquor; after you have strain'd it through a Hair-sieve, tun it up, and bung it, leave out the Spile-pin till it has done fomenting, and in six Months Time it will be fit for Use; but if not fine in that Time, if you have half a Hogshead of Wine, take an Ounce of Ising-glass, cut it with a Knife, and put it into a Quart of rough Cider; cut the small End off a Whisk, and beat this up every Day with the Whisk, till all the Glass is dissolved, it will be all thick as Calf's Feet Gelly is when it is cold; then strain it through a fine Wood-sieve, draw out a little of the Wine and mix with it, and as much more of the Wine as the Cider and Ising-glass; then pour in the Ising-glass and Wine, stirring it with a Stick not above a Quarter of a Yard within the Cask, and round the Cask; then bung it close down, and it will be fine in forty-eight Hours: This Method will fine any of the above Wines.

To make Orange Wine.

TO six Gallons of Water take three Dozen of Oranges, and squeeze out their Juice; take the Rind of twelve Oranges and put into the Water with the Juice, and let it stand two Days, stirring it every six Hours; then strain it through a Hair-sieve, and press the Juice of the Oranges all through the Sieve; to every Gallon of Liquor add four Pound of Loaf-sugar, and put two Spoonfuls of Yeast fresh off the Gile-fat to it; tun it up, put a Quart of Brandy thereto, leave the Spile-hole open till it be done working, and it will be fit for bottling in four Months.

To make Cherry Wine.

TAKE twenty Pounds of *Morella* Cherries full ripe, and bruise them; take two Gallons of red Currants stripp'd from the Stalks, and bruised with a

Wooden-pestle, and put them in a clean Vessel open headed; to every Gallon add a Gallon of boiling Water, stir all together, and let it stand forty-eight Hours, stirring it up every six Hours; then strain it through a Hair-sieve, and to every Gallon of Liquor add three Pounds of double-refined Sugar; put it into a Brandy-cask, leave the Spile-pin open till it be done working, and in three Months you may bottle it off.

To make Elder Wine.

STRIP your Elder-berries off the Stalks, put them into a large deep Earthen-pot, cover it close, and set it in an Oven all Night; then take it out of the Oven, and strain off the Juice into a clean Pot; to every Gallon of Juice put a Gallon of Water, and to every Gallon of Liquor put three Pounds of Loaf-sugar; put it into a Cask that has had Brandy in it, bung it down, leaving the Spile-hole open, and when it has done fomenting, close it up.

To make Bramble Wine.

INFUSE your Bramble-berries as above directed; to every Gallon of Juice add two Gallons of Water, and to every Gallon of Liquor put three Pounds of Loaf-sugar; stir it well till all the Sugar is dissolved, and let it stand twenty Hours in the Tub you mix it in; then tun it up into a Cask, leaving your Spile-hole open, and when it has done fomenting close it up; it will be ready for bottling in six Months, and fit for drinking.

To pickle Mushrooms.

TAKE the close Buttons, cut off their Stalks, and put them into Water an Hour; then take a Brush made of Rice, strain and wash your Mushrooms with this Brush, and put as much Water as the Mushrooms require to cover them, so that this Brush takes the Scurf off the Mushrooms; then give them plenty of clean Water, and wash them with the Brush as before; then take them into a clean Cullender, having a clean Pan that just holds the Mushrooms, put them into it, and cover it close; set it on a clear Fire with nothing but the Mushrooms, which will discharge as much of their own Liquor as will cover them, and let them boil in this Liquor five Minutes; in which Time make a Brine of Salt and Water so strong as to bear an Egg, then drain the Liquor from the Mushrooms, put them into this Salt-brine, and let them stand five Days, stirring them every Day; make another Brine as strong as the former, put in the Mushrooms, let them stand a Week longer, and this is physicking the Mushrooms; then add to them some distilled Vinegar, and let them lie fourteen Days, after all bottle them; every Bottle will take a Jill of distilled Vinegar, and put two Blades of Mace into each Bottle: This will keep either close or open in Bottles or Jarrs; now the Juice that the Mushrooms discharges in the Pan, is the best of Catchup; if you have a Pint of it, add three Spoonfuls of Beef-brine, if it be fresh and perfectly sweet, also Mace, Nutmeg, Cloves, and Pepper powdered, and boil it, filtering it through a Flannel-bag: This will be proper for White-sauces.

To pickle Walnuts.

TAKE Walnuts when they are almost at their full Growth, but that a Pin will run through them; then pick off their Stalks, rub them with a coarse Cloth, make a Brine of Salt, and let it be so strong as to bear an Egg; then put in your Walnuts and lay a Board upon them to keep them under the Brine, and let them lie in this Brine six Days; then make a fresh Brine, pour off this from them and put in the fresh Brine, let them stand ten Days longer, and then take and dry them with a coarse Cloth: To every Hundred of Walnuts take a Jill of Mustard-seed, lay your Walnuts in Lairs, and upon every Lair strew your Mustard proportionably, and when your Jar is full have some of the best Beer-Vinegar and put in; for every Hundred of Walnuts have *Jamaica* and Black-pepper of each an Ounce, Mace and Nutmeg of each half an Ounce, and boil up in the Vinegar, pour it boiling upon the Walnuts, and put a Bladder over them; don't use them till the Bitter be overcome by the Pickle and hot Spices: This Pickle make Sauces richer than Catchup made of Mushrooms.

To make Walnut Catchup.

TAKE four Hundred of Walnuts, such as before described, and with a sharp Penknife cut off all the pulpy Part till you are at the Inner Shell, and be careful to keep that whole, beat the green Pulp in a Mortar, and to every Pint of the Pulp add a Spoonful of fresh Beef-brine, and let it lie 20 Hours; then take the Shells that you cut the green Part of the Walnut from, and put them into a Jarr, make a Brine of Milk-whey, pour it boiling hot upon the Shells, and let them stand twenty-four Hours; then take your Walnut-pulp and strain it through a clean coarse Linen-cloth, squeeze all the Juice you can possibly get out of it, and to every Pint of this Juice add Nutmeg, Mace, and Black-pepper of each a Quarter of an Ounce, and half that Quantity of Cloves; then boil it up, but do not make any use of it till the Bitter is gone off: A Tea-spoonful of this will make Sauce rich for Fish or any Made-dish, nor is there any Thing so agreeable to the Taste, for I never knew that the most delicate Palate objected it, nor the tenderest Stomach was offended therewith: Then you take the Walnut out of the Whey, and with a Flannel-rag wash all the Scurf off them into clear Water; then put them into Bottles with wide Mouths, fill them up with distill'd Vinegar that has been distill'd from Beer-vinegar, and hot Spices: This is a delicious pretty Pickle that very few are acquainted with.

To pickle Onions.

TAKE Onions no larger than small Nutmegs, pour boiling Water upon them, and take off their brown Coat; put the Onions into a Brine of Milk, with Salt and Water into a Pan, and take the Onions out of the Milk-brine into a Cullender; when the Salt and Water boils put them in, and let them boil two Minutes; then take them out of the Water and lay them on a Cloth to cool; put them into Bottles with distill'd Vinegar, and keep them for Use.

To pickle Colliflowers.

LET your Colliflowers be very white and without Frickles, and let them be close; cut them into Buds and boil them in a Brine of Salt and Water one Minute; then take them out and lay them to cool, when they are cold put them into Jarrs, and fill them with distill'd Vinegar; then tye them down close with a Bladder and Pack-thread for Use.

To pickle Turnips.

CUT your Turnips into various Shapes, that you may have them for Garnishing, and cut them a Quarter of an Inch thick; let your Turnips be clear of Worm-eaten, and let them boil a Minute in Salt and Water; then take them out into a coarse Cloth, and when they are cold and all the Water drain'd out put them into a Glass-jar, fill them up with distilled Vinegar; cover them close with a Bladder, and keep them for Use.

To pickle Kidney Beans.

TAKE Whey after it is scalded and the Curds from it, make a Brine so strong as to bear an Egg, let your Beans be young and dry pull'd, put them into the Whey-brine till their Colour is discharg'd; when they are of a bright Yellow, take them out of the Whey into a Cullender, and dry them with a coarse Cloth; then put them into a Brass-pan and cover them with Beer-Vinegar, put in some Dill, and cover them close down, put Paper round the Edge of your Cover, and set the Pan a good Distance from the Fire, if it be hot; but if slow, it need not be at so great a Distance, and let it stand till the Beans turn grass Green; then take them out of this Vinegar and put them into a Jarr, and make Pickle of fresh Beer-vinegar, *Jamaica* and Black-pepper, and Race-ginger boil'd up, pour it upon your Beans, and keep them for Use. The aforesaid Receipts is a Rule to Pickle Girkins, Cucumbers, Parsley, Reddish-pods, Aftertion-buds [sic], Broom-buds, or Burtree-buds: So there is no need of telling the Tale oftner than is necessary.

To mango Cucumbers.

TAKE large Cucumbers and cut a long narrow Piece out of each, with the Mouth of a Teaspoon pick out all the Seeds and Pulp of it, gather out all the Seeds and mix them with white Mustard-seed, Astertion-buds, Shalot, and some Salt; fill the Cucumbers with this Mixture and put them close down in a Jarr, boil up Beer-vinegar, Salt, *Jamaica* and Black-pepper, with Race-ginger, and pour upon the Mangoes, cover them close and let them stand two Days; then boil up the Pickle again, and repeat it till your Mangoes are green, and keep them for Use.

To mango Apples.

THERE is a long green Apple call'd a Finger, take of this Sort, and with a Penknife cut a round Piece out at each End, with an Apple-scope take out all the Core, and fill the Place with Horse-radish, White-mustard, and a little Mace; put the Pieces on at each End from whence they were taken, and sew it up with a Needle and Thread, pack them close up into a Jarr, and boil Beer-vinegar with *Jamaica* and Black-pepper, Race-ginger and Salt, and pour it boiling hot upon the Mangoes; let them stand, and repeat the boiling of the Vinegar till you see your Mangoes turn green; then cover them with a Bladder, and keep them for Use.

To mango Millons.

TAKE little Millons of the latter Growth, when the first Growth is over, and cut a long Piece out of the Side; take out the Seed, and put your Millons in Whey till they have discharg'd their Colour; then take as much Vinegar as you have to Cucumbers to green them, and cover the Millons with it, place them at a little Distance from the Fire till they are green; then take them up, and when they are cold, take the Seeds you took out of them, and mix with white Mustard, Horse-radish cut small, and Afterson-seed; mix all well, fill up your Millons, and put the Pieces you cut out into their proper Places; take four Yards a Penny Tape to to roll up the Millons, and put them into a Jarr; boil up Beer-vinegar, *Jamaica* and Black-pepper, and Race-ginger, and pour boiling upon the Millons; cover them with a Paper, and keep them close for Use.

To pickle Dutch Cabbage.

TAKE a red Cabbage, cut it into four Quarters, take out the Core, with a sharp Knife cut your Cabbage, lay it into a Wooden-dish, mix it with Salt, and let it lie five Days, turning it with your Hands every Day; when it has lain the above Time, take up a Handful and squeeze with all your Strength, and when one Handful is done take another, till you have squeezed it all; then set upon a clear Fire a broad Pan, and boil as much Beer-vinegar as will cover the Cabbage, and have *Jamaica* and Black-pepper, and Race-ginger; when it boils put in the Cabbage, and let it not boil above a Minute; then take it up, put it into a Jarr, and keep it close covered for Use: You may put into it some red Beat Root.

To pickle Pumpkins.

TAKE a Pumpkin and cut into half Inch Slices, after you have taken out all the Seed, cut it into various Forms, so as to make ornamental for garnishing such as carved Work, *&c.* the Outside is a bright rich yellow; boil White-wine Vinegar and hot Spices, and pour upon your Mango into a Jarr three sundry Times, and keep for Use.

To pickle Barberry-berries.

TAKE Barberry-berries when they are full ripe, pick all the Leaves from off the Stalks, take all the small Barberry-berries and beat in a Mortar; then make a Brine of Salt so strong as to bear an Egg, and boil the beaten Barberry-berries in it, put them through a Flannel-bag, and boil it up again; powder Two-pennyworth of Cocheneal and put to it; then put the Berries into a Jarr, and pour this Brine boiling upon them, and lay a Piece of Flannel over the Barberry-berries within the Jarr; cover the Jarr, and keep them for garnishing Fish, Fowl, Rabbets, or any other Made-dish.

To make Mackroons.

TAKE a Pound of *Jourdon* Almonds, blanch and beat them in a Marble Mortar to a Paste, take the Whites of five Eggs, and a Pound of beat and sifted Loaf-sugar, and mix with the Whites of the Eggs; beat the Sugar and Whites one Quarter of an Hour with a Whisk, before you mix it with the Almond-paste; then add to it a Glass of Orange-flower Water, and beat all well with a Wooden pestle a Quarter of an Hour; lay some Wafer-paper upon Wires, and drop the Mackroons on the Paper: Set them in a sharp Oven, and a Quarter of an Hour will bake them.

To make Ratafia Drops.

TAKE a Pound of *Jourdon* Almonds and half a Pound of bitter Almonds, blanch and beat them to Paste; take a Pound and a half of beaten and sifted fine Loaf-sugar, add three Eggs, and beat the Eggs, Sugar and Almond-paste all well together till they become a very stiff Paste, add to it a Glass of Ratafia or *French* Brandy: You must have a Marble Mortar for your Purpose, and observe to have your Ingredients not only work'd to a proper Stiffness, but also to a very fine Smoothness; then drop it on Cap-paper in Drops as big as large Nutmegs, bake them brown in a sharp Oven, and keep them for Use.

To make a Biscuit Cake.

BEAT and sift a Pound of Loaf-sugar, take a Pound of Eggs and beat with the Sugar till it is thick, add to it a Pound of fine *London* Flour; put it into a Cake-pan, after you have rubb'd the Pan with Butter; and bake it in a slow Oven.

To make Biscuit Drops.

TAKE a Pound of Loaf-sugar well beat and sifted through a Hair-sieve, beat four Eggs with the Sugar till it is very white and thick; take a Pound and a Quarter of the finest *London* Flour, and let it stand drying before the Fire a Quarter of an Hour; then mix it with the Eggs and Sugar, adding a Glass of Orange-flour Water to it, and when it is well mix'd drop it on Gray-paper, and bake them in a slow Oven: Be exceeding careful to take your Papers off whilst hot, for if they are suffered to cool, they will by no Means part with their Paper.

Appendix

Pigeons *paradised*.

PICK, singe, and wash six Pigeons, cut up their Backs and take out the Bones; then cut the Livers small with a Quarter of a Pound of Beef-suet, pounding them well in a Mortar, steep the Crumb of a Halfpenny Roll in Cream and beat with it; add to it the Yolks of four Eggs boiled hard; and season it with Mace, Nutmeg, Pepper, and Salt; add green Thyme, Sweet-marjoram, and Parsley; break two Eggs and mix it well together; then divide it equally amongst the Pigeons, after you have dried them well with a clean coarse Cloth; put the Stuffing equally within them, and put them in the Form they were before you boned them; lay them in a flat-bottomed Earthen-dish, and rub the Breast of each Pigeon with Butter, throwing over all some grated Bread and green Parsley; then rub some Butter on white Paper and lay over them, and set them an Hour in an Oven; then take a Quarter of a Pound of Rice, boil, and drain it dry in a Hair-sieve; colour one Half of it Green with the Juice of Sorrel, and the other Half let be White, and lay it round the Dish-rim in various Forms; and have half a Hundred Asparagus boiled, and cut the green Tops, and stew in good Gravy thickned [sic] with Butter and Flour, pour it on the Dish; lay on the Pigeons with Sippets and green Parsley, and serve it up.

Pigeons *in Blankets*.

PICK and wash your Pigeons clean, and dry them: For three Pigeons, take the Yolks of six hard boiled Eggs cut small, add green Thyme, Sweet-marjoram, and Parsley shred fine, and take the Bulk of a Hen's Egg of Butter, and work up all the Ingredients, which divide equally amongst and put into the Pigeons; then roll out three Sheets of cold Paste, into each Sheet roll a Pigeon, and tie it tight in a Cloth: Boil them an Hour and a Half; then take off the Cloths, and lay them in a Dish. For Sauce, Gravy and Butter.

A savoury Pigeon Pye.

MAKE a raised Crust, that is, a standing Crust; for four Pigeons, make three Corners and one in the Middle, and when it is cold, take some savoury Force-meat and draw all over the Inside; bone the Pigeons, and rub them on the Inside with Yolk of Egg, and lay on some of the Force-meat; put them as for baking, and let their Breast be uppermost; then put on the Lid, and let them stand two Hours in a moderate Oven: Then have a Jill of Gravy and Butter, and pour into it.

Another Pigeon Pye.

TAKE six Pigeons, pick and wash them clean, cut off their Feet and Pinions; take half a Pound of Butter, and work up in it as much Pepper and Salt as you think reasonable to season them; then make a Sheet of cold Paste, and lay a Rim round the Edge of the Dish, and lay in your Pigeons, after you have put an equal Quantity of Butter and Seasoning within each, put the Gizzards, Livers, and Pinions into the Dish, add a Pint of Water, and lay a Sheet of Paste over all: Bake it an Hour and a Half in a moderate Oven; when it is drawn, put half a Jill of good Gravy into it.

A white Fricassey of Eggs.

BOIL six Eggs hard, and take out their Yolks, cut the Whites very small; take a clean Frying-pan and heat some Butter hot, but take Care not to brown it; then drop in six Eggs and fry them White, lay them on a clean Tin-pan and set them before the Fire; rub your Frying-pan clean, and put more Butter into it, and fry as many more Eggs in the above Manner, and lay them into the same Pan, then take a Knife and cut off all the Rags; when you have trimmed them, take half a Wine-pint of sweet Cream and a Quarter of a Pound sweet Butter, wrought in Flour; put your fried Eggs into a Hash-pan, add to them the Cream and Butter, with a little powdered Mace, grated Nutmeg, and Salt; then toss it up, and when it boils take it off the Fire, and squeeze the Juice of a Lemon; toss it up, and lay the Whites round the Dish; cut some Parsley, then pour in the Fricassey; lay the hard Yolks over it, and serve it up.

A brown Fricassey of Eggs.

TAKE six Eggs, break and separate the Yolks from the Whites; tie the Yolks in a Linen-rag and boil them hard, cut them small, and grate the Crumb of a Halfpenny Roll, and mix with the shred Yolks; add Nutmeg, Pepper, Salt,

Thyme, and sweet-Marjoram cut small, and rub the Bulk of a Nutmeg of Butter into the Mixture; take a raw Egg and work it up, dusting a little Flour over it, roll it into small Balls, and rub a Plate with Butter, then set them to brown before the Fire or in an Oven: Beat the Whites with a Spoonful of Cream, add Nutmeg, Salt, and Parsley cut very small; then take a very small Bladder and pour in the Whites, leaving a little for them to rise in boiling; then take a thick Slice of sweet Butter in a Frying-pan over a sharp Stove or clear Fire, brown the Butter, and drop six Eggs, fry them brown on both Sides; then pour out the Eggs and Butter into a clean Hash-pan, and fry six more Eggs in the above Manner, and put them to the other Eggs; then half a Jill of Water, of Walnut Pickle, Catchup, and Mushrooms, each a Spoonful. Thicken it with Butter and Flour.

A Pallateen *of* Eggs.

BEAT twelve Eggs, and take out the Crumb of a Penny Loaf, add to it a Jill of Rhenish Wine, and mix it well with the Eggs; boil six Artichokes, take the Buttoms and cut small, and mix with the Eggs; season them with Mace, Nutmeg, and Salt, and mix them all well together: Grease a round Bason that will just hold them, and pour them into it, lay three thin Slices of Butter over all, and set it an Hour in a slow Oven; then take half a Hundred fresh Oysters and wash them clean in Water, lay them on a clean Board, and season them with Black-pepper and Salt, and drudge some Flour over them; then take a Quarter of a Pound of Butter in a clean Frying-pan over a clear Stove or brisk Fire, let the Butter be brown when you put in the Oysters, and turn them; then add to them half a Jill of Water, a Spoonful of Catchup, and thicken it with Flour and Butter; then turn the Eggs out of the Bason on the Middle of the Dish, pour over it the Ragoo: Garnish with Barberry-berries and Parsley, and send it up.

Eggs *a la Mode.*

TAKE ten Eggs and beat them well, soak the Crumb of a Penny Loaf in Cream and beat with them, boil a Hundred of Asparagus, cut the green Ends small, and mix with the above, add Nutmeg, Pepper and Salt; when you have mixt them well, butter a Tin-pan, and lay a thin Sheet of Puff-paste in it, pour on your Eggs, and throw over them some grated Bread and melted Butter, set it in an Oven; then take a Quart of Water, slice a Carrot, and put to it a Faggot of sweet Herbs, Horse-radish and Shalots, let it boil to half a Pint; then strain it in a clean Pan, add to it two Spoonfuls of Catchup; and take a

Slice of Butter in a Frying-pan, brown it over a clear Fire, toss up the Sauce in the Frying-pan, and so put it in the Sauce-pan; thicken it with Butter and Flour, and have some Force-meat Balls as before directed; then take out your Eggs and cut them into Dices, leaving a large One for the Middle; then dish it up, pour over the Sauce, strew over the Force-meat Balls, and some pickled Mushrooms. Garnish with green Parsley.

Another Way to a la Mode Eggs.

BREAK sixteen Eggs, and take out all the Yolks with a Spoon, lay them upon a Plate, and take great Care not to break any; then beat the Whites very well, and boil a Quarter of a Pound of Rice in Water till it is tender; then mix the Rice and Whites together, season it with Nutmeg and Salt: Grease a Cloth with Butter, and pour this into the Cloth, then boil it an Hour: In the mean Time, take a clean Frying-pan and a thick Slice of Butter over a quick Fire, make the Butter brown; then put in the Yolks and fry them whole, turning each separate very carefully; then add to then a Jill of Water, two Spoonfuls of Catchup, one of Walnut Pickle, and toss it up, pour it on the Dish, and throw the Balls over it; take the Whites out of the Cloth, and cut into thin Slices, and lay round them. Garnish the Dish with fried Parsley.

To ragoo Eggs.

BEAT ten Eggs, and take the Crumb of a Penny *French* Roll soak'd in Cream, and mix it well with the Eggs, add green Thyme, Sweet-marjoram, and Parsley cut small, Nutmeg, Mace, Pepper and Salt, boil this in a Calf's Bladder; take a Pint of fresh Mushroom-buttons, and fry them brown in Butter, add to them a Pint of fresh Water, and boil half a Hundred Asparagus, cut off the tender Part of the Tops into Half-inch Lengths, and stew amongst the Mushrooms, add Walnut Pickle and Verjuice of each a Spoonful, let it boil till the Liquor is half consumed; then thicken it with half a Jill of plain Butter-sauce, and take the great Egg out of the Bladder, cut it down the Middle, and lay the one Half in the Middle of the Dish; cut the other Half in two, and lay on each Side, pour the Ragoo all over them. Garnish with Sippets, Barberry-berries and Capers.

Plumb Pottage.

TAKE two Houghs of a Bullock, break and put them into a Pot and fill it with Water, and when it boils skim it well, add Thyme and Sweet-marjoram, Cloves, Nutmeg, Pepper and Salt; so let it boil, close covered, till it is a strong

Soop: Then take up the Houghs, whose Sinews will be as tender as Marrow, strain the Soop into an Earthen-pot and let it stand to cool; then take off all the Fat and put the Soop into a large Hash-pan, grate the Crumb of a Two-penny Loaf and add to it, sweeten it with Sugar to your Taste; then take two Pounds of the best Raisins, a Pound of Prunes, and a Pound of Currants, boil them in the Soop a Quarter of an Hour, and so send it up.

To make Pork Sausages.

TAKE a Hind-chine of Pork, skin it and shred it very fine, as above directed; season it with Pepper, Salt, and dried Sage, mix it well, and when it is beat fine fill your Skins, and they will keep as long as Beef Sausages. But all Sausages are to be put into the smallest Skins, Sheeps Guts are fittest for them; but if you cannot get Sheep Skins, the smallest of the Beef or Hog Skins, which must not be filled above half full.

To make Sausages *without Guts.*

TAKE a Pound of lean Mutton, and a Quarter of a Pound of Beef-suet shred very small, and beat it in a Mortar to a fine Paste, season it with *Jamaica* and Black-pepper, Nutmeg, Salt, Thyme, Sweet-marjoram and Parsley; then drudge Flour on the Table, and roll the Sausage with your Hands into Rolls the Thickness of Sausages, and make them into various Shapes, as O, S, C, X, or in any other Shape as your Fancy directs; And when you have Turkey-pouts or Chickens roasted or boiled, lay these Sausages on a Tin-pan and set them in a quick Oven, or before the Fire and broil them, and lay round and over the Fowl or Fowls, with Gravy on the Dish.

To stew Pigeons.

PLUCK and singe the Pigeons clean, and wash them, stuff their Crops with Force-meat, cut off their Legs and turn up their Thighs, put under the Wings as for Baking; then put them into a Stew-pan, and cover them with Water, set them on a slow Stove close covered, and let them stew till they are tender, turning and skimming them often; when their Liquor is almost consumed, add to it a Pint of Veal-gravy, Force-meat Balls, and Catchup, let them stew till there is but what is sufficient for Sauce; then add to it a Spoonful of pickled Mushrooms, a Spoonful of Walnut Pickle, a little Butter, and toss all together: Lay Rashers of Bacon all over them on the Dish. Garnish with Lemon and green Parsley.

A *Sham* Pig.

BOIL and peal as many Potatoes as will be the Bulk of a little Pig, which you must take while they are hot, and beat a Quarter of a Pound of Butter in them, break six Eggs (leaving out the Whites of four) very well, and mix with the Potatoes; add to them Sugar, Nutmeg and Salt, to your Taste; let them stand to cool, and then make it up in the Form of a roasted Pig; make a Skin to cover it of Paste as for a standing Pye; let it have Head, Ears, and Mouth in the Form of a roasted Pig; let it be set in an Oven and baked brown: Then take a little clarified Butter, and a few clean Feathers, dip their Ends in the Butter, and whisk all the Pig with it, just as it is taken out of the Oven; this will make the Paste shine as a natural Pig's Skin. For Sauce, have melted Butter, Sugar and red Wine, then serve it up.

A *Sham* Turkey.

TAKE half a Pound of Butter and a Jill of sweet Cream, boil it till the Butter is melted, then take two Pounds of Flour, add a grated Nutmeg, a little Sugar and Salt, and pour your Cream and boiled Butter into the Flour, and make it into a Paste. Pick and wash clean half a Pound of Currants, stone and cut small a Quarter of a Pound of Rasins, cut an Ounce of Orange-peel very small, and work all into this Paste, making it up in the Form of a boiled Turkey; take a Sheet of Puff-paste and lay over the Breast, Wings and Thighs, as the natural Shape of a Turkey, set it on a flat-bottomed Dish, and bake it in a slow Oven an Hour; make some Balls of Puff-paste and bake them; lay boiled Rice round the Dish; and for Sauce, plain melted Butter, sweeten'd with Sugar and two Spoonfuls of Rhenish; set this Turkey on the Dish, pour the Sauce round, and the Balls, so serve it up.

N.B. If the Reader is a good Mechanick, may with the above, sham any Sort of Wild or Tame-fowl, and it may perhaps be a great Disappointment to Gormandizers, and a very agreeable one to others.

To make Sausages *of* Beef.

TAKE two Pounds of the Inside of a Surloin of Beef, and half a Pound of Beef-suet cut very small on a Shreading-board; add *Jamaica* and Black-pepper, Salt, Sweet-marjoram, and Thyme; beat this well in a Marble Mortar, with half a Jill of Red-wine or old Beer; then fill the Guts, and hang them in the Kitchen: When they are to be used broil them on the Cranks, with two

Spoonfuls of Water in a Plate or Tin-pan under them, to intermix with their Gravy.

To make Sausages *of* Mutton.

TAKE a Loin of fat Mutton, skin it and take out all the Sinews, shred the Fat and Lean very small on a Shreading-board; add half a Jill of Water to it, and season with *Jamaica* and Black-pepper; the small Skins to be filled for Present Use, and broil them as above directed.

To make Puff-paste.

MIX the Flour with cold Water, and weigh the Paste; to every Pound of Paste put half a Pound of butter, roll out the Paste and divide the Butter into three Parts, laying one Part on each Sheet, throwing Flour on every Time, and roll it three Times after all the Butter is laid on; if it is frosty, mix the Flour with Water Milk-warm.

P.S. Be sure to roll the Paste 'till all the Butter is well mixed, or it will run out in the baking. This Paste is for Puddings, Pasties, Dish-pyes, Florentines, or Minced-pyes.

Paste *for standing* Crusts.

TO seven Pounds of Flour take three Pounds of Butter and three Pints of Water, boil the Butter and Water till it is melted, then skim off the Butter and mix it with Flour, likewise the remaining Flour with Water, and the Paste all together with your Hands; when it is well mixed, cut the Paste into little Pieces and lay on the Table to cool; then work them all together, and raise it into a Pye or Pyes.

Another Paste *for standing* Crusts.

TAKE some Beef or Sheep-suet, which cut small and put into a Brass-pan, set it on a clear Fire at a good Distance, if it stands over hot it's in Danger of burning the Fat; and when it is discharged, take it off the Fire, and drain all the Fat into a Sieve, letting it run into a clean Earthen-pot; when it is cold, to a Pound of this Fat take a Pint of Milk, a little Salt, and boil and mix it with the Flour as above: This makes a much better Crust in Winter, when Butter is strong, than Butter does. There are a few Criticks can discover the Taste of the Fat, for the Milk diverts it, and likewise hinders the Paste from cracking.

Lent *minced* Pyes.

TAKE a Pound of Apple-pulp, half a Pound of Lemon-peel cut small, half a Pound of hard boiled Yolks of Eggs chopped small, and a Pound of Currants clean picked and washed, half a Pound of Raisins stoned and cut small, with half a Pound of Sugar; mix all together, and bake it with Puff-paste in Pans, or in standing Crusts.

Another Way for Fast *minced* Pyes.

TAKE a Pound of boiled Potatoes, beat into it a Pound of sweet Butter, with a Pound of Apple-pulp; also Mace, Cinnamon, Cloves, and Nutmeg pounded, half a Pound of Sugar, a Pound an a Half of Currants, a Pound of Raisins stoned and cut small, and half a Jill of Sack; mix them well together, and bake it as above.

Another Sort of minced Pyes.

TAKE a Pound of Calf's Feet shred very small, with two Pounds of Beef-suet, but all the Skin must be taken from it; add two Pounds of Currants clean picked and washed, a Pound of Prunes scalded, stoned and cut small, half a Pound of Apple-pulp, a Pound of Almonds blanched and beat to a Paste, half a Pound of Lemon-peel cut small, half a Pound of moist Sugar, of Red-wine and Sack each half a Jill: Season to your Taste with an equal Quantity of Cinnamon, Mace, Nutmeg, and Cloves; mix all well together, and bake as you knead the Pyes.

Another Way to make minced Pyes.

TAKE a Pound of the fattest of Beef, and two Pounds of the Kidney-suet, shred them together till both are so small as you cannot perceive the least Bit of the Beef, only it gives a carnation Colour to the Suet; then add two Pounds of well picked Currants, a Pound of Stoned Raisins, and half a Pound of Prunes scalded, stoned, and cut small with the Raisins; season with the above-named Seasonings: Also the Wine, Sack, and the above Quantity of Sugar, with four Ounces of Lemon, and three Ounces of Citron-peel cut small, and to be all well mixed together.

A Trennill Pye.

TAKE a Trennill of a good fat Calf, open and wash it in many Waters very clean, let it lie all Night in Salt, and boil it till it's tender; then shred it as small as minced Pye-meat, and season it, with *Jamaica*-pepper and Salt; take Prunes, Raisins, Currants, and Sugar, of each half a Pound; pick the Currants, stone the Raisins and Prunes, cut and mix them all together. They that will be thrifty, may skim the Trinnill well in Time of boiling, and it will discharge as much Fat as will make a Standing Crust for it, instead of Butter; and if cleanly done, it will be as sweet as Butter.

How to dry Plumbs.

TAKE large white *magnum bonum* Plumbs; and to every Pound of Plumbs take two Pounds of Sugar; and to every Pound of Sugar add a Pint of hard Water, and boil it ten Minutes: Rub every Plumb with a clean Cloth, and put them into an Earthen flat-bottomed Mug; pour over them the boiling Syrup, and cover it with Paper close, let them stand twenty-four Hours; then take the Syrup from them, and boil it a Quarter of an Hour: In which Time, take the Skin off the Plumbs, and set each Plumb upon its End with the Stalk upper-most; and when the Syrup hath boiled the above Time, pour it upon the Plumbs, and so repeat it six Times in the above manner; then let them stand a Week without boiling the Syrup, and then boil it till it is ropey, pour it on the Plumbs, let them stand three Weeks, then boil the Syrup again; and let them stand a Month, in which Time they will have a soft Candy; then take them out of the Pot, and lay them on an Earthen-dish, and sift a little double-refined Sugar over them: Let them dry in the Sun or before a Fire, and so keep them for Use.

How to make Wormwood Drops.

BEAT the Whites of two new laid Eggs on a Pewter-plate with the Back of a Case-knife, till the Froth is so stiff, that you may cut it into Parcels; then beat and sift through a Tiffany-sieve a Pound of double-refined Sugar, which beat with the Eggs, add a Spoonful of Orange-flower Water, and beat it to the Stiffness of light Paste; then drop on it three Drops of the Oil of Wormwood, and mix it well: Lay a little of this on a square Pane of Glass, or a Holland glazed Brick, powder a Penny-worth of Cocheneal, and mix with the Bulk of an Egg of this beat-up Mixture, and marble the other with the red Colour; but you must mix it so as to make the White and Red transparent. Drop them upon glazed Paper, that is, white Paper glazed with a Sleek-stone; let not each be above the Size of a Filberd, and set them in the Sun or before a Fire to dry. Put them on clean Paper into a Paper-box, and keep them for Use.

To make Lemon Drops.

PARE the yellow Skin of a fresh Lemon, cut it small, and put it into a Quarter of a Jill of the best Brandy, let it stand twelve Hours; then take the Whites of two new-laid Eggs, and mix with the same Quantity of double-refined Sugar, beat and sifted as in the above Manner: When it is done, beat into it a Spoonful of the Brandy that the Lemon Skin lay in, mix it well, and dry them as above; then drop it on glazed Paper, and dry it as before directed. Box them up, and keep them for Use.

To make Jumballs.

INFUSE an Ounce of Gum-arabick, put to it a large Wine-glass of Orange-flour Water, the same Quantity of Rose-water, and let them stand twenty-four Hours; then take the Whites of three fresh Eggs, with a Pound and a half of double-refined Sugar sifted, beat them to a Stiffness; then take the Gum, which must be as thick as clear boiled Starch, beat it with the Eggs, blanch and beat two Ounces of *Jourdon* Almonds, with a Spoonful of Rose-water, and the above Ingredients all to a fine Paste: Then roll it into Balls and flatten them a little, lay them on glazed Paper and Wires, and set them in an Oven to bake; when they are enough, keep them for Use.

To make Currant-paste.

TAKE two Quarts of pick'd ripe Red-currants, and put them into Jars, cover them close and set them into an Oven two Hours; then strain them through a Flannel-bag, and take two Pound of Loaf-sugar, wet it with Water and boil it to Candy-height; then put to it a Pint of Currant Juice, but don't let it boil after it is in, stir it well together, and put it into an Earthen-mug till the next Day; then drop it in little Cakes on Wafer-paper, and dry it in the Sun, or in a very cool Oven.

Marmalade *of* Orange.

BOIL twelve thin skin'd *Seville* Oranges, that is fresh, three Times, removing them out of the boiling Pot each Time, till they are so tender that a Straw will run through them; then take them out, and to every Pound of Oranges take two Pounds of double-refined Sugar, to every Pound of Sugar add half a Pint of Water, and boil it in a clean Brass-pan on a clear Stove: In the mean Time, cut each Orange, and take out the Insides (take Care of the Juice and

Meat) and Seeds; cut the Orange Skins into very thin Slices, and put into the boiling Sugar, let it boil till the Skins are clear, keep stirring it; then put all the Insides into the Marmalade, and boil it till it begins to spark and fly, but be sure to keep it stirring all the Time; so put it into Glasses or Jelly-pots, laying white Paper over it dipped in Brandy, and tie over it Bladders; then keep it for Use.

To preserve Oranges *whole.*

TAKE six of the beautifullest large *Seville* Oranges to be got, and lay them in Salt and Water three Days; then boil them in Water, and shift them as above; and when they are so tender that a Straw will run through them, take them out and cut out a round Piece off each Top of the Oranges, not to exceed the Breadth of a Shilling, and with a Tea-spoon take out all the Seeds, but none of the Meat; then take six Pounds of double-refined Sugar, put to it two Quarts of Water, and boil it ten Minutes; set each Orange on its End in a flat-bottomed Pot, and put within them the Round Piece you cut out; then pour upon them the boiling Syrup, and lay a Delf-plate over to keep them down. Thus boil it once every Day for 12 Times, after put each Orange into a Gally-pot just fit for it, to be covered with Syrup, and tie a Bladder over each Pot, so keep them for Use.

How to make Orange Chips.

TAKE the fresh Skin of *Seville* Oranges, whose Juice has been used for Punch, and lay them in Salt and Water three Days; then boil them tender, shifting them as above, and take out all the Strings of the Insides; put them into an Earthen-pot, make a Syrup of common Lump-sugar, and boil it three Times a Week the first Fortnight; then let it stand a Month longer, and take the Skins out of the Syrup and wash them in clear Water, turn them down on a Sieve, and so dry them in a slow Oven; then cut them into Chips, and according to the Quantity, if three Pounds of Chips, two Pounds of Sugar, wet it with Water and boil it Candy-height; then put in your Chips and let them boil, dip a Slice into the Syrup and blow it through, if it flies like Snow, you must take them out and spread them on an Earthen-dish to cool, so keep them for Use.

Red Marmalade of Quinces.

PARE, core and slice your Quinces, and to every Pound of Quinces take a Pound and a Half of Loaf-sugar, and to each Pound of Sugar a Jill of Water;

set them on a Stove in a clean Pan, and heat all together slowly till it comes to a red Colour; then sharpen the Fire, boil it to a stiff Gelly, and pot it for Use.

To make white Marmalade of Quinces.

PARE and quarter your Quinces, and have ready a Pan, to every Pound of Quinces take a Pound and a half of double-refined Sugar, wet it with fair Water; put your sliced Quinces into boiling Water, and boil the Sugar Candy-heighth; when the Quinces are tender, drain the Water from them thro' a Hair-sieve, put it into the Sugar, and let all boil till the Quinces be clear; then put it into Pots or Glasses for Use.

To make Rasberry Cakes.

TO every Pound of Rasberries take a Pound of double-refined Sugar, mix and put into a Preserving pan; boil it on a clear Stove, keep it stirring all the Time, let it boil till it is a thick strong Stiffness, and set it by till it is cold; then make it into little Cakes, lay them on a Paper to dry, and keep them for Use.

To dry red Currants *in Strops.*

PICK out all the Seeds of the Currants on the Stalks, boil Loaf-sugar Candy-heighth, and put in your Currants; boil and take them out Stalk by Stalk, and lay them on a large Stone-dish separate to cool; dust grated double-refined Sugar, and turn them every Day till they are dry: So box them up for Use.

To make Gingerbread.

TAKE four Pounds of Treacle into a Pan, and set it on a clear Fire till it is scalding hot; then stir into it half a Pound of Sweet-butter and a Jill of Brandy, and pour it into a Bowl; add to it two Ounces of beat Ginger, the same Quantity of powdered *Jamaica* Pepper, an Ounce of Coriander Seeds, the same of Carraway Seeds, all well beat, and beat four Pounds of Flour into it very well; when the Lumps are very well beat out, cut half a Pound of Lemon-peel into long Pieces, grease a large Cake-pan with Butter, and divide it into four Loaves, laying the Fourth Part of the Lemon-peel on each Lair: it will take six Hours Baking.

The Cordial Hunters Gingerbread.

TAKE three Pints of red Port, and four Pounds of Loaf-sugar; boil them in a broad Brass-pan, let it boil till it is a Syrup, and take it off the Fire; add to it a Pint of Brandy, Cinnamon, Race Ginger, Mace, Cloves, and Nutmeg, of each half an Ounce finely beat to a Powder, grated Manshet Bread dried in an Oven or before the Fire four Pounds, three of which put to the above Ingredients, and boil it till it is thick; then let it cool, work up the other Pound of dry grated Bread, and make it into various Shapes, as Prints, small Rolls, and little Cakes: Lay it on white Paper to dry, and keep it for Use. A small Piece of this is a Dram in the Morning.

Glossary

A la mode — "A *buttock or Rump of Beef in Pieces,* stov'd and larded." *CC* 209

Ale — "A liquor made by infusing malt…in hot water and then fermenting the liquor." *SJ* n.p. Although beer and ale were brewed differently in the 18th century, they are interchangeable today

Ale-yeast — "The frothy mass of fungi produced during the alcoholic fermentation of ale." *JN* 16; "…the frothy mass produced on top of ale during fermentation." *HG 1747 fac.*47; also, "barm"

Alio — olio? "…a Portuguese Dish of all Kinds of Flesh, Fowls, Greens, *&c.* blended together." *CC* 211

Almonds, bitter — variety of almond, similar to sweet almonds but containing substantial amount of cyanide so must be used with care

Almonds, *Jourdon* — "Jordan is a corruption of gardin, garden." *JN* 24; sweet almonds "…annually brought to *England*.…" *NB* n.p.; NOT those in a thin candy shell

Alum — "…a powerful kind of salt…[used] in medicine, [it] is a powerful astringent. In dyeing, it fixes the colours upon the stuff." *EB* I, 129; also "allum"

Amalet — omelet; "…the principal Composition whereof is *Eggs*." *CC* 209 also "amlet," "amulet"

Anchovy liquor — the juice or brine from anchovies, used as salty flavoring

Apple scoop — tool similar to modern utensil used to core apples, etc.

Arian — var. spelling of aryan "…pertaining to or holding to the doctrine of Arius…who denied that Christ was consubstantial [of one and the same] with God, 1642." *OED*; use here is unclear

Astertion seed — "…an odd way of spelling nasturtium…" *HG 1747 fac.*176; often pickled and used as a substitute for capers; also "stertion"

Bacon hog — "Those hogs that are generally put for bacon, being generally older than those that are fed for porkers,…" *NB* n.p.

Baker — "A small portable tin oven." *OED*; in receipts, sounds more like a baking dish. See "A Chicken Pye." *AC* 104

Barberry-berries — "Small translucent red fruit of *Berberis vulgaris*, an ornamental garden shrub." *JN* 17

Baum — variant of balm, *Melissa officinalis*; also called lemon balm

Bay salt — "salt of seawater…" *ES* glossary; "…made by evaporating Sea water in Pits, clayed on the inside, only by the heat of the Sun… The Bay-Salt is preferable to the others for most Uses." *MB* II, 120; "…very large or coarse-grained in consequence of the slowness of the evaporation, and more or less impure…" *HG 1747 fac.* 198

Bear an egg — a way of measuring the strength of salt solution by dissolving enough salt in water so that a raw egg in its shell will float

Beef brine — salt liquid used to pickle or preserve beef

Beef suet	fat surrounding kidneys in cattle; NOT tallow, which lies between the skin and the muscle, often sold as "suet for the birds"
Beer vinegar	vinegar resulting from souring of beer or ale; also called alegar; today called malt vinegar
Berries of lobster	lobster coral, red matter found inside the body of a lobster
Bill-knife	bill: "…an instrument, made of iron, edged in the form of a crescent, and adapted to a handle." *EB* I, 553; "…an Edg-tool at the end of a stake or a handle." *JW* 314
Bird-lime	"A glutinous substance, which is spread upon twigs, by which the birds that light upon them are entangled: *SJ* n.p.
Bladder	animal organ that holds urine until discharged. Note: information in HG 1747 glossary is incorrect. It is also incorrect in *A Glossary of Cookery*…by Prospect Books.
Blades of mace	whole membrane of mace removed from nutmeg and dried
Boiler	"The vessel in which any thing is boiled." *SJ* n.p.
Bolognia sausage	large sausage made with beef and pork
Bottom dish	dish set in front of the hostess at the lower end of the dining-table
Bramble-berries	blackberries, *Rubus* sp.
Bran water	"…*the sour waters*, with which they [cloth-dyers] prepare their several dyes." *EB* I, 660
Bread sauce	"CUT out a large Piece of Crumb of Bread, rub it in a Cloth till it is as small and fine as if it had been grated; set on a Sauce-pan with some Butter, when it is well melted throw in the Crumbs of Bread, and stir them about at

	Times till they are thoroughly brown; then pour them into a Sieve, and let them stand some Time to drain…" *MB* II, 239
Brine/salt brine	"…water replete with saline particles or pickle." *EB* I, 679
Brush made of rice	rice: "The shrouds or tops of Trees, or fellings of Coppices." *JW* 321
Bullock	"…young bull or bull calf…" *OED*
Burnt butter	"*To burn* Butter…SET your Butter on the Fire and let it boil till it is brown, then shake in some Flour, and stir it all the Time it is on the Fire till it is thick. Put it by, and keep it for Use. A little Piece is what the Cooks use to thicken and brown their Sauce…" *HG* 19
Burn-trouts	burn: "A brook." *OED*; trout caught in fresh water
Butt	"A name of various flat fish, as sole, fluke, plaice, turbot, *&c*." *OED*
Butter-deshes	variant of butter-dishes; but may refer to pots or dishes in which butter was packed for sale *JN* 18
Cabbage lettuce	headed lettuce, such as today's Bibb or Boston; NOT iceberg
Cake pan	baking-dish for cakes; see illus. in *JC,* 2
Canary	"Wine brought from the Canaries; sack." *SJ* n.p.; use sherry
Candy height	"When your sugar is at a candy height, which is the second height it comes to, it will draw between your fingers in great flakes like bird lime, and then it is at a height eyther to candy or for any other things." *MW* 227
Canteen	"A small tin or vessel for water or liquor." *OED*

Cap paper	"1. A kind of wrapping paper. 2. A size or kind of writing paper." *OED*
Case-knife	"A knife carried in a case or sheath." *OED*
Catchup	highly seasoned liquid added to various dishes and sauces to enhance flavor; also catsup, katchup, ketchup; NOT today's tomato ketchup
Cat's collop	not found in sources consulted
Caudle	"A mixture of wine, and other ingredients, given to women in childbed, and sick persons." *SJ* n.p.; "…a general term for a kind of thick drink." *HG 1747 fac.* 179; "a gruel made from oatmeal or other farinaceous substance boiled in milk or water (or wine or ale) and used as a thickening or as a drink for invalids." *ES* glossary
Cheshire cheese	cheese made in Cheshire, in northwest England; for a detailed description of the process, see *WE* 411–412; can sometimes be purchased at gourmet or specialty shops
Chine	"The part of the back, in which the spine or backbone is found." *SJ* n.p. "The whole or part of the backbone of an animal with the adjoining flesh." *ES* glossary
Cider vinegar	vinegar made from apple cider
Citron	"a fruit larger, less acid and thicker in rind than a lemon…" *ES* glossary; rind from citron melon was used as a substitute
Claret	"…red wine imported from Bordeaux." *OED*
Clarified butter	butter melted, with impurities skimmed off; liquid butter then poured off milk solids at bottom and allowed to solidify
Cloves of mace	would appear to be AC's error; mace is the lacy membrane around a nutmeg, often

called blade mace in period receipts as in HG's receipt

Cochineal — "An insect gathered upon the *opuntia*, and dried; from which a beautiful red colour is extracted." *SJ* n.p.

Cockles — "A small testacreous fish." *SJ* n.p.

Codling — -ling is a suffix meaning small or little, according to *SJ*; "a young cod." *ES* glossary; NOT to be confused with codlin/codling meaning "A variety of apple…" *OED*. Consider context to determine meaning

Collar — a method of cooking meat, involving rolling a long thin piece of meat around savory stuffing and tying with a strip of linen, then cooking it in wine

Cook's perquisities — "perks" or benefits above and beyond wages available to cooks, such as money from sale of leftovers

Copper — "A vessel made of copper; commonly used for a boiler larger than a moveable pot." *SJ* n.p. Often built into a brick or stone frame-work, with a fire built below it, sometimes called a set-kettle

Cordial — restorative or healthful alcoholic drink

Crank — "Any bending or winding passage…" *SJ* n.p.

Cullis — "…a strained liquor, made of any sort of meat or other things pounded in a mortar and passed through a hair sieve; of which there are various sorts." *NB* n.p. "…they are essential to Made Dishes, and will be found very useful on many other Occasions; they are Things that should be kept in the House ready for different Purposes." *MB* III, 331 "These may be considered either as a rich Kind of Sauce, or as the Essence of Soups; they serve to

GLOSSARY • 169

	improve or enrich both the one and the other, and on some Occasions may be eaten as Sauce alone." *MB* V, 171
Currants	1. fruit of *Ribes* sp.: red, white, and black, product of the kitchen garden and used fresh in fools, jellies, jams, wines; NOT used in baked goods or like raisins 2. small dried raisins from the Mediterranean used in baked goods and puddings; also called *corinths*
Cypher pye	cypher/cipher: "A symbolic character." *OED*; perhaps a pie with a decorated crust? For illustrations of what such a pie might be like, see *RM*, 144–147
Delf[t]-bowl/dish	china from the Netherlands in a blue and white pattern
Distilled vinegar	vinegar run through a still to purify; colorless, often used where the color of pickle is desirable, like cauliflower or mushroom pickles; today's white vinegar
Double-refined sugar	sugar that is "…particularly white," *JE* 195; made with several additional steps in refining; today's granulated white sugar
Double-round	"possibly honeycomb tripe, the second stomach [of bovine] or reticulum." *ES* glossary
Dov'd beef	Beef a la Dobe: beef forced [stuffed], larded, and stoved [cooked] *CC* 210; also sometimes *a la daub*
Dresser	"The bench in a kitchen on which meat is drest or prepared for the table." *SJ* n.p.
Drunk the wine well up	absorbed the wine
Earthen dish/mug/ pan/pot	utensil made of redware; may be glazed or unglazed
Elder vinegar	vinegar in which elderflowers have been infused

Essence of ham	"These may be considered either as a rich Kind of Sauce, or as the Essence of Soups; they serve to improve or enrich both the one and the other, and on some Occasions may be eaten as Sauce alone." *MB* V, 171; see *HG* 102 and/or *AC* 35
Family standing pie	meaning unclear; would seem to be a pie lasting more than one meal for a family. See "*A Standing* Crust *for* Great Pies." *HG* 145
Farce/force	verb: stuff; noun: stuffing
Fillet	"The fleshy part of the thigh: applied commonly to veal." *SJ* n.p.
Fish-kettle	"...oval in shape and deeper than the kind now sold." *HG 1747 fac.* 184
Fish Sauce	would seem to be a sauce made with fish rather than a sauce for fish
Flannel	"A soft nappy stuff of wool." *SJ* n.p.
Flannel-bag	a bag made of flannel, for straining jellies, wines, or other things
Flummery	"A kind of food made by coagulation of wheatflour or oatmeal." *SJ* n.p.
Force meagre	stuffing made without flesh
Force-meat	"Meat chopped fine, spiced and highly seasoned, chiefly used as stuffing or as a garnish." *OED*
French barley	pearl barley: "...barley as being skinned, with the ends ground off." *JE* 18; "...(barley which has been husked and milled)..." *HG 1747 fac.* 176
French rolls	"...presumably a small round loaf of French bread [likely enriched with milk and eggs]." *JE* 182; "...rolls made from yeast-leavened dough, enriched with eggs, butter, and milk,..." *JN*, 18

Fricasee	"A dish made by cutting chicken or other small things in pieces, and dressing them with strong sauce." *SJ* n.p.; "meat sliced and fried or stewed and served with a sauce." *ES* glossary; also spelled fricassy
Gang of [hog's/calves'] feet	"a number [of feet] herding together…" *SJ* n.p.
Gelly-bag	cloth bag through which liquid jelly is poured to clarify it; also spelled jelly-bag
Gherkins/girkins	kind of cucumber, pickled in brine; "*very small pickled Cucumbers.*" *CC* 210
Gile-fat	large container "…in which wort is left to ferment [when making beer or ale]." *ES* glossary; also guile-vat, gyle-vat
Gile yeast	yeast from brewing-vessel
Girdle	another spelling for griddle
Glanders	a distemper affecting horses, characterized by "matter…discharged from the nostrils…" *EB* II, 557; one of "…seven different kinds… four of which are incurable." *OED*
Glazed paper	coated paper that is smooth and glossy, *SJ* n.p.
Gore	name of a kind of bird
Grate-iron	another name for gridiron
Gravy	a well-seasoned liquid made to add to stews, soups, and other dishes "…to render them more succulent, and to heighten their relish." *NB* n.p.; may also refer to the liquid that runs from cooking meat
Green gages	a kind of plum with green skin and yellow pulp
Green wheat	unripe wheat; juice often used as food coloring
Greens	"Among the principal Greens may be reckoned the *Cabbage, Brocoli, Cauliflower*

and *Spinage*, to which we may add *Celeri, Lettuce, Radish*, and *Salleting; Asparagus, Beans, Pease*, and *French Beans.*" MB I, 5

Groats — "oats after the Hulls are off or great Oatmeal." *JW* 317; "...sometimes wheat, barley or maize." *HG 1747 fac.* 186

Hair-bag — coarse bag made of horsehair, used for straining

Hair-sieve — "A sieve with the bottom made of hair finely woven: esp. for straining liquids." *OED*

Half a crown — a silver coin worth 2s6d; size used as measurement in cookery

Half-penny roll — a bread roll purchase for 1/2d; size and weight would have varied depending on the price of wheat

Ham cullis — a rich addition to sauces

Hand-meat — not found in sources consulted

Hard water — water in which soap does not lather or form suds because of mineral content; pump water was considered hard

Hartshorn — "...the whole horns of the common male deer, which fall off every year." *SJ* n.p.; "...shavings of a stag's antlers...used to set a jelly." *JE* 51

Hash-pan — pan for cooking chopped or shredded meat with vegetables and seasoning

Head-dish — dish placed in front of the host at the head of a dining-table

Hodgepodge — "A medley of ingredients boiled together." *SJ* n.p.

Hot spices — cinnamon, cloves, ginger, peppers

Hough — "The lower part of the thigh." *SJ* n.p.

Isinglass	jelling agent made of cleaned, dried lining of air-bladders of certain freshwater fish; cf. *JQ* 75; NOT to be confused with the mineral mica
Jagger iron	also called jagging iron; "an instrument for ornamenting pastry; a pastry-wheel." *ES* glossary; see illustration of pastry wheel in *JC* 21
Jamaica pepper	allspice
Jar	meaning not found in sources consulted; from context, it would seem to be a kind of fish; see receipt for "Potted Jars," p. 165
Jill	one-half cup or four liquid ounces; sometimes spelled gill
Kell	"The omentum; that which inwraps the guts." *SJ* n.p.
Kidney fat	very high-quality fat surrounding the kidneys of an animal; sometimes called suet
Kitchen of-falls	"Waste meat; that which is not eaten at table…thrown away as of no value." *SJ* n.p.
Kitchen stuff pies	not defined in sources consulted; may mean pies suitable for servants but not for family or guests
Lamb-stones	testicles of an immature sheep; "lamb's testicles" *ES* glossary
Lard	noun: pig fat; verb: to insert thin pieces of fat or other things under the skin to add moisture or flavor during cooking
Laurel-leaves	bay leaves; NOT laurel leaves, which are poisonous
Lights	"The lungs; the organs of breathing." *SJ* n.p.; "the lungs of an animal." *ES* glossary
Ling	"A kind of sea-fish." *SJ* n.p.
Liquor	"A liquid." OED; not necessarily alcoholic

Loaf sugar	"sugar refined and moulded into loaf [cone] shape." *ES* glossary; See *MB* II, 12 for various sugars available
Loin	"The back of an animal carved out by the butcher." *SJ* n.p.
London butter pound	not found in sources consulted; from context, would appear to be half an ordinary pound. Stead, on p. 31, does not comment on the 3 pounds in Glasse's receipt and the 6 then mentioned by Cook
London flour	would seem to mean the quality of flour sold in London
Mace	see blades of mace above
Made dishes	wide variety of well-seasoned prepared dishes, such as fricasees, ragoos, stews, etc. based on meat, poultry or game
Magnum plums	Magnum Bonum Plum variety "…excellent for making Sweet-meats…" *PM* 1125
Maiden skate	skate: "…a very large, flat, cartilaginous fish much used for food." *OED*; maiden: meaning unclear; perhaps immature female
Marrow	fatty substance inside bones, used to thicken or enrich dishes; NOT a vegetable
Marrow peas	"The best of all the large [early] Kinds is the Marrow-fat, which, if gathered young, is a well-tasted Pea…" *PM* 1089
Milk-whey	the liquid remaining after milk has curdled and the curds [milk solids] have been removed
Millons	melons: cantaloupes, musk-melons, water-melons *PM* 890–891
Morella/Morello cherries	"…a very good Fruit for the Table…" *PM* 305

Mushroom flaps	large mushrooms, like Portobellos; small mushrooms were called buttons
Mutton	meat of an adult sheep; so hard to find that it is all right to use supermarket lamb, which is similar in texture and taste
Naples biscuits	"plain biscuits of a particular shape, used as a substitute for breadcrumbs." *ES* glossary "To make Naples Biskets. TAKE a Pound and half of fine Flour, and as much double-refined Sugar, twelve Eggs, three Spoonfuls of Rose-water, and an Ounce and half of Carraway-seeds finely powdered, mix them all well with Water, then put them into Tin-plates, and bake them in a moderate Oven, dissolve some Sugar in Water, and glaze them over." *JN*, N 1. Note: it is almost impossible to powder caraway seeds; purchase them already powdered if you can find them
N.B.	*nota bene*; Latin phrase meaning note well
Neat	"A Heifer, or any of the kinds of Beeves." *JW* 319; also "an Ox" *JE* 189
Nectars	nectarines
Offal	internal organs of an animal, such as liver, kidneys, etc.
Oranges	usually meant Seville oranges, which are bitter
Pack-thread	"Strong thread used in tying up parcels." *SJ* n.p.
Pail	"A wooden vessel in which milk or water is commonly carried." *SJ* n.p.
Paste	pie or pastry crust; may also occasionally refer to a substance like Vermicelli; also the cover seal around the edge of a lid with a flour-water mixture to prevent steam from escaping; may be a confection made of fruit and sugar

Pasty pan	pan for baking pasties or turnovers in an oven or over the fire
Pearl barley	"…barley which has been husked and milled…" *HG 1747 fac.* 176; also called French barley, dry measure of eight quarts
Pen-knife	"A knife used to cut pens [quills]." *SJ* n.p.
Penny loaf	loaf of bread purchased for 1d; weight or size might have varied, depending upon the price of wheat *JE* 17
Pennyroyal	*Mentha pulegium,* a member of the mint family; be very cautious in using this because it can affect pregnant women
Pennyworth	"The amount which may be bought for a penny; as much as is worth a penny." *OED*
Penny tape	narrow woven strip, used to tie clothing, shoes, Etc.; this kind would seem to have been tape of a certain size or quality known by its cost
Petre salt	also spelled peter-salt; unpurified nitre *JQ* 144; see *MB* II, 100
Pickle	brine for preserving meats, fruits, and/or vegetables; often a salt solution
Pinion	"The [endmost] joint of the wing removed from the body." *SJ* n.p.
Pippin	"A sharp [tart] apple." *SJ* n.p. "seedling apple." *ES* glossary
Pluck	"the heart, liver and lungs." *ES* glossary
Pokey [tongue]	meaning not found in sources consulted; perhaps imitation
Poor man's spit	"a little Iron…with six Hooks to it…fasten one End of a String to the Chimney, and the other End to the Iron (this is what we call the poor Man's Spit)…" *HG 1747 fac.* 43

Pope's Eye	"The lymphatic gland surrounded with fat in the middle of a leg of mutton; regarded as a tit-bit." *OED*
Pot dripping	fat from animal as it cooked, collected and kept for use
Pouts	"1. A kind of fish; a cod-fish. 2. A kind of bird." *SJ* n.p.; "…a term for young birds." *HG 1747 fac.* 195
Powder sugar	white sugar ground to powder with a pestle in a mortar; NOT today's powdered or confectioner's sugar, which has been adulterated with cornstarch
Preserving-pan	pan used to preserve fruits with sugar to make marmalades, jams, sweetmeats, etc.
Pudding-cloth	linen cloth gathered to form a bag, into which pudding-batter was put; after being tied, the bag was plunged into boiling water where it remained until the pudding was cooked through
Pump water	water from a pump, usually in a city; considered hard
Queen-cake pan	pan for baking Queen-cakes
Queen's Cakes.	"BEAT one pound of butter to a cream, with some rose-water, one pound of flour dried, one pound of sifted sugar, twelve eggs; beat all well together; add a few currants washed and dried; butter small pans of a size for the purpose, grate sugar over them; they are soon baked. They may be done in a Dutch oven." *CM* 404
Race ginger	sold today as ginger root; not actually the root, but the rhizome of ginger *HG 1747 fac.* 195

Ragoo	"Meat stewed and highly seasoned." *SJ* n.p.; also spelled "ragout; a seasoned stew or thick sauce or relish." *ES* glossary
Raisins stoned	raisins that have had the seeds removed before being used; if Thompson seedless raisins are purchased, stoning is unnecessary
Rashers	slices of bacon
Raspings	breadcrumbs
Rasps	raspberries
Reddish pods	radish pods; "…the seed-pods of the radish plant." *HG 1747 fac.* 196
Rhenish [wine]	Rhine wine; white wine
Rice-sauce	not found in sources consulted; would seem to be a sauce made of rice
Roch allum	"rock alum." *ES* glossary; alum "…prepared from stones … contradistinguished from the common alum…" *EB* I, 129; also roach- or roache-alum
Rock codling	"A cod found on rocky sea-bottoms or ledges." *OED*
Rough cider	harsh or coarse cider *OED*
Rubber	"A hard brush, a cloth or the like used for rubbing in order to make clean." *OED*
Sack	fortified grape wine from Spain; English imitation made with honey; "a generic name for a class of white wine formerly imported from Spain and the Canary Islands…" *ES* glossary
Sal prunella	"Fused nitre cast into moulds." *OED*
Salt-fish	dried and salted fish, usually cod
Saltpetre	"…potassium or sodium nitrate." *JE* 93; used as a preservative for animal products, such as meats and butter

Savoury meat	meat that has been well-seasoned; could also mean any solid food
Sagoe, Sego	"…an invalid food…" *HG 1747 fac.* 199; made from the "inward pith of a species of palm tree…" *JQ* 78
Sellery	celery
Seville orange	bitter orange, originally from Spain
Shredding-board	possibly another name for a cutting-board, or for a utensil similar to that, used to shred cabbage
Sippet	"A small sop." *SJ* n.p.; small pieces of bread, often toasted, used under various foods on a plate or as garnish
Skate	"A flat sea fish." *SJ* n.p.
Small birds	birds like larks or sparrows, formerly eaten
Small wine	wine with a lower alcohol content than usual
Soft water	water in which soap lathered easily; see *MB* IV, 735; rainwater was considered soft
Sourtout	var. spelling of surtout [q.v.] "A large coat worn over all the rest." *SJ* n.p.
Sparling	"The common European smelt." OED
Spav'd quay	not found in sources consulted; Barbara Corson, DVM, says quay may be a variant spelling of quey, an old term for a heifer. Spav'd may be a misprint for spay'd: "spay: castrate a female animal" *SJ* n.p.
Spring-water	fresh water from a source upwelling from the ground
Sprouts	the small knobs of cabbage that appear on the stalk when the head has been cut off; NOT today's Brussels sprouts
Standing crust	"…standard pastry for dishes baked in a crust." *HG 1747 fac.* 193

Stew-pan	round or oval pan used for long cooking; see illustration in *JC,* 13
Stone	weight for meats, flour, etc., 14 lbs *SJ* n.p.
Stoned raisins	dried grapes from which the seeds have been removed; if using Thompson raisins today, the raisins do not need to be stoned. You can make raisins with seeds by purchasing grapes with seeds and hanging them in a cool, shaded place until they are completely dry
Stove	"A apparatus for heating…to contain burning fuel…" *OED* NOT what is mean by "stove" in the 19th–21st century; see illustration in *ER*, 1782 ed.
Strong as to bear an egg	salt solution in which a raw egg in its shell will float
Strop	"A band, thong; a loop or noose…" *OED*
Suckles	noun not found in sources consulted; may mean breast tissue or nipples
Surtout	"Coat; surcoat." *JN*, 35; "Literally covered all over." *HG 1747 fac.* 201
Sweetbreads	the thymus gland of a calf
Sweet herbs	a mixture of some or all of the following: chervil, parsley, summer/winter savoury, sweet marjoram, thyme
Sweet sauce	"To make a sweet Sauce. SET a Sauce-pan over the fire, with Vinegar or White-wine, Sugar, a Stick of Cinnamon and a Bay-leaf; boil these together very well, then strain it for use." *JN*, S 50
Tart-pan	small pan for baking tarts
Tiffany sieve	sieve made with fine silk

Tincture of saffron	an infusion made by soaking saffron threads in wine; see *MB* IV, 568; sherry works well
Top dish	dish set in front of host at the head of the dining-table; also called head dish
Trails	"Entrails, intestines, collectively; esp. those of certain birds, as woodcock and snipe, and fishes as red mullet, which are cooked and eaten with the rest of the flesh." *OED*
Trennill	not found in sources consulted; possibly another term for entrails
Twining band	would seem to be the doubled string twisted when using a string-spit to roast meat or poultry
Twitchbells	not found in sources consulted; possibly part of twitch grass: "A weed that…draws away the virtues of the ground." *SJ* n.p.
Two penny loaf	"…cost twice as much [as a penny loaf] and was twice as large [12–16 oz. depending on price of wheat]." *JE* 182
Veal and ham cullis	a rich flavorful thickener for ragoos, etc., based on veal and ham
Veal olives	"…inside of a…[fillet], roll'd and forc'd." *CC* [beef] 209
Veal pluck	"The heart, liver and lights of an animal [here, from a calf]." *SJ* n.p.
Vent	"1. A small aperture; a hole; a spiracle; passage at which any thing is let out." *SJ* n.p.
Verjuice	"Acid liquor expressed from crab-apples." *SJ* n.p. "The acid juice of green or unripe grapes, crab-apples or other sour fruit, expressed, formed into liquor and used in place of vinegar." *SJ* n.p.

Vermicella/vermicelli	"A paste rolled and broken in the form of a worm." *SJ* n.p.; often imported; made at home: "...take the Yolks of two Eggs, and mix it up with just as much Flour as will make it to a stiff Paste; roll it out as thin as a Wafer, let it lye to dry till you can roll it up close without breaking, then with a sharp Knife cut it very thin, beginning at the little End...." *HG* 137; also "...a composition of flour, cheese, yolks of eggs, sugar, and saffron, reduced to a paste, and formed into long slender pieces like worms..." *JQ* 78
Wafer-paper	"a preparation of paste in very thin sheets." *ES* glossary
Walnut liquor	juice or liquid from pickled walnuts
Water-glass	"A glass vessel to contain water..."; NOT the gummy substance used to preserve eggs in the 19th century
Weather/wether heads	"A ram castrated." *SJ* n.p. "The males that are gelt will be larger than those that are not..." *NB* n.p.
Well-cresses	watercress, *OED*
Whelm a dish	whelm: "1. To cover with something not to be thrown off; to bury. 2. To throw upon something so as to cover or bury it." *SJ* n.p.; "...to turn [a hollow vessel] upside, or over." *OED*
White pepper	black pepper with the black outer coating rubbed off
Wigs	"buns or small cakes made from fine flour." *ES* glossary
Wine pint	16 oz. or 2 cups *JQ* 8
Wormwood drops	sweetmeat/meringue flavored with oil of wormwood, which had a variety of medicinal uses

Bibliography

Bain, Priscilla. "Recounting the Chicken: Hannah further Scrutinized," *Petit Propos Culinaire 23*. London: Prospect Books Ltd, 1980.

Bailey, N. *Dictionarium Domesticum,*…London: Printed for C. Hitch…1736; facsimile reprint by ECCO from Amazon Books on Demand. (Abbreviated as *NB*)

Bradley, Martha. *The British Housewife*…in 2 vols. London: Printed for S. Crowder and H. Woodgate…[1756]; facsimile reprint in 6 vols by Prospect Books, Totnes, UK, 1998. (Abbreviated as *MB*)

Burnet, Regula (ed.). *Ann Cook and Friend*. London: Oxford University Press in Humphrey Milford, 1936. (Abbreviated as *ACF*)

Carson, Jane. *Colonial Virginia Cookery*…Williamsburg, VA: The Colonial Williamsburg Foundation, 1985. (Abbreviated as *JC*)

Carter, Charles. *The Complete Practical Cook*:…London: Printed for W. Meadows…1730; facsimile reprint by Prospect Books Limited, London, 1984. (Abbreviated as *CC*)

Cook, Ann. *Professed Cookery*:…3rd ed. London: Printed for…the Author…c. 1760; scanned copy from The New York Public Library. Also, 1st and 2nd eds from Newcastle-on-Tyne. (Abbreviated as *AC*)

Ellis, William. *The Country Housewife's Family Companion*:…London: Printed for James Hodges…1750; reprint by Prospect Books, Totnes, UK, 2000. (Abbreviated as *WE*)

Encyclopaedia Britannica:…in 3 vols. Edinburgh: Printed for A. Bell and C. Macfarquhar…1771; facsimile reprint by Encyclopaedia Britannica Inc., Chicago, 1979. (Abbreviated as *EB*)

Glasse, Hannah. *The Art of Cookery, Made Plain and Easy*. London: Printed for the Author…1747; modern glossary in facsimile reprint by Prospect Books Ltd, London, 1983. (Abbreviated as *HG 1747 fac*.)

Glasse, Hannah. *The Art of Cookery, Made Plain and Easy*. 2nd ed.: London: Printed for the Author…1747; scanned copy from The Library of Congress, Washington, D.C.

Glasse, Hannah. *The Art of Cookery, Made Plain and Easy*. 5th ed.: London: Printed, and sold at Mrs. Ashburn's, 1755, in the collection of The Historical Society of Pennsylvania, Philadelphia. (Abbreviated as *HG*)

A Glossary of Cookery…by Prospect Books, 2003. http://www.kal67.dial.pipex.com/index.htm

Heinrichs, Christine. *The Backyard Guide to Chickens*. Minneapolis: Voyager Press, imprint of Quarto Publishing Group USA, Inc., 2016. (Abbreviated as *CH*)

John Evelyn, *Cook*, ed. by Christopher Driver. Modern glossary. Totnes, UK: Prospect Books, 1997. (Abbreviated as *JE*)

Johnson, Samuel. *A Dictionary of the English Language*:…in 2 vols. London: Printed by W. Strahan…1755; facsimile reprint by Longman Group UK Limited, Harlow, UK, 1990. (Abbreviated as *SJ*)

Maclean, Virginia. *A Short-title Catalogue of...Cookery Books...1701–1800*. London: Prospect Books, 1981. (Abbreviated as *VM*)

Mason, Charlotte. *The Lady's Assistant*...London: Printed for J. Walter...1787; facsimile reprint by Applewood Books, Bedford, MA, n.d. (Abbreviated as *CM*)

May, Robert. *The Accomplisht Cook*...4th ed. London: Printed for Robert Hartford...1678; reprinted by Falconwood Press, Albany, NY, 1992. (Abbreviated as *RM*)

Miller, Philip. *The Gardeners Dictionary*, abridged 1754 ed. Codicote, UK: Wheldon & Wesley Ltd., 1969. (Abbreviated as *PM*)

Nott, John. *The Cooks and Confectioners Dictionary*...3rd ed. London: Printed by H.P. for Charles Rivington, 1726; facsimile reprint with modern glossary by Lawrence Rivington, London, 1980. (Abbreviated as *JN*)

Peckham, Ann. *The Complete English Cook*...2nd ed. Leeds: Printed by Griffith Wright, 1771; scanned copy from The New York Public Library, New York. (Abbreviated as *AP*)

Quincy, John, M.D. *Pharmacopoeia Officinalis*...15th ed. London: Printed for T. Longman...1782. (Abbreviated as *JQ*)

Raffald, Elizabeth. *The Experienced English Housekeeper*...A New Ed. London: Printed for Millar...1782. (Abbreviated as *ER*)

Shorter Oxford English Dictionary...in 2 vols., prep. by William Little, H.W. Fowler, J. Coulson; 3rd ed., rev. and ed. by C.T. Onions. Oxford, UK: The Clarendon Press, 1964. (Abbreviated as *OED*)

Smith, E. *The Compleat Housewife*...15th ed. London: Printed for R. Ware...1753; modern glossary in facsimile reprint by Literary Services and Production Limited, London, 1968. (Abbreviated as *ES*)

Stead, Jennifer. "Quizzing Glasse: or Hannah Glasse Scrutinized, Part I." *Petits Propos Culinaires 13*, London: Prospect Books Ltd, March 1983. (Abbreviated as *JS*)

Washington, Martha. *Martha Washington's Booke of Cookery*...transcribed by Karen Hess. New York: Columbia University Press, 1981. (Abbreviated as *MW*)

Worlidge, John. *Systema Agriculturae*...2nd ed. London: Printed by J.C. for T. Dring...1675; facsimile reprint by Sherwin & Freutel Publishers, Los Angeles, 1970. (Abbreviated as *JW*)

Index of Recipes

Almond pudding	128	fruit	136
Apple,		pound	136
custard pie	104	Queen	136–37
dumplings	130	Calf,	
fritters	131	foot, to collar	119
to mango	143	soup	124
pudding	126	flummery	132–33
		jelly	132
Barberries, pickle	146	pudding, boiled	127–28
Bath cakes	136	Calf head,	
Baum wine	140–41	a la mode	89–90
Beans, French,		to dress	95
pie	105–06	hashes	82–83
pudding	129	to marble	119
Beef,		stews	81, 88
a la mode	85	Carrot pudding	125
to collar	118	Catsup, walnut	143–44
collops, broiled	91	Celery soup	120
dov'd	85–86	Cherry,	
minced	91	pie	105
heart, ragoo	89	wine	141–42
pot	117	Cheshire cheese soup	122
ragoo	85	Chicken,	
rump, stewed	86	a la Royal	93
sausages	154–55	fricasees	75–79
steak pie	100	pye	99–100
Birds, alio	99	Christmas goose pie	101
Biscuit cake drops	147	Clary pancakes	131
Bread puddings	126–27	Cocks-combed tripe	94
Bramble wine	142	Cod,	108
Butts, to stew	109	to boil	108
		head	105
Cabbage,		tail	105
Dutch pickle	146	Colliflowers, pickled	144
soup	120	Collops,	
Cake,		beef	91
Bath	136	ling	106–07
biscuit	147	Scotch	79–80

stuffed	79–80
Cowslip wine	140
Crawfish soup	123–24
Cream,	
currant	134
to fry	132
lemon	134
rasp[berry]	133
steeple	133
Crow crant	134
Cucumbers, to mango	143
Currants,	
jelly	138
paste	158
to preserve in stalks	139
in strops	139, 160
wine	140
Custard, boiled pudding	127
Cutlets, veal	94–95
Drops,	
lemon	158
wormwood	157
Duck,	
pie	100
ragoo	93
Dumplings,	
apple	130
spice	130
Ears, hogs	89
Eel pye	103
Eels, Lampar	116
Eggs,	
a la mode	151–52
amalet	170–01
Fricasseys	150–51
pallateen	151
ragoo	152
Elder wine	142
Feet,	
calves, to collar	119
flummery	132–33
jelly	122
pudding, boiled	127–28
Feet, hog's and ears	89
Fish soup	123

Florentine	98
Flounder, to fry	109
Flummery,	
calves' feet	132–33
hartshorn	133
Fowls,	
a la mode	92
boiled with onions	97
Fritters, apple	131
Gelly, tansy	129
Goose,	
a la mode	92
Christmas pie	100
Gingerbread	160–61
Gooseberry,	
preserve	139
pudding	128
Gore, to pot	116
Green Gages	137–38
Haddocks, to boil	108
Ham pie	101
Hare,	
jugged	93–94
to pot	117
pye	99
Head, lamb's and pluck	81
Herby pudding	129–30
Herring, to pot	118
Hodge-podge	121
Hog's feet and ears	89
Hunter's pudding	126
Jars, to pot	115
Jelly,	
calves' feet	132
currant	139
hartshorn	132
tansy	129
Jumballs	158
Lamb,	
in blankets	90
made dish	87
shoulder, to ragoo	90–91
Lamb head, to stew	83, 87
Leach	133

Lemon,	
drops	158
puddings	125
Ling,	
to boil	107
to collar	119
fricassey	104
to ragoo	106
Scotch collops	106–07
Liver pudding	130
Lobster, to pot	116
Mackerel, to boil	110
Mackroons	147
Mango,	
apples	145
cucumbers	145
millions [melons]	145–46
Marmalade,	
orange	158–59
quince	159–60
Marrow pudding	128
Moor-fowl, to pot	116–17
Mushroom, to pickle	142–43
Mutton,	
pasty	98
pye	99, 102
steak pye	100
Neat's feet, to fry	94
Olives, veal	80–81
Onion,	
to pickle	141
soup	122–23
Orange,	
chips	159
marmalade	158–59
to preserve	159
puddings	124
wine	141
Ox,	
cheek pie	101–02
head, to stew	86
Oyster,	
pye	103–04
sauce	97

INDEX OF RECIPES • 187

Pallateen	82, 176
Pancakes,	
wafer	131
ratafia	131
Paste,	
crisp for tarts	134
currant	158
puff-paste	155
for standing crust	155
Pasty,	
beef steak	100
venison	97–98
Peaches, to preserve	139
Pease, soups	122
Pellow	91–92
Pickle,	
barberries	146
kidney beans	143–44
pompion	146
turnip	144
walnut	143
Pie,	
beef steak	100
cherry	105
chicken	99–100
Christmas goose	101
French bean	105–06
ham	99
hare	99
minced	156
mutton	99, 102
ox cheek	101–02
oyster	103–04
pigeon	150
salmon	103
trennil	156–57
turbot	102–03
sweet veal	88
Pig,	
to collar	118
to roast like lamb	95
sham	154
Pigeons,	
in blankets	149
Paradised	149
pie	150
to stew	153

Pike, to dress	112–13	Salmon,		
Plumbs,		to bake	112	
to candy	137	to boil	112	
to dry	157	olives	111	
pottage	152–53	pie	103	
to preserve	137	to pot	115	
Pokey tongue	82	ragoo	110	
Pompion, to pickle	146	Scotch collops	110–11	
Pork sausages	153	Sausages,		
Portable soup	121–22	beef	154–55	
Posset, whip	134	mutton	155	
Prune pudding	128	pork	153	
Pudding,		without guts	153	
almond	122	Sego pudding	125	
apple	126	Sellery soup	120	
calves' foot	127–28	Sham pig	154	
French bean	129	Sham turkey	154	
gooseberry	128	Sheep heads and tongues	96	
herby	129–30	Sheep rumps	88–89	
hunter's	126	Skate,		
lemon	125	to boil	109–10	
liver	130	to crimp	109	
marrow	128	Soles	109	
orange	124	Soup,		
prune	128	portable	121–22	
ratafia	129	sellery	120	
rice	126	veal	117–20	
sego	125	white	121	
tansy	129	without water	120–21	
Pye, *see* Pie		Sparlings	113	
		Spice dumplings	130	
Queen cakes	136–37	Sweetbreads	96	
Quince marmalade	159–60	Sweetmeat tarts	134	
Rabbit, fricassey	76–77	Tansy,		
Raisin wine	141	gelly	129	
Rasp[berry],		pudding	129	
cakes	160	Tarts,		
cream	133	crisp paste for	135	
jam	138	glazed	135	
to preserve whole	138	puff-paste for	135	
Ratafia,		sweetmeat	134	
drops	147	Tench, to stew	112	
pancakes	131	Tongue, pokey	82	
pudding	125	Tripe,		
Rice pudding	126	cocks-combed	94	
Rumps, sheep's	88–89	to fry	94	

INDEX OF RECIPES • 189

Trout,
    Burn 113
    to fry 113
    potted like Jars 115
Turbot,
    to dress 111
    pie 102–03
Turkey,
    a la Royal 92
    to boil 96–97, 97
    with oyster sauce 97
    with rice 97
    sham 154
Turnip,
    to pickle 144
    soup 123

Veal,
    in blankets 80
    breast ragoo 79, 81
    cutlets 94–95, 97
    fillet 81
    fricasee 77
    olives 80–81
    pluck 84
    to pot 117

    rolled 88
    soup 119–20
    sweet pie 98
Venison pasty 97–98

Walnut,
    catchup 143–44
    to pickle 143
Water pancakes 131
Whip posset 134
Whitings,
    to boil 108
    to fry 108–09
Wigs 135
Wine,
    baum 140–41
    bramble 142
    cherry 141–42
    cowslip 140
    elder 142
    gooseberry 140
    orange 141
    raisin 141
    red currant 140
Woodcocks 116
Wormwood drops 157